Ferries

Compiled by Nick Widdows

Ferry Publications, PO Box 33, Ramsey, Isle of Man IM99 4LP

Email: ferrypubs@manx.net   Website: www.ferrypubs.co.uk

Europe's **leading** guide to the ferry industry

Contents...

CONTENTS

© Ferry Publications 2022
Produced and designed by Ferry Publications trading as Lily Publications Ltd
PO Box 33, Ramsey, Isle of Man, British Isles, IM99 4LP.
Tel: +44 (0) 1624 898446
www.ferrypubs.co.uk e-mail: info@lilypublications.co.uk
ISBN: 978-1911268-659

Introduction

This is the thirty-fifth edition of this book, which first appeared in 1983 as the 24-page 'home published' *'Car Ferries from Great Britain and Ireland'*. This year's edition has a Baltic theme. The book aims to list every passenger/vehicle ferry in Great Britain and Ireland, ro-ro freight vessels which operate regular services between Great Britain and Ireland and to nearby Continental destinations and major passenger/vehicle ferries in other parts of Northern Europe. The coverage of Northern Europe is not fully comprehensive (to make it so would probably double the size of the book). Major passenger only operators are also included in abridged form.

Each operator is listed alphabetically within sections - major operators, minor operators, freight-only operators, chain, cable and float ferries, passenger-only ferries, other North European passenger operators and vehicle/passenger vessels owned by companies not currently engaged in operating services. After details relating to each company's management, address, telephone numbers, email, website and services, there is a fleet list with technical data and then a potted history of each vessel with previous names and dates.

Nick Widdows

Whitstable, Kent

September 2022

Early 2022 saw a major industrial dispute in the UK between the unions and managment of P&O Ferries. *(Gordon Hislip)*

Foreword

The thirteenth edition of this book at the turn of the millennium was sponsored by P&O Ferries, who were then by far the dominant force in the UK ferry industry. The challenges of the opening of the Channel Tunnel, the loss of duty-free sales income, and the difficulties of adapting vessels to meet emerging SOLAS regulations, had forced consolidation within the ferry industry in the closing years of the last century, with the loss of several routes and operators. Few industries in the pre-Covid era had faced upheaval on this scale, but in his Foreword to the book, Graeme Dunlop, Chairman of P&O Ferries, predicted that "the fittest will survive as ferry travel will remain an integral part of our transport infrastructure.

P&O Ferries' operations were spread across a range of subsidiary companies in 2000. The 60% owned P&O Stena Line was the market leader on the short sea routes, facing up to the Channel Tunnel with a finely honed operation. P&O North Sea Ferries had a stranglehold on services across the North Sea, with the popular daily passenger services from Hull to Rotterdam and Zeebrugge, backed by a fleet of thirteen freight vessels serving Rotterdam and Zeebrugge from Middlesbrough, Hull and Felixstowe. On the Western Channel, P&O Portsmouth operated 5-star cruise ferries to Le Havre and Bilbao, with fast craft and a comparatively ageing service to Cherbourg. P&O Irish Sea – formed from the merger of the Felixstowe and Pandoro operations in 1998 – employed fast craft and conventional vessels on the Cairnryan-Larne route, and a fleet of eleven freight vessels on a portfolio of routes that linked Larne with Cairnryan and Fleetwood, Dublin with Liverpool, and Rosslare with Cherbourg. In a nod to the parent company's heritage, P&O Scottish Ferries still served Orkney and Shetland from Aberdeen.

The company stood ready to welcome four new vessels to the fleet. At Hull, the *Pride of Hull* and *Pride of Rotterdam* were set to transform capacity and quality on the Hull-Rotterdam route, bringing about economies by replacing two cruise ferries and two freighters. The Japanese-built *European Causeway* was to become the biggest and fastest conventional vessel on the Cairnryan-Larne route, the first time that the company would employ a new purpose-built vessel on the North Channel – one capable of knocking 30 minutes off the crossing duration. Meanwhile, the larger *European Ambassador* was heading for the Liverpool-Dublin route, acknowledging the impact that Merchant Ferries' increased competition was having on the business. The arrival of these vessels enabled a shuffling of older resources to generate benefits across a wider range of routes.

There was an air of confidence, despite the impact of the Channel Tunnel on the 'cash cow' short sea business. The Group's fleet of 51 vessels operating on 20 routes stood ready to face the new century. The management team was strong, the brand well respected. However, the search for profit was to lead to a succession of rationalisation projects and the shedding of vessels, routes, and jobs.

In spring 2002 P&O was invited to purchase Stena Line's 40% interest in P&O Stena Line for £150m, with the former partner absorbing P&O's freight operations at Felixstowe, thus improving its North Sea freight business. The deal was concluded in October 2002. This prompted the consolidation of the combined operations of P&O Stena Line, P&O Irish Sea, P&O North Sea Ferries and P&O Portsmouth into the single P&O Ferries brand, with management centralised in Dover, thereby eliminating local teams with their specialist market knowledge.

The long association with Orkney and Shetland came to an end in September 2002, when P&O Scottish Ferries was unsuccessful in its bid to retain the tendered service. The Dover-Zeebrugge freight service closed in December that year.

Although the Portsmouth routes stood as a useful bulwark against encroachment up the Channel by Brittany Ferries and were the closest that the company came to having a 'cruising' product on the English Channel, they had been consistently loss-making since the charter of the *Pride of Le Havre* and *Pride of Portsmouth* from Olau Line in 1994. The charter of the *Isle*

Pride of Kent and Pride of Canterbury lie alongside the Eastern Arm at Dover Western Docks during the dispute. *(George Holland)*

Pride of Canterbury, Pride of Kent and Spirit of Britain await their next duties on the Admiralty Pier at Dover. *(George Holland)*

Irish interlopers – Isle of Innisfree enters Dover whilst Isle of Inisheer loads a full freight deck.
(George Holland)

of Innisfree as the *Pride of Cherbourg* in 2002 saw the end of the 27-year-old 'Super Vikings' on the Cherbourg route, and the fast craft *Caen Express* brought direct competition to Brittany Ferries' Portsmouth-Caen route for a single season in 2004. Consolidation of management to the Dover team did not address the sector's financial difficulties, which included the high charter costs of the fleet's three cruise ferries. The new management team's 2004 business review resulted in the closure of the Cherbourg route in January 2005, with the Le Havre route following in September; the remaining single cruise ferry service to Bilbao could not be made to pay as a standalone operation, and the *Pride of Bilbao* was withdrawn in 2010.

Difficulties with handling the *European Ambassador* in Liverpool after she entered service to Dublin in January 2001 prompted a move to Mostyn later that year, but this proved no panacea, and the service returned to Liverpool in 2004. The addition of the freighters *Norbank* and *Norbay* allowed expansion from 2002 but attempts to sell the Liverpool and Fleetwood operations to Stena Line were thwarted by the Competition Commission in 2003. Eventually Stena Line took over the Fleetwood-Larne route and the three-year-old *European Ambassador* joined Stena Line as the *Stena Nordica*. The Rosslare-Cherbourg link closed in 2005.

In March 2006 the P&O Group was acquired by DP World, primarily to gain control of the extensive portfolio of ports. The new owners promised investment, and this materialised in the form of a €360m order with Aker Yards of Rauma, Finland for two new vessels in August 2008. The 'Super-Spirit' class vessels *Spirit of Britain* and *Spirit of France* entered service on the Dover-Calais route in January 2011 and February 2012 respectively.

Meanwhile, the North Sea operations failed to respond to the growing threat posed by DFDS at Newcastle, Superfast's route from Rosyth to Zeebrugge (2002-9), and the expansion of Cobelfret, DFDS and Stena Line's interests on the Humber. A route from Tilbury to Zeebrugge opened in July 2007, and the London port was connected with Calais in 2019. The Covid lockdown period prompted a focus on the Hull-Rotterdam service, and on 1st January 2021 the Hull-Zeebrugge passenger route was closed, with the *Pride of Bruges* and *Pride of York* sold to GNV for their Naples-Palermo overnight route.

P&O Ferries record across the first two decades of the 21st century was one of retrenchment and restructuring in the constant pursuit of profit, characterised by the closure, withdrawal from, or sale of some fifteen routes in this period. Twelve of the current 20 ships in the fleet were in service in 2000; the newest vessel – *Spirit of France* – is over a decade old. (In contrast, only seven of DFDS's 33 ship fleet were operational in 2000; just four of Stena Line's 20 ship fleet were operational in 2000). This will be partly remedied by the arrival of the *P&O Pioneer* and *P&O Liberté* from the Chinese Guangzhou shipyard in 2023, which will reintroduce the concept of double-ender vessels to the Dover Strait. These represent significant investment of €260m at a time when competition on the short sea routes has been ignited by the introduction of Irish Ferries' three-ship operation. But spread over the last two decades, this represents a limited outlay across the portfolio of routes compared to their competitors; Brittany Ferries, DFDS, Irish Ferries, Seatruck, and Stena Line, for example, have all made notable investments in new tonnage in recent years.

P&O Ferries track record has long been punctuated by attempts to change crew working practices, terms, and conditions, dating back to the protracted and bitter strikes at Dover shortly after the takeover of Townsend Thoresen. P&O European Ferries proposed to cut their cost base by £6m in December 1987 to remain competitive with the forthcoming Channel Tunnel, eliminating 500 jobs from a workforce of 2,300 seafarers, reducing earnings, and extending working hours. National Union of Seamen members stopped work on 6th February 1988 and a bitter dispute ensued. Suspension of services from Dover was accompanied by mass picketing; it was some two months before sailings resumed with employees on new contracts, and the dispute was only formally abandoned 16 months later.

Crew costs have continued to vex the company, despite several rounds of redundancies. The Group made small profits of £34.8m in 2017, and £8.9m in 2018, but losses of £39.8m in 2019 and £105m in 2020 as Covid restrictions began to bite. These losses were covered by its parent, DP World, but this position was unsustainable. P&O received almost £15m in government grants in 2020.

Cutbacks had already been made. The Cypriot flag appeared at the stern of a once proud British icon. Some 440 staff left the business in 2020, the Hull-Zeebrugge passenger route was closed, waiter service disappeared in restaurants on the Dover-Calais route, the *Pride of Bruges, Pride of York,* and *European Seaway* were sold and the *Pride of Burgundy* laid-up. The company entered a space charter arrangement with DFDS after scrutiny by the UK Competition and Markets Authority. P&O Ferries remained tight lipped about the launch of the first of their new fleet on 2nd January 2022, refusing to release images and supressing YouTube coverage of the event. Rarely, if ever, can the floating out of a landmark vessel have been heralded by such limited publicity. Perhaps they were anticipating trouble ahead.

Meanwhile Irish Ferries' *Isle of Inishmore* began to provide competition to the flagship Dover-Calais route, operating on a low-cost crewing model; their ambitions to operate a three-ship service on the route were quickly realised in 2022. Irish Ferries had experienced a protracted dispute with trade unions when they addressed the issue of crew costs by unilaterally proposing to replace 543 directly employed seafarers with agency crew in 2005, and to reflag their fleet to Cyprus. Ships were laid up in port for almost three weeks. When the dispute was finally resolved, Irish Ferries achieved its objectives and secured annual cost savings of €11.5m, with new – predominantly Latvian - entrants being paid the Irish minimum wage and working for longer periods of time than the staff they displaced. Irish Ferries entered the Dover market with a lean, competitive cost base consistent with a widely established crewing model prevalent in 80% of the maritime industry.

In November 2021 Sultan Ahmed bin Sulayem, Head of P&O Ferries' parent DP World, told the then UK Transport Secretary Grant Shapps during a meeting in Dubai, that Irish Ferries' low-cost operation posed "challenges in respect of P&O's operations", to which Shapps was recorded as responding "I recognise you will need to make commercial decisions." The resultant strategy, which was said to be devised and implemented by P&O Ferries independently of its owner, was drastic.

In a move which sent shock waves across political and media circles, P&O Ferries tied up their fleet on Thursday 17th March 2022 and dismissed some 786 crew without notice in a message delivered by Zoom call. Security staff and replacement crew boarded vessels as the redundant crews departed.

 An "enhanced offer" was made available to employees who complied with the requirements set out in the redundancy package and completed a non-disclosure agreement. There was a narrow window for response. P&O Ferries claimed that the £36.5m settlement with its workers was the largest compensation package ever made in the British Maritime Sector. Shore staff, the small numbers of seafarers directly employed by the company's French and Netherlands subsidiaries, and existing agency crews on the North Sea and Irish Sea routes were not affected. Advertisements were placed by Clyde Marine Recruitment to join vessels 'on a new venture, operating between the UK and Northern Ireland', with similar adverts by Columbia Shipmanagement for a new ferry sailing between the UK and Continental Europe.

A company spokesperson justified the decision by saying "This has been an incredibly tough decision for the business: to make this choice or face taking the company into administration. This would have meant the loss of 3,000 jobs and the end of P&O Ferries. In making this hard choice, we have guaranteed the future viability of P&O Ferries, avoided large-scale and lengthy disruption, and secured Britain's trading capacity." The absence of any attempt to negotiate with trade unions and the sudden and impersonal way crew lost their jobs was condemned by politicians of all hues, trade unionists, and by business and community leaders alike. P&O Ferries' carefully crafted reputation was instantly trashed on television, in social media and across the press.

The RMT reported that P&O Ferries' crews at Dover were replaced by Indian seafarers being paid $2.38 an hour. P&O Ferries responded that the *average* wage was £5.50/hour. But the issue was about more than salaries, with the company implementing their new crewing model with crews paid for time worked, rather than an annual salary.

There is little doubt that conventional consultations with trade unions would have been protracted, and unlikely to fully yield the desired outcome. Nonetheless there is a requirement

Still going strong. The 35-year-old GNV Aries (former Norsea/Pride of York) alongside in Napoli. *(Philippe Holthof)*

GNV Antares (former Norsun/Pride of Bruges) in Palermo alongside Tirennia's Rubattino. *Philippe Holthof*

to consult with both unions and staff about potential dismissals, with flag governments given appropriate notice that jobs are at risk. P&O Ferries' CEO Peter Hebblethwaite, the company's third CEO in eighteen months, admitted in parliament that the company had knowingly broken the law, and that he would do the same again in similar circumstances, adding fuel to the flames. The Prime Minister backed calls for his resignation.

Shapps set out several measures in response to the P&O Ferries sackings, including plans to create 'minimum wage corridors' on ferry routes between the UK and other countries. Yet the government proved powerless to prevent the changes, and an ultimatum to reinstate sacked workers or be threatened with legislation received a strong rebuttal from P&O. The redundancy offer was legally irreversible, and the terms were accepted by virtually all affected individuals. The company pointed out that they "had called for a level playing field regarding salaries on British ferry routes." Tackling a global phenomenon with a unilateral political response is fraught with difficulty. The days of a strong British flagged and crewed ferry industry are long gone.

The Maritime & Coastguard Agency proved more effective than politicians in ensuring that services met the appropriate standards before they could resume, yet P&O Ferries gradually, but rather more slowly and no doubt at greater cost than originally anticipated, resumed operations across its route portfolio. The company's tarnished reputation was not enhanced by the repeated failure of vessel safety inspections.

Whilst early reports suggested that carryings on P&O Ferries' resumed sailings were significantly below the norm on cross-Channel crossings, freight hauliers are pragmatic and will be tempted back by available capacity, rates, and the space sharing arrangements with DFDS. Peak season problems with immigration delays at Dover in summer 2022 illustrate the continuing national dependence on the short sea routes.

Hebblethwaite retains the support of Ahmed bin Sulayem who, speaking to the Financial Times, praised the actions of the company and said it had to make its own business decisions, emphasising that the chief executive had "done an amazing job" saving P&O Ferries. The company remains upbeat; a spokesman noted that "As part of our long-term commitment to the business, we are investing in a new generation of fully efficient, low impact ships on Dover to Calais. In addition, a new class of ship - due to enter service in 2023 - will reduce turnaround time in the ports, reducing operating costs and emissions. Our newly formed and forward-looking operational relationship with DFDS is also focused on customer service through delivering greater flexibility, more frequency and easier travel."

The brutal implementation of these changes cynically and unrepentantly placed profit above the law, but the long-term damage to the P&O brand will take time to assess. P&O Cruises (owned by Carnival Cruise Corporation of the USA) was quick to distance itself from the former sister company, nervous of the commercial consequences of association. The UK government may yet implement more controls on crewing arrangements for ferries using the country's ports, and this will deliver the 'level playing field' craved by P&O Ferries, albeit at greater cost and therefore consumer prices. Whether this latest in a long sequence of cutback and service reductions delivers the levels of profitability desired by the parent group remains to be seen. There is still a long outstanding need for significant investment to replace ageing tonnage and address the green agenda across the fleet, to test the patience of DP World further. This year's changes are just one step in a long and continuing journey if P&O Ferries is to be fit enough to survive.

Richard Kirkman
Editor of Ferry & Cruise Review

Surplus to requirements - Pride of Burgundy remains unused by P&O Ferries in 2022, laid up in Dunkerque Est. *(George Holland)*

Spirit of France made a belated return to traffic in 2022 after protracted repairs in Rotterdam. *(Richard Seville)*

The Viking Glory – A Cruise Ferry for the Twenty-First Century

The period since the early-1990s has been one of a general decline of cruise ferry operations – routes dependent on the passenger mini-cruise trade with duty-free shopping as the big attraction. Nearly 30 years ago, the loss of the Baltic ferry *Estonia* dented public faith in such vessels and led to a hiatus in the placement of further orders for new examples. Thereafter, the ending of duty-free shopping between EU member states considerably reduced their market potential and on many routes they were superseded by ro-pax-type tonnage. As the Åland Islands in the middle of the Baltic Sea managed to achieve an exemption from the EU's mandate banning duty-free sales, the mid-Baltic routes connecting Sweden and Finland remained as one notable exception to the otherwise greatly reduced market for cruise ferries. On the Stockholm-Turku route in particular, on which 22-hour return mini-cruises operate, the established business model involved bringing large numbers of Swedes and Finns by coach from small towns and villages in the near and distant rural hinterlands. Their aim was to eat, drink and party – and the model continued to be successful into the 2000s, Tallink Silja Line placing on the route its former Helsinki-Tallinn vessels *Galaxy* and *Baltic Princess*, which superseded the *Silja Festival* and *Silja Europa* and had the benefit of being nearly identical and with a larger vehicle capacity. Topsides, these cruise ferries' passenger accommodations were merely another iteration of the established formula of Las Vegas-style glitz with numerous bars and entertainment facilities – but they had pathetically little outside deck space from which to view the attractive passing archipelago scenery and such sun decks as there were served as 'smoker's corners' on account of the public smoking ban inboard. These were ferries on which it was really only possible to fill one's stomach with food and drink and partake of synthetic entertainments inboard.

In the wider culture, however, profound changes were underway as a result of a generational sociological shift from the baby-boomers and generation X/Y, many of whom sought to find their leisure through imbibing intoxicating substances, to the emergent generation Z, who were much more likely to have gym memberships and to eat organic foods. Viking Line, Tallink Silja's rival between Stockholm and Turku, traditionally had attracted the former clientele – but in the early-2010s observed that henceforth it would be more lucrative instead to seek out the latter. The outcome was the innovative cruise ferry *Viking Grace*, which combined greener propulsion technologies using liquefied natural gas for fuel with a very stylish and aspirational passenger accommodation, designed by the noted Finnish interiors specialist Vertti Kivi and containing numerous novel features intended to attract a more diverse clientele than hitherto. The *Viking Glory* introduced to Baltic cruise ferries the innovation of the entire public room accommodation being in the topmost decks, a feature previously found on a couple of Norwegian Hurtigruten coastal vessels. The *Viking Glory* represents a further development of this approach which has enabled many striking spaces to be developed inboard.

When Viking Line began design development work in 2015, the initial thought was that an only slightly modified sister ship to *Viking Grace* would be required, but as discussions progressed amid a shifting legislative landscape, it became clear than an entirely new design would be needed. Forthcoming damage stability legislation affecting ferries, coupled with a desire to carry an even bigger payload of freight and also to optimize further the efficiency of the hull form would necessitate different overall dimensions. Whereas *Viking Grace* measures 218.8 by 31.8 metres, *Viking Glory* is 222.59 by 35.61 metres, the substantial extra width providing space for an extra vehicle lane, there being 1,500 lane metres, as opposed to the 1,275 on the slightly older ship. (By comparison, the *Amorella*, which *Viking Glory* has replaced, offered a mere 970 lane metres). To maintain a satisfactorily low centre of gravity, the superstructure is narrower than the hull with external walkways running the length of deck 6 on either side.

Mechanically, *Viking Glory* looks forward to future fuels, its propulsion plant comprising six state-of-the-art Wärtsilä W10V31DF engines, generating 33,000 kilowatts, which are capable of burning LNG and also methanol.

Viking Grace under construction (*Viking Line*)

Viking Grace (*Viking Line*)

Torget Café and bar, Viking Glory *(Viking Line)*

Mimmi's restaurant, Viking Glory *(Viking Line)*

Restaurant Kobba, Viking Glory *(Viking Line)*

Torget, Viking Glory *(Viking Line)*

When it came to building *Viking Glory*, Viking Line had a dilemma; the potential European shipyards already mostly had well-filled order books and, besides, the likely cost would be very high. As with several other Nordic ferry operators, Viking Line decided instead to have the ship built in China. The others, however, had ordered ro-ro freight and ro-pax tonnage; Chinese shipyards had no experience whatsoever of building a large cruise ferry with complex passenger accommodation of the kind that Viking Line wanted. On the other hand, as far back as over half-a-century ago, the company had commissioned new tonnage from another emergent shipbuilding nation, Yugoslavia (the *Amorella* was also built there and, back in 1986-1988, represented a major challenge for the Brodosplit shipyard). Viking Line has a skilful and experienced technical team and a lot of in-house know-how concerning every aspect of ferry design and operation – and it also has good long-term relationships with a range of ship designers, design analysts and suppliers throughout the Nordic region and beyond.

When a contract was signed with Xiamen Shipbuilding Industry of Xiamen in China, however, nobody could have foreseen that in late-2019, the terrible Coronavirus pandemic would arrive, fragmenting communications and travel possibilities between China and Europe. Viking Line's shipyard project team thus spent unexpectedly lengthy periods effectively 'trapped' in Xiamen while they worked on the project, communicating with headquarters in Mariehamn and with the many Nordic and European suppliers of a vast and diverse inventory via the internet. To build a large, modern passenger ship is an incredible achievement of human ingenuity – but to build one on the other side of the world at an inexperienced shipyard during a pandemic is one of a whole other magnitude. The realization of the amazing outcome that is *Viking Glory* in such unpropitious circumstances is indeed a very great credit to all involved.

Externally, the *Viking Glory* is a notable design success. It is arguably one of the best-looking passenger ships to have been completed for many a long year. Although at a glance having a familial resemblance to *Viking Grace*, it is evident that that the cheaper Chinese labour producing the metalwork has allowed much more to be done by way of bending and cutting plates and so there is a great deal extra visually satisfying detailing. The design also shows some similarity in forms and proportions to the much smaller *Viking XPRS*, another aesthetically effective solution.

In silhouette, the tinted glass screens protecting the aft sun decks form the beginning of an arc that curves gently up, over and into the top of the midbody. This is surmounted by the funnel, which is another, much smaller arc with the base of the mast being a further arc that is smaller still. The forward superstructure has its own more spectacular character, it being of faceted form with the three levels of public rooms above the bridge stepped in as a series of tiers with tinted glazing flowing around the front and sides in a succession of slanted folds. On the exterior, there are clues regarding the novel disposition of the spaces within the shells of the upper decks, most notably bulges on either side and a break in the deck line aft of amidships.

A great deal of fresh thinking has indeed been expended inboard and the outcome is a vessel with a strong and unique personality. In 2015 Viking Line assembled an in-house project development team comprising shore-based department heads and ships' hotel staff to work out a specification for the eventual interior architects, using *Viking Grace* as the starting point for their deliberations. A well-developed brief was thus produced which would be built upon further by the appointed designers, Concept Stockholm. This firm had no prior experience of shipboard work, meaning that they could bring fresh thinking and inspiration, rather than merely producing a derivation of previous designs. Concept Stockholm are noted for their trendy restaurant, bar, nightclub, retail and boutique hotel interiors, a project portfolio that made them ideal appointees.

The Stockholm-Turku route is a very busy one, carrying a wide variety of passengers; some are going from A to B, but most are making return mini-cruises. The ferries operating on the route thus need to be designed to function equally well in overnight and daytime use and to accommodate and cater to very large throughputs. *Viking Glory* can accommodate 2,800, there being 922 en-suite cabins. These are all located on decks 5, 6 and 7. On the former, there is in addition an upper car deck, while on the latter two, many of the crew cabins are placed inboard of very commodious and well-arranged lifeboat embarkation areas. Forward on Decks 6 and 7 are four thematically-designed, multi-room suites, inspiration for which comes from

Algoth's, Viking Glory *(Viking Line)*

Algoth's, Viking Glory *(Viking Line)*

Viking Glory *(Kenneth Karsten)*

the environment through which the vessel sails. These are named 'Sunset', 'The Forest', 'The Cliffs' and 'Blue Water' – and very beautiful they are too. The ordinary cabins also are nicely appointed and I particularly liked the corridor carpeting, the witty design of which shows diagrammatic aerial views of *Viking Glory* creating patterns in its wake. The cabins were made in China on a production line basis – a new skill for shipbuilding there. Lying in bed, one experiences silent stillness, just like in a business hotel.

The main public room decks are 9, 10 and 11. Whereas most ferries since the 1960s have used asymmetrical layouts with a starboard arcade typically connecting the spaces, on *Viking Glory*, by contrast, a single big central focus has been developed. Known as 'Torget' (Swedish for 'town square'), it is two decks high and fills the full width of the superstructure. To reach it, embarking passengers need to ascend one or two decks via smartly detailed stairways. On Deck 9, the vestibule ceiling has groups of suspended brass lanterns, the expanded metal mesh used for their shades being a motif used throughout the accommodation to achieve various glittery and feathery illumination effects. This is a first clue as to what lies beyond the dark gold panelling of the elevator block. Turning the corner into Torget, one is met with a visual feast of attractive scenography and activity. At one end, there is a bandstand for jazz music with a huge LED screen behind showing soothing imagery. Surrounding this is a semi-circular open void to the deck above. A variety of different types of café furniture is interspersed with more lanterns at table height, all on an expanse of parquet-style flooring from which rise tree-like structures containing concealed illumination. These spread across the ceiling and their form is another motif that appears in various ways at other points in the accommodation.

In the background, there is a café serving counter, filled with delicious-looking sandwiches and cakes and from which wafts an enticing aroma of cinnamon – a smell I greatly associate with being in Sweden. With its visual, olfactory and musical delights, the Torget space can be considered a big success and it is full of happy passengers from early in the morning until late at night. Some older couples were sitting on rattan chairs, drinking coffees from little round tables with polished green centres and brass rims, feeling something of the atmosphere of a Parisian café. The floor-to-ceiling windows on either side let light flood in during the day, but provide a shiny black backdrop by night, when the beautiful artificial illumination really comes into its own.

One deck up – reachable via a curved feature stairway above which is suspended a shiny fish sculpture, one reaches the 'balcony' level, which is called 'Market' and which features a range of open-fronted food outlets serving slightly more substantial snacks and light meals than from the Torget café counter below. The concept is derived from the kinds of 'Saluhall' found in Swedish and Finnish cities, where delicious eats can be bought from deli counters. There are, in addition, some unstaffed counters from which pre-packed snacks can be bought and, along one wall, bottles of good quality olive oil and other nice deli condiments to buy and take home. Surrounding the balcony void and on either beam are commodious seating areas, comprising café-style groups and some high tables with stools. Altogether, the 'Market' concept is very attractive and so much more appealing than a boring old ferry cafeteria.

The many sources of food on *Viking Glory* emanate from a three-deck service island of galleys, sculleries and stores, located forward of the Torget and Market complex. In addition to these outlets, it serves the conference department forward on Deck 9, The Buffet and Mimmi's Restaurant, forward on Deck 10, and the Kobba Restaurant & Bar forward on Deck 11. These all offer spectacular panoramas ahead and to the sides through great expanses of glazing. The Buffet is bright and spacious with plenty of circulation space, but is otherwise the most conventional of the dining concepts. Mimmi's – which takes its name from a pioneering woman seafarer from the Åland Islands – is contrastingly dark-toned and offers a short menu of beautifully-cooked fish and meat dishes which are ordered from the bar and delivered to the table by a waiter. There are intriguing spherical lights in wire cages suspended overhead, maybe somewhat reminiscent of lobster creels. I ate Arctic char which came with a fresh salad, which was delicious. The details of the food service have been considered in great detail – the colour and texture of the napkins, the 'distressed' finishes of the boxes holding the cutlery and the matching cruet sets on each table – oh, and there are more little brass lanterns along the window sills, framing the views of the passing archipelago.

Saltö Bakery, Viking Glory *(Viking Line)*

The Market, Viking Glory *(Viking Line)*

Up another level to Deck 11, Kobba seeks to be a fancy, yet informal bistro restaurant with its own very stylish long bar. The space, which fills the forward starboard quarter, looks its best at night when shiny metal mesh lampshades and back-lit layers of metal chainmail above the bar and over some of the tables provide most of the illumination. Some of the tables and seating, incidentally, are inside metal 'cages' from which lighting is suspended, making for a slightly more intimate experience. Up a feature stairway to Deck 12, at the base of the mast, is a very special 'hidden' feature – a revolving private dining space with a single circular table and with floor-to-ceiling windows around two-thirds of the perimeter. Bookable in advance, it offers a dining experience that is not only unique on the Baltic Sea, but – so far as I am aware – is the only one of its kind on any passenger ship anywhere.

The portside half of Deck 11 contains the Archipelago spa and fitness centre, which is equally distinguished by its fine views outward. Facing forward, there is a relaxing pool with loungers in warm water to ease away aches, pains and stresses as the islands slip by. Behind a large window is a unisex sauna, enabling the same vistas to be enjoyed while being steamed. In the aft section there are more traditional single-sex saunas, a yoga room, treatment rooms and a gym. These facilities are indicative of the generational change that has occurred with health and fitness now an intrinsic part of the modern lifestyle.

If the front half of *Viking Glory* is mostly about eating and health, the aft half is about shopping and entertainment. Back on Deck 9, astern of Torget, the aft half of the deck is entirely occupied by a vast shopping complex called 'Shopping World' that comprises a succession of distinct 'departments', forming a U-shape around the funnel casing. En-route, there are places for drinks tastings and, at the exit, self-service check-outs – perhaps another 'first' on a ferry. On the exterior, incidentally, the blank sides of Shopping World are disguised by dark grey paint, giving the illusion that the glazing of the spaces forward and amidships continues all the way to the stern.

Above Shopping World on Deck 10 is another of the *Viking Glory's* outstanding design successes. The Vista Room is the main nightclub and entertainment space and it is here that the bulging sides occur. Not only that, but the space is one-and-a-half decks high, making it immediately impactful upon entering. The extra height not only lends grandeur and avoids claustrophobia but also enables the seating to be slightly tiered, meaning that everyone can have a good view of the stage and dance floor. There are no steps, however, and so all of the changes in level are accessible to the disabled.

Concept Stockholm have not missed the opportunity presented to make a bold design statement, which is achieved by dramatic 'fountains' of lighting strips that emerge from the centres of the drinks racks behind the two circular bar counters. Emulating on a big scale the forms of the 'trees' in Torget, the strips rise towards the ceiling, then radiate out across the space. As its name suggests, the Vista Room has large windows – but it also has glazed areas of flooring in the side overhangs, through which a drop of nine decks down to the sea can be viewed. Adjacent to the main Vista Room space are a smaller bar, separated by a sound-proof plate glass partition, with its own stage where a troubadour can play, and a further bar for conference guests called 'Algot's', where a wide range of drinks are kept in a big cupboard which opens to reveal them and where a 'mixologist' can prepare cocktails to order at a long table.

As well as viewing the beautiful natural surroundings that are such a feature of the Stockholm-Turku route from indoors, *Viking Glory* had very extensive outside deck areas that have also received very careful design attention. The Vista Deck is aft of the Vista Room and is laid in teak-effect cladding with comfortable patio furniture and has a counter for beverages and snack foods. Amidships, above the Vista Room, is 'The Terrace', a sheltered outdoor deck area with a stage for performances in summer weather and this has an adjacent Terrace Bar, decorated with festive red and white stripes. Overhead, there is another big metal fish sculpture. The Vista Deck and The Terrace will each appeal to a particular clientele and they set an exceptional standard for the important but too often neglected 'outdoor' aspect of ferry interior design.

Altogether, *Viking Glory* is undoubtedly the most magnificent new ferry to have entered service anywhere for many a long year. The only problem with taking a mini-cruise from Stockholm to Turku and back is that 22 hours is insufficiently long enough to enjoy all of the myriad attractions. In the first months after the vessel entered service, Viking Line could claim a 70 per cent market share. Now, Tallink Silja Line has announced the withdrawal of its *Galaxy*, which shadows *Viking Glory's* departures, and its redeployment as a floating hostel for Ukrainian refugees in the Netherlands. Viking Line's investment would therefore appear to have paid off handsomely and the company is now the dominant operator between Stockholm and Turku.

Bruce Peter

Shopping World - Viking Glory *(Viking Line)*

The 'Aura' and the 'Luna' – DFDS Upgrades in the Baltic

2022 marked the arrival of two significant new ro-pax ferries for DFDS Seaways' Baltic routes, their first designed-from-scratch passenger new buildings for a remarkable 40 years. Employed between the company's Baltic hub of Klaipėda, Lithuania and the southern Swedish port of Karlshamn, the *Aura Seaways* and her younger sister, the *Luna Seaways*, have a garage capacity of 4,500 lane metres and spacious, comfortable accommodation for 600 passengers. The 56,043t twins are 230m in length and, with a 23 knot service speed, have also been designed to serve on the parallel service from Klaipėda to Kiel in Germany.

First for 40 Years

DFDS were in the middle of their disastrous flirtation with the US and Caribbean market when the ahead-of-her-time cruise ferry *Scandinavia* was delivered in 1982 - now seemingly a world away. Since then DFDS as a total company has changed almost beyond recognition with the significant transformation and expansion of their ferry route network. In the early 1980s, who would have predicted that the company would be a major player on the Dover Strait, for example? Since that time, while numerous freight ro-ro freighters have been designed and built to their order, any new passenger ships have either been acquired second-hand or purchased "off the stocks", having been originally ordered by, or designed for, other operators. The 2021-new build *Cote D'Opale*, from the Dover to Calais route, arguably comes the closest to a purpose-built passenger ferry since 1982, although even she was an amended design from the prolific Stena Line e-flexer-series. The delivery of the *Aura Seaways* is therefore an event worth celebrating.

Development of the former LISCO Network

DFDS' presence at Klaipėda essentially dates from 2001, with the company's acquisition of LISCO (the Lithuanian Shipping Company) whose network included links to both Sweden and Germany operated by six ferries. At the time, this eclectic fleet comprised three train ferries built for service between Lithuania and East Germany, two former Soviet ro- ro freighters and intriguingly the former French ferry *Palanga*, which built for SNCM as the *Monte Stello*. DFDS quickly moved to modernise the fleet, as well as disposing of the general cargo vessels which they had also acquired in the deal. Across the subsequent 20 years, traffic on the former LISCO routes has grown considerably and February 2018 saw an order confirmed with the Chinese Guangzhou Shipyard International (GSI) for the two new ferries. The yard was founded in 1954 and relocated to a large, modern new site in 2018. The company builds a wide portfolio of vessel types, including both chemical and oil tankers, bulk carriers and specialist ships including semi-submersibles. In addition to the order for DFDS, GSI is also currently building the new *P&O Pioneer* and *P&O Liberté* for P&O Ferries' Dover to Calais service and the huge *Moby Fantasy* and *Moby Legacy* for Moby Lines' routes to Sardinia.

The crossing between Karlshamn and Klaipėda typically takes 11 hours, with the majority of sailings undertaken overnight. The two ports offer quite a contrast; with Klaipėda being a major industrial town, with a significant port complex and where the DFDS berth is reached only by a lengthy navigation of the Kursiy Marios Bay, whilst Karlshamn is a sleepy Swedish town with a modern but relatively small harbour. The route attracts a mix of both accompanied and unaccompanied trailers as well as vans and private cars. Cargo-wise, a wide variety of products are carried, with furniture and construction material two of the bigger sectors. The crossing's main passenger traffic comprises emigrant Lithuanian workers travelling to and from Scandinavia, along with limited tourist traffic to the Baltic states. The Russian invasion of Ukraine certainly poses challenges for the route, although the long-term effects remain to be seen. The *Aura Seaways* and her sister are significantly bigger both in terms of both trailer capacity and passenger capacity than the ships being replaced, the largest of which were the Italian built "Apuania"-class *Athena Seaways*, *Regina Seaways* and *Victoria Seaways*. The *Aura*

Aura Seaways (DFDS)

Lighthouse Café (Richard Seville)

Mare Balticum à la carte *(Richard Seville)*

Road Kings *(Richard Seville)*

Seaways' new 600-passenger capacity represents double that of her predecessors, and DFDS set out not only to increase the passenger capacity but also to improve the experience onboard. The result is an expanded range of comfortable public facilities and an increased number of 250 passenger cabins.

Passenger Facilities

Accommodation is arranged on Decks 8 and 9, with public facilities located forward and sleeping accommodation aft, the former all featuring DFDS' regular on-board facility brand names. The interior design, the work of Steen Friis Design of Denmark, is completed in a modern-Scandi style, in line with recent refurbishment projects across the passenger fleet, creating a house-style that stretches from Klaipéda in the East to Calais in the West. On the *Aura Seaways*, amenities start at the front of the Deck 8 with the Seven Seas restaurant, boasting panoramic views across the bow. The restaurant is fitted out in light wood and pastel shades of lilac, grey and light orange. It usually operates in a single-price buffet format, though can alternatively be configured as a self-service. Moving astern, the Navigator Bar is located to port, finished in darker tones, with a grey and burgundy-red palate. Here, the impact of the pandemic can be seen in the room's layout, with the seating areas permanently broken up into smaller clusters and separated with mid-height transparent dividers, although the overall effect is unobtrusive. To starboard is a small conference room followed by the Mare Balticum à la carte restaurant and fitted out with shades of blue. The conference room is designed so that it can easily be converted to serve as an extension to either restaurant, as demand requires.

The full-width reception hall follows, complete with information desk, with a walkway then leading astern to starboard into the Lighthouse Café Lounge, where pink and grey pastel colours dominate. The walkway is lined with bookshelves, giving the impression of a library. A walk-around shop and the Pirates' Island children's play area can also be found adjoining the café, although the positioning of the shop unfortunately means the café facility lacks windows for much of its port side. The layout could perhaps have been better resolved if the shop has been located centrally, surrounded by glass-bulkheads, with the café servery adjoining the shop aft, thus giving the café a u-shaped configuration with access to natural light on both sides. Such a configuration has been successfully used on various Stena Line vessels, for example, although of course the detailed technical requirements governing the layout on the *Aura Seaways* are not known. The dedicated Road-Kings facility for freight drivers with their own, private, self-service restaurant and lounge area is housed forward on Deck 9, with a similar colour scheme to the Seven Seas restaurant below. The remainder of both decks is given over to passenger/driver cabins. Unfortunately, the Road Kings facility can only be accessed from the forward stairwell by walking through cabin corridors, meaning some disturbance to occupants may be caused. External deck space is generous, although lacking any form of seating, but does include smoking shelters at the after end of both Decks 8 and 9.

Technical Configuration

The new sisters are stern-loading only and to facilitate the smooth loading/unloading of the vast 4,500 lane metre garage, the *Aura Seaways* has three stern ramps, comprising a centre ramp serving Deck 3 (and the lower hold on Deck 1) and side ramps serving Decks 5 and 7 (and Deck 8). This contributes. The main propulsion plant consists of two sets of Wartsila 6 and 8-cylinder engines, generating up to 33,600 KW, an arrangement which provides substantial flexibility in terms of operating with the most optimum engine set-up and load in order to keep the fuel consumption lowest possible. Typical service speed is 18 kn. Eschewing the trend for LNG power, the sisters are nonetheless equipped with scrubbers. With a profile best described as bulky rather than elegant, a notable of the vessel's external appearance is that one of the twin funnels is located further forward than the other. This unusual characteristic is because the vessel has two separate engine rooms, in order to comply with 'Safe Return to Port' legislation requirements.

Initial customer reaction to the *Aura Seaways* has been highly favourable, with freight clients appreciating the loading capacity and ramp configuration that allows a smooth loading and discharging process as well as the dedicated driver area, Road Kings. From a passenger

Seven Seas Restaurant *(Richard Seville)*

Information Desk *(Richard Seville)*

viewpoint, the enhanced passenger facilities have received much positive feedback along with the raised on-board standards; during the author's voyage on board, the quality in the Mare Balticum à la carte restaurant was, in particular, exceptional and offered at very reasonable prices. The all-inclusive buffet option in the Seven Seas restaurant appeared the most popular option, but for passengers not wishing to partake of a full meal, however, a range of hot bar snacks was also available in the Navigator Bar.

Despite the shadow of the Ukraine crisis, the arrival of these two substantial new sisters represent a major milestone for DFDS Seaways and their Baltic network, significantly raising the bar in terms of both passenger comfort and on-board standards, as well as technical innovation. Only time will tell whether DFDS need to wait another 40 years for their next purposely designed passenger vessels, but in the meantime passengers and drivers heading for Lithuania will benefit from two highly impressive new ferries.

Richard Seville

Luna Seaways *(DFDS)*

Nils Holgersson – TT-Line's Seventh Generation Baltic Ferry

2022 not only marks TT-Line's 60th anniversary year, but also 30 years of service on the Rostock – Trelleborg line, the company's secondary route established in 1992. Founded in 1962 as "TT-Linie" (for Travemünde – Trelleborg), the German company has sailed through both calm and stormy seas over the course of 60 years to welcome in March this year a new NILS HOLGERSSON, the 7th ferry to proudly bear this name.

Among the many changes adopted by TT-Line over those 60 years is the fact that their ships are no longer assigned to a particular route. Also the new *Nils Holgersson* rotates between the Travemünde – Trelleborg, Rostock – Trelleborg and Swinoujscie – Trelleborg routes and between day and night sailings as well. Add to this the need for cost-effectiveness and versatility, the new TT-Line flagship has (necessarily) emerged as a highly flexible ferry adapted to a wide variety of requirements in terms of passenger and cargo mix, load factor and not least fuel availability.

We embark the ship on a sunny July forenoon in Trelleborg for a day sailing to Travemünde, TT-Line's core route when established in 1962 by the small *Nils Holgersson* (1). At 10:30 am, a mini-van collects the 7 or 8 foot passengers at the terminal building in Hamngatan and drives them to Trelleborg's new Eastern harbour where at berth no. 10 *Nils Holgersson* is busy loading bow-in, in true Baltic RoRo style.

Foot passengers are released on the vessel's upper cargo deck 5 to make their way via the lift (or stairs) to the ship's public rooms. What impresses at first glance is not only the fresh smell even of the cargo deck itself, but the latter's sheer size. The ship's cargo capacity is one of the main differences between the 7th and 6th generation TT-Line ferries. While the passenger and cabin configuration has remained largely the same (800 vs. 744 passengers), the new *Nils Holgersson* features cargo holds measuring 4,600 lane metres in length (300 trailers) compared to 2,400 lane metres (160 trailers) on her namesake predecessor (in February 2022 renamed *Akka*). Four cargo decks (1, 3, 5 and 7) on the newbuilding compare to three (1, 3 and 5) on the present *Akka*, so basically the public rooms begin on deck 9, with most amenities spread over the decks 10 and 11.

With us in port and also docked in the new harbour extension are TT-Line's 1995-built *Nils Dacke* (bound for Rostock) and the "ugly duckling" *Marco Polo* (bound for Klaipeda) as well as Unity Line's RoRo cargo ferry *Galileusz*, the latter berthed at TT-Line's old city berth no. 5 near the terminal building. After a safety announcement at 11.00 am, the *Nils Holgersson* does not lose time and departs for Travemünde at 11:05 am, ten minutes ahead of schedule.

On a sunny day like this, *Nils Holgersson* easily plays out one big advantage her designers have thought of. Unlike many other contemporary RoPax vessels (and even cruise ships), the new TT-Line ferry is blessed with ample open deck space. Despite the aft part of the vessel behind the funnel taken by the open weather deck, the sun deck "Havsilver" (deck 11) is both large and unobstructed and furthermore fitted with a flat wooden pyramid on which people can sit, stretch, relax, unfold blankets or take a nap. One could argue that this place could have benefitted from a more refined design approach (like on Stena Line's recently rebuilt *Stena Scandica* with her sun deck terrace and comfortable lounge chairs), but the adjacent bar serves the sun deck and pyramid perfectly. Furthermore, stairs lead from here to the upper sun deck (deck 12) where passengers can enjoy a perfect view over the ship's bow and to both sides.

With Sweden imposing no strict restrictions on pets travelling with their families, these two sun decks are also ideal for dogs in need of walking space. Of course there is a dedicated dog toilet in a more remote corner of the deck as well while TT-Line also offers dedicated pet-friendly cabins.

Going indoors from the sun deck, deck 11 serves as the ship's main passenger deck. Sailing year-round to Sweden, the *Nils Holgersson* is not only pet-friendly, but also family-friendly. This is strikingly visible in the "Little Pixie Playland" on deck 11, the ship's large children's playroom.

Nils Holgersson *(Kai Ortel)*

Nils Holgersson *(TT Line)*

Captain Akka's Restaurant (Deck 11 aft) *(Kai Ortel)*

Atrium and stairs (Deck 10) *(Kai Ortel)*

Uppsala Bar (Deck 11 forward) *(Kai Ortel)*

Lookout Café (Deck 11 forward) *(Kai Ortel)*

Looking aft over the upper freight deck *(Kai Ortel)*

The upper passenger deck area *(Kai Ortel)*

The latter not only functions to "drop" your kids for the duration of the voyage, but TT-Line crew members even do some pirate animation with the kids. The activity spreads over the whole duration of the eight hour sailing and also includes a rally of the ship as well as games being played in one the adjacent conference rooms (which for business purposes are named "Travemünde", "Rostock" and "Trelleborg"). Opposite the conference rooms on portside is "Nils' Lounge" where passengers with or without children can spend the crossing between meal times or deck walks. Some of the Nils' Lounge tables are designed with Chess and Ludo playing fields painted on the plate, so the lounge can also be regarded as an extension of the children's playroom. On the other hand, the sun deck bar nearby is designed so flexibly that it can serve customers on both sides – on the sun deck outdoors and in Nils' Lounge indoors.

On a different note, TT-Line has not forgotten the needs of the 21st century traveller and inserted USB and power sockets both under the tables and above the sofas. There are also large TV screens on the walls which display the ship's position and voyage data, somewhat euphemistically titled "Cruise Show". By the way, after routinely switching my mobile phone to flight mode after departure from Trelleborg, it took me four hours to discover that TT-Line offers free wifi onboard. Clearly, a bit of information regarding these and other details of the trip would have been helpful if provided in advance.

The front stairwells separate the children's play area and Nils' Lounge aft from the restaurant and lounges in the forward part of deck 11. These comprise of "Captain Akka's Restaurant" (Akka being the leader goose in Selma Lagerlöf's "Nils Holgersson" tale), the "Sunnerbo" shop (at Sunnerbo in the tale, little Nils helps find a treasure), a truckers' lounge and the two passenger lounges "Uppsala Bar" and "Lookout Café". The latter two are situated next to one another right in front of the deck and overlook the bow. In fact, it is these two rooms that hide behind the upper row of large panoramic windows above the bridge which make the new *Nils Holgersson* appear somewhat boxy externally, resembling the much-debated exterior style of the cruise ship *Norwegian Epic*. The Uppsala Bar even incorporates a little stage for some low-key onboard entertainment while the counter at the aisle serves as a cash desk for the shop, as a bar for the two lounges and as the onboard reception desk for all general inquiries from passengers and drivers. Another clever layout detail which allows for a minimal deployment of staff.

Internally, both the "Uppsala Bar" and "Lookout Café" are appointed quite nicely – the former fitted with furniture and carpets in green tones and the latter with bright blue chairs, orange lamps and wooden floors. The public lounges on deck 11 also benefit from sunlight coming through windows in the ceiling – the same circular glass inlets on the upper sun deck which are marked "Do not step". TT-Line had outsourced the design of the *Nils Holgersson* and her upcoming sister ship *Peter Pan* to two firms: While the Danish OSK Group (OSK ShipTech and Sten Friis Design) had been in charge of the concept, tender, contract and basic technical design, the German enterprise Ocean Architects of Waren-Müritz (*Hanseatic Nature* and *Hanseatic Inspiration*) has been responsible for the final interior (re)design of the two vessels.

In fact, not only the public rooms onboard are spoilt with sunlight, but also the forward stairwell which is fitted with panoramic windows at both sides of the ship. Large signposts help passengers find their way onboard, and the whole area is laid out very spaciously. The stairs lead to the second passenger deck below (deck 10) where the public rooms are restricted to the forward part of the ship. (The latter part, just like on deck 9, is taken up by passenger cabins.) The selection of public rooms here is similar to deck 10 – a lounge ("Smygehuk Bar"), a restaurant ("Sailaway Restaurant") and, in addition to those, a room with Pullman chairs (strangely named "Sunrise") and the drivers' diner.

The wall of the corridor leading to the lounge and restaurant is decorated with a large illustrated timeline depicting the 60 years history of TT-Line and its ships. This table could be an interesting eye catcher for passengers to spend a few spare minutes during the crossing. But the problem is that on my sailing (and probably on many others to follow) the public rooms on deck 10 were sealed off after lunchtime and remained closed until the ship's arrival in Travemünde in the evening. So basically, the facilities on deck 11 were all that was left for the passengers to spend the greater part of the trip in. This may be regarded as another clever design feature to adapt the ship to the actual passenger number travelling on board, but from a passenger point of view, it would be nicer of course to have a broader variety of public rooms to chose between. On sailings when the Uppsala Bar and Lookout Café are fully occupied quickly and the weather less friendly than today, all that will remain to await the ship's arrival will be Nils' Lounge with the prospect of spending one's time amidst dozens of crying and screaming children simultaneously for hours. Not really a notion to look forward to.

On the other hand it can be argued if the passenger in the Uppsala Bar were better off when at 4:30.pm that day, a solitary troubadour arrived in order to sing German shanties to music played from his music machine. Those songs were targeted to an older clientele even when they were released 50 years ago, so it can be questioned if this was the perfect entertainment on a 21st century ferry. Half of the guests left after the first song, and the fact that those were performed in front of a giant screen where a news channel broadcast the latest horrible scenes from the Ukraine war did not make things better. Perhaps someone at TT-Line should have a second thought regarding the onboard entertainment concept?

The same can be said for the company's determined emphasis on their new vessel being a "Green Ship" (as marked so in giant letters on the hull). Technically, the *Nils Holgersson* is fitted with dual fuel engines, being able to run on ultralow-sulphur marine diesel oil (ULSD) or LNG. However, TT-Line on the occasion of the introduction of the vessel in service remarked that for the time being, LNG was too expensive to be used permanently. After all, neither Travemünde, Rostock (*Nils Holgersson*'s home port) nor Trelleborg do possess LNG terminals, so even if used, the gas would have to be shipped to the ports via lorries or tanker ships which is not feasible (save ecologically sensible) either. So the lettering on the hull may say the ship was "LNG-powered", but in reality, it isn't (yet).

Nevertheless, TT-Line with the new *Nils Holgersson* has conceived a beautiful RoPax ferry which will serve her customers well in the years to come. The public rooms of the vessel have been given interesting Swedish names derived from Selma Lagerlöf's "Nils Holgersson" saga, and her layout is clear and efficient. Passengers willing to spend the crossing the "classic" way rather than just staring on his or her cell phone display for hours will be delighted by the ample outdoor deck space the vessel has to offer and by the vast amount of natural light floating her public rooms. *Nils Holgersson* will be followed by her sister ship *Peter Pan* in October which at the time of writing is nearing completion at China Merchants Jingling Shipyard.

Kai Ortel

NILS HOLGERSSON

IMO:	9865685
Class:	DNV
Shipyard:	China Merchants Jingling Shipyard, Nanjing/Jiangsu
Length oa:	229.40 m
Beam:	31 m
Draft:	6.70 m
GT:	56,138t
Main Engines:	2 MAN 6L51/60DF and 2 MAN 8L51/60DF dual fuel engines
Output:	29,400 kW
Service Speed:	22 knots
Passengers:	800
Berths:	644
Cabins:	239
Crew:	66
Freight Capacity:	4,600 lane metres (or 300 trailers)

Review 2021/22 - UK & Ireland

The following is a review of passenger and freight ferry activities during 2021 and the first half of 2022. Some events occurring in the first half of 2021 will have also been mentioned in 'Ferries 2021..

2021 and 2022 continued to be dominated by Covid 19 and Brexit. The gradual recovery of tourist traffic was matched by a restoration of services, in some cases not fully and direct freight services between the Republic of Ireland and other EU countries continued to develop.

EAST COAST & THAMES

P&O Ferries' sacking of its entire UK based staff in March 2022 caused the Hull - Rotterdam service to be suspended for 9 days before a single ship operation could be started using the Netherlands based *Pride of Rotterdam*, whose crew were unaffected. A full service, following the eventual granting by the MCA of a licence to operate the *Pride of Hull* with the new crew, after a four week gap. Freight services, with vessels time chartered from Bore Shipowners of Finland were unaffected.

In January 2022 Stena Line moved their Rotterdam - Killingholme service to the inner docks at Immingham. The two Polish owned vessels *POL Maris* and *POL Stella* were replaced by the smaller ex DFDS vessels *Hafnia Sea* and *Fionia Sea*. However it was later announced that Associated British Ports were to build a new river berth in conjunction with Stena Line which will enable larger ships to be used.

Also in January, perhaps designed to stop a new operator moving in to use the berth at Killingholme vacated by Stena Line, DFDS and CLdN launched an additional joint service between Killingholme and Rotterdam calling at both the DFDS facility at Vlaardingen and the CLdN berths at Rozenburg. Although expected to be operated by a vessel from each company, the service was, from the start, operated by two CLdN Kawasaki class vessels and, in March, it

Stena Hollandica and Stena Transporter *(Rob de Visser)*

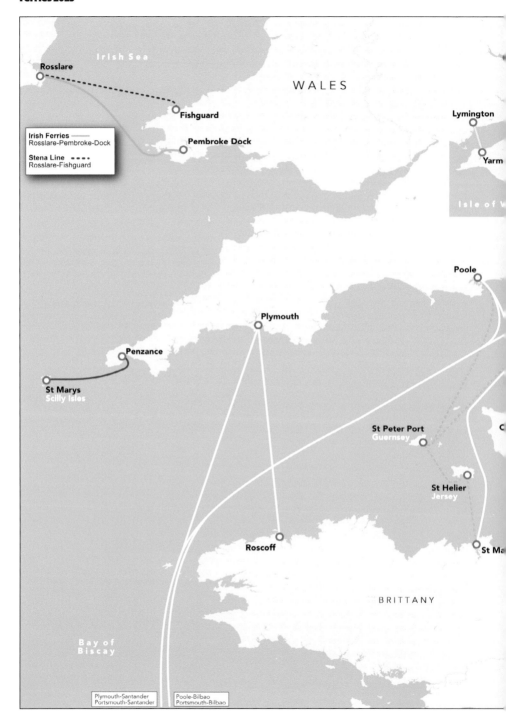

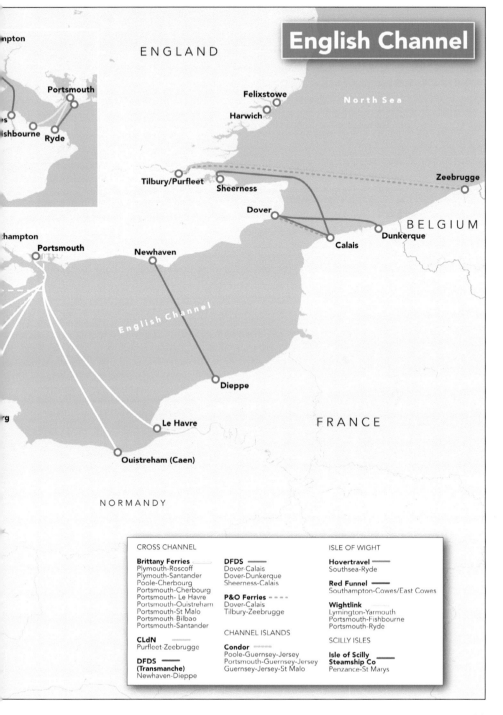

English Channel

ENGLAND

North Sea

Portsmouth
Ryde
shbourne
npton

Felixstowe
Harwich

Tilbury/Purfleet
Sheerness

Zeebrugge

Dover

BELGIUM

Calais
Dunkerque

hampton
Portsmouth
Newhaven

English Channel

Dieppe

Le Havre

FRANCE

Ouistreham (Caen)

rg

NORMANDY

CROSS CHANNEL

Brittany Ferries
Plymouth-Roscoff
Plymouth-Santander
Poole-Cherbourg
Portsmouth- Le Havre
Portsmouth-Cherbourg
Portsmouth-Ouistreham
Portsmouth-St Malo
Portsmouth Bilbao
Portsmouth-Santander

CLdN
Purfleet-Zeebrugge

DFDS
(Transmanche)
Newhaven-Dieppe

DFDS
Dover-Calais
Dover-Dunkerque
Sheerness-Calais

P&O Ferries
Dover-Calais
Tilbury-Zeebrugge

CHANNEL ISLANDS

Condor
Poole-Guernsey-Jersey
Portsmouth-Guernsey-Jersey
Guernsey-Jersey-St Malo

ISLE OF WIGHT

Hovertravel
Southsea-Ryde

Red Funnel
Southampton-Cowes/East Cowes

Wightlink
Lymington-Yarmouth
Portsmouth-Fishbourne
Portsmouth-Ryde

SCILLY ISLES

Isle of Scilly
Steamship Co
Penzance-St Marys

was announced that the service would become a solely CLdN operation and Vlaardingen would no longer be served. In April 2020 DFDS purchased the *Meleq* from CLdN and renamed her the *Acacia Seaways* and, at the same time, CLdN purchased the *Gothia Seaways* from DFDS and renamed her the *Maxine*. Both ships were initially chartered back and were not delivered to their new owners until the end of the year. DFDS also chartered the Maxine's sister vessel, *Belgia Seaways* to CLdN who used her mainly on services to Ireland. On her return she was moved to the Baltic.

Although continuing to use the word 'Seaways' in their ships' names, DFDS dropped this branding and simply became DFDS, the logo displayed on both the side of ships and funnels. DFDS stands for 'Det Forenede Dampskibs-Selskab' (The United Steamship Company) something that few users will probably know and even fewer non-Danes would be able to pronounce properly!

During 2021 and 2022 CLdN took delivery of the *Faustine* and *Serphine* from the Hyundai Mipo Shipyard in South Korea. Similar to the earlier *Laureline* class they are designed to run on both conventional diesel fuel and liquid Natural gas (LNG). Two new ships were ordered from the same shipyard for delivery in 2024. These vessels will be similar to the 2017 built *Celine* and *Delphine* but with hybrid engines able to run on battery electricity as well as carbon based fuels.

During 2021 Flensburg built *Alf Pollak* and *Maria Grazia Onorato* were sub-chartered from Tirrenia of Italy. In November 2021, the *Valentine* was sold to Rederi AB Gotland of Sweden and immediately chartered to KiwiRail of New Zealand to operate between Wellington and Picton. She was the first of the 20 year old Kawasakis to go and others are likely to follow in the coming years.

In June 2021 Tirrenia of Italy decided not to exercise the purchase option on the *Massimo Mura* which they had had on charter from an associated company of CLdN since 2016. She returned to the fleet as the *Caden 3*, having been transferred to a Swiss based associated company Cadena Shipping. She was found to be in poor condition and spent a lot of time out of service before returning to service. In January she was chartered to Wallenius SOL and returned in August.

In May 2021 Grimaldi Lines of Italy started a twice weekly ro-ro service between Antwerpen and Cork, in competition with CLdN's twice weekly Zeebrugge route. The vessel used was the 2021 built *Eurocargo Bari*. It later become One sailing per week serving Zeebrugge and Antwerpen and the other only serving Zeebrugge. In July 2022 associated company Finnlines launched a twice weekly Zeebrugge - Rosslare service and the Grimaldi route reverted to its original format..

Operators of service from the Baltic to North Western Europe - Finnlines and Wallenius SOL - both had large environmentally friendly freighters under construction in China during 2021 and the first half of 2022. The first of these - the *Finneco I* arrived at Zeebrugge in mid-June and the second, the *Botnia Enabler* to Wallenius SOL at the end of the month. The rest, the *Finneco II*, the *Finneco III* and the *Baltic Enabler* followed shortly after having been built simultaneously. None of these vessels are due to serve UK ports for the time being.

In order to enhance their services Wallenius SOL chartered the former DFDS vessels *Fionia Sea* and *Jutlandia Sea* from January 2021. The one year charter could not be extended as a charter to Stena Line from the start of 2022 had been agreed. So instead a charter of CdN's *Cadena 3* and *Catherine* was arranged, ending when the new ships arrived in summer 2021.

Brand new cruise ferry services in the North Sea are rare these days but in April 2022 Holland -Norway Lines began operating between Eemshaven and Kristiansand April 2022. The18hour service operates three times a week. This ship used is the chartered *Romantika*, first of a large batch of cruise ferries built for Tallink in the 2000s. The service is aimed at passengers rather than freight, deigned to tap into Dutch and German tourists' love of the Norwegian mountains and fjords.

In January 2021 Transport for London took over the operation of the historic Woolwich ferry from the contractor Briggs Marine.

North Sea

NORWAY

Oslo

Fredrikstad

Brevik

Halden

Kristiansand

SWEDEN

Göteborg

Hirtshals

DENMARK

Esbjerg

Torshavn-Hirtshals

CLdN
Killingholme-Rotterdam (Rozenburg), Zeebrugge
Purfleet-Rotterdam (Rozenburg), Zeebrugge
Zeebrugge-Esbjerg, Göteborg

DFDS
Felixstowe-Vlaardingen
Göteborg-Brevik, Gent, Zeebrugge
Immingham-Brevik, Cuxhaven, Esbjerg, Fredrikstad,
       Göteborg, Halden, Hamburg, Oslo,
       Vlaardingen, Zeebrugge
Newcastle-IJmuiden
Zeebrugge-Fredrikstad, Göteborg

Holland-Norway Line
Eemshaven-Kristiansand

P&O Ferries - - - - -
Hull-Rotterdam (Europoort)
Middlesbrough-Rotterdam (Europoort), Zeebrugge
Tilbury-Zeebrugge

Smyril Line
Torshavn-Hirtshals

Stena Line ▪ ▪ ▪ ▪ ▪
Harwich-Hoek van Holland, Rotterdam (Europoort)
Immingham-Rotterdam (Europoort)
Killingholme-Hoek van Holland

Newcastle

Middlesbrough

Hull

Killingholme
Immingham

Cuxhaven

Hamburg

Eemshaven

IJmuiden

NETHERLANDS

Rotterdam (Europoort/Rozenburg), Vlaardingen

Hoek van Holland

Felixstowe

Harwich

Tilbury

Purfleet

Zeebrugge

Gent

GERMANY

BELGIUM

FRANCE

Humbria Seaways *(Peter Therkildsen)*

Pol Stella *(Rob de Visser)*

Thames Clippers did not acquire any new vessels in 2021 but did acquire a new sponsor in the form of the 'app hailing' taxi operator Uber, becoming 'Uber Boats by Thames Clippers'. The decline in tourism and the 'work at home' policy seriously affected traffic and services were cut back but expansion resumed in 2022 including serving the new Barking Riverside development on the north bank of the Thames.

EASTERN CHANNEL

Ramsgate continued to be an 'ex-ferry port' with visits from car carriers conveying import cars having dried up and part of the marshalling area being used as a temporary home for travellers.

During 2021 P&O gradually restored services following substantial cuts in 2020 due to Covid and some loss of freight traffic due to Brexit. However, it was not the high class service as before. The excellent waiter service 'Brasseries' did not reopen and the 'International Food Court' cafeterias were re-equipped for self service 'grab and go' microwaved meals in cardboard boxes. By early 2022 even that had closed and hot meals were only available in Club Class. The bombshell came in March when the three Dover ferries then in service (another was in dry dock and a fifth laid up) were moved to the cruise berths on the Western Docks and all the crew-officers and ratings, were advised by a recorded video that they were being made redundant forthwith and would be replaced by cheaper agency crews. Security staff then boarded the ferries and escorted everyone off, Anyone wanting to to return to their cabins to retrieve their belongings had to escorted and many did not bother.

The government huffed and puffed but in the end found there was very little they could do and most staff accepted the redundancy terms. No sanctions were applied to the company for breaking the law by not consulting with the trades unions. All but one of the staff accepted the redundancy which included additional compensation equal to that which a tribunal would have awarded for unfair dismissal. However the 'few days' suspension of services announced to passengers and freight operators proved rather optimistic as the ships continually failed inspection by the Maritime and Coastguard Agency under their new crews. Eventually the *Pride of Kent* re-entered traffic in early May, initially freight only, but later for passengers. The other two vessels - *Pride of Canterbury* and *Spirit of Britain* - re-entered service over the ensuing weeks. The *Spirit of France* remained at the shipyard at Rotterdam until July.

The effect of the sudden withdrawal of the P&O fleet (plus some DFDS ships being in dry dock and only two Irish Ferries vessels operating) led to a massive backlog of (mainly freight) traffic and the introduction of Operation Brock (holding freight traffic on the M20 and Dover TAP (holding traffic on the A20 outside Dover). With P&O ships returning to traffic and a third Irish Ferries ship entering service the problems gradually abated and Operation Brock was withdrawn in June but had to be restored again in July (start of the school holidays) when enhanced French passport checks and a lack of French border police led to massive queues of this time passenger traffic for several days.

DFDS's new Stena RoRo 'E-Flexer' *Côte d'Opale* was delivered to the company in May 2021 and arrived at Calais from China in July, entering service in August and replacing the *Calais Seaways*. In July 2021 DFDS launched a ro-ro service between Calais and Sheerness using the *Maxine*, chartered from CLdN. The idea was to divert unaccompanied traffic from Dover where new Brexit inspired customs controls could have resulted in a backlog of such traffic. At the start of 2022 she service was suspended and the *Maxine* was re-delivered to CLdN. However it resumed in March 2022 using the *Botnia Seaways*.

In May 2021 P&O Ferries and DFDS announced an arrangement by which they would sell capacity on each other's ferries - not a joint service as such but purchasing capacity on a day to day basis. This briefly ceased in 2022 following a decision by the Monopolies and Mergers Commission to investigate whether it was anti-competitive, but was later restored.

A surprising new arrival at the end of June 2021 was Irish Ferries, who deployed their *Isle of Inishmore* on the Calais route with the aim of providing a through facility for truckers using the 'land bridge' from Holyhead and Pembroke Dock to Dover. Rather than enhancing their direct serves from Ireland to France to a major degree, they concluded that the faster route via GB would still be attractive if it could be made as seamless as possible. With only one ship and therefore low frequency traffic was slow to build up but this increased following the introduction of a second ship - The Isle of Innisfree, formerly Calais Seaways of DFDS, which entered service in December 2021 - and a third - the Isle of Inisheer which entered service in March 2022. Then came the P&O hiatus which meant ships sailing full all the time. Many users stayed with Irish Ferries even when P&O services gradually resumed.

Following the opening of the new Commercial Port at the Western Docks, the quay between ferry berths 1 and 2 which handled reefer traffic from South America was, during 2020 and 2021, cleared of cranes and transit sheds to make more space for trucks. The passenger services facilities adjacent to berth 2 were also demolished, leaving only the more recent facilities between berths 8 and 9 - a long way to walk! Also in July 2021, berth 1, a basic ro-ro berth suitable for freighters, was removed.

The berths at Calais which have been used by ferries for the last 40 years or so are on reclaimed land in an outer harbour. Over 2020 and 2021, the port constructed an 'outer-outer' harbour, initially with two berths. Trials were conducted during spring 2021 and in spring 2022 the new berths came into full use.

WESTERN CHANNEL AND SOLENT

In 2016 Brittany Ferries ordered a new vessel from FSG in Flensburg for delivery in 2019. However the Honfleur, as she was to be called, was seriously delayed and in 2020 all work stopped. In June 2020, it was announced that the order had been cancelled. However, the building of three 'E-Flexer' vessels chartered from Stena RoRo, continued apace. The first of these vessels, the Galicia, arrived in France in October 2021 and entered service in December. The second, theSalamanca, entered service in March 2022, The third, the Santoña, will enter service in March 2023.

In August 2021 Brittany Ferries announced the order of two more E-Flexers to be chartered from Stena RoRo for the Portsmouth - St Malo and Portsmouth - Ouistreham routes. To be delivered in 2024 and 2025, the new ships will be shortened versions of the original design at 194 metres long. It was later announced that the first of these will be called the Saint Malo and will be deployed on the St Malo route. The much loved Bretagne will probably be sold.

The Étretat concluded her charter at the end of March 2021 and was chartered to Stena Line for Baltic service, being renamed the Stena Livia. In February 2022 Cap Finistère was sold to GNV of Italy.

In 2021, Brittany Ferries' Normandie Express was transferred to the Condor fleet and renamed the Condor Voyager. She replaced the Condor Rapide which was sold.

In spring 2022 Wightlink introduced a new timetable on the Portsmouth - Fishbourne route. Instead of a basic hourly service with extra sailings at the peaks, an all day 40 minute frequency came into operation meaning that the 33 year old St. Faith - the last British Rail Sealink designed vessel (albeit built under Sea Containers ownership) still operating in UK waters - had a full daytime schedule - although the two newer units usually took over in the evening when the service was reduced. An hourly service was due to resume in October. Unlike the other two vessels she cannot use the upper deck loading facilities at both ports. The three 'Wight Class' vessels remained allocated to the Lymington - Yarmouth route, although a maximum of two vessels - and sometimes only one - were in use at any one time.

In 2021 the Portsmouth - Gosport passenger service operated at an all-day 15 minute frequency with a single ship. There was no rush hour doubling to the pre-Covid two ship 7½ minute pattern. This continued into 2022.

IRISH SEA

In January 2021 the third Stena Line E-Flexer - the Stena Embla arrived from China. Although initially used between Dublin Cherbourg, she then moved to her regular route - Birkenhead - Belfast. This arrival - and that of the Stena Edda the year before - enabled the Stena Mersey and Stena Lagan to depart for Turkey for lengthening and ultimate deployment in the Baltic.

Spirit of Britain *(Andrew Wood)*

Isle of Inisheer *(George Holland)*

Normandie (Darren Holdaway)

Stena Estrid (Miles Cowsill)

The ending of the UK's membership of the European Union on 1 January 2020 did not cause any problems as there was a one year transition period. However from January 2021 a multitude of documentation was required by Irish truckers transiting the UK. Shipping companies responded in different ways. Stena Line supplemented their passenger vessel, the *Stena Horizon*, on Rosslare - Cherbourg, with the freighter *Stena Foreteller* giving a daily service (although only 12 drivers could be accommodated on the latter vessel). The *Stena Estrid* started undertaking a weekend trip from Dublin to Cherbourg and then, in February swapped roles with the *Stena Horizon*, the older vessel replacing her on Holyhead - Dublin. In May the two vessels returned to their normal routes.

Irish Ferries - whose genesis goes back to Irish Continental Line which established direct Ireland - France services in 1972 - took a more cautious approach in terms of direct services. Although operating the three times a week Dublin - Cherbourg service with the *W B Yeats*, they believed that the 'land bridge' would continue as the preferred choice for many freight operators if made simple enough and launched their own Dover - Calais service in June 2021 with the *Isle of Inishmore*. To replace her on Rosslare - Pembroke Docks the *Blue Star 1* was chartered from Blue Star Ferries of Greece.

DFDS took more drastic measures with the launch of a three ship direct service from Rosslare to Dunkerque. The service started with their *Optima Seaways* and *Kerry* plus the *Visby* chartered from Destination Gotland. After three weeks, the *Optima Seaways* was replaced by the *Visby's* sister vessel, *Drotten*. In March, the *Drotten* was needed back on the Baltic and the *Pelagos* (formerly DFDS's *Liverpool Seaways*) was chartered from La Méridionale of France. In late May, the *Pelagos* was needed by her owners and the service was reduced to two ships but, using her higher speed, the *Visby* undertook three return sailings per week. In April, the freighter *Ark Dania* was moved to the route to convey unaccompanied traffic but was withdrawn in May. Over the ensuing months the service settled down to a mainly two ship, five sailings per week service with the *Visby* - renamed the *Visborg* in February 2022 - complemented by a ship from the company's Baltic fleet. In May 2022 the route briefly became

Ben-my-Chree *(Darren Holdaway)*

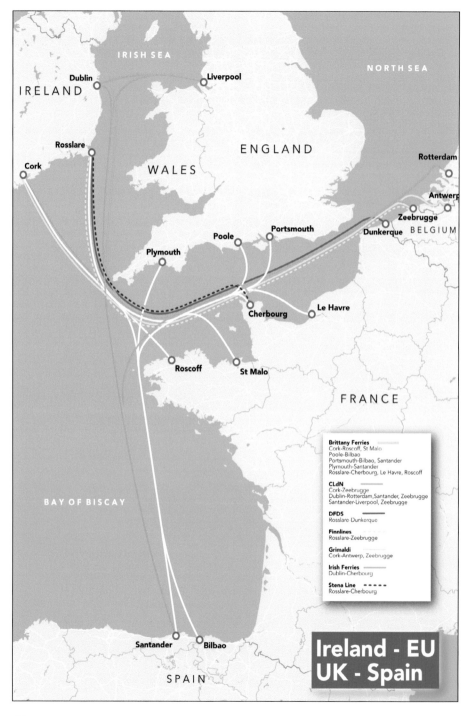

Brittany Ferries
Cork-Roscoff, St Malo
Poole-Bilbao
Portsmouth-Bilbao, Santander
Plymouth-Santander
Rosslare-Cherbourg, Le Havre, Roscoff

CLdN
Cork-Zeebrugge
Dublin-Rotterdam, Santander, Zeebrugge
Santander-Liverpool, Zeebrugge

DFDS
Rosslare-Dunkerque

Finnlines
Rosslare-Zeebrugge

Grimaldi
Cork-Antwerp, Zeebrugge

Irish Ferries
Dublin-Cherbourg

Stena Line
Rosslare-Cherbourg

Ireland - EU
UK - Spain

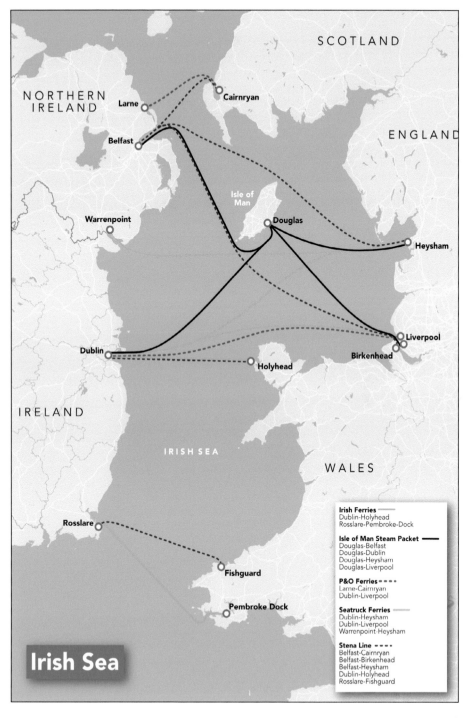

SCOTLAND

NORTHERN
IRELAND

Larne

Cairnryan

Belfast

ENGLAND

Warrenpoint

Isle of
Man

Douglas

Heysham

Liverpool

Birkenhead

Dublin

Holyhead

IRELAND

IRISH SEA

WALES

Rosslare

Fishguard

Pembroke Dock

Irish Sea

Irish Ferries ——
Dublin-Holyhead
Rosslare-Pembroke-Dock

Isle of Man Steam Packet ——
Douglas-Belfast
Douglas-Dublin
Douglas-Heysham
Douglas-Liverpool

P&O Ferries ━ ━ ━
Larne-Cairnryan
Dublin-Liverpool

Seatruck Ferries ——
Dublin-Heysham
Dublin-Liverpool
Warrenpoint-Heysham

Stena Line ━ ━ ━
Belfast-Cairnryan
Belfast-Birkenhead
Belfast-Heysham
Dublin-Holyhead
Rosslare-Fishguard

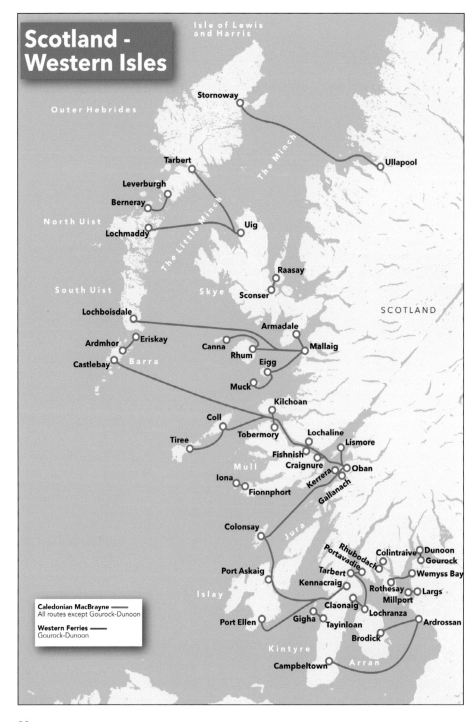

Scotland - Western Isles

Isle of Lewis and Harris

Outer Hebrides

The Minch

Stornoway

Ullapool

Tarbert

Leverburgh

Berneray

The Little Minch

North Uist

Uig

Lochmaddy

Raasay

South Uist

Skye

Sconser

SCOTLAND

Lochboisdale

Armadale

Ardmhor · Eriskay

Canna

Mallaig

Castlebay

Barra

Rhum

Eigg

Muck

Kilchoan

Coll

Lochaline

Tiree

Tobermory

Lismore

Fishnish

Mull

Craignure

Oban

Iona

Kerrera

Fionnphort

Gallanach

Colonsay

Jura

Rhubodach

Colintraive

Dunoon

Portavadie

Gourock

Port Askaig

Tarbert

Wemyss Bay

Kennacraig

Rothesay

Largs

Islay

Millport

Claonaig

Lochranza

Port Ellen

Gigha

Tayinloan

Ardrossan

Brodick

Kintyre

Arran

Campbeltown

Caledonian MacBrayne ——
All routes except Gourock-Dunoon

Western Ferries ——
Gourock-Dunoon

Isle of Lewis and Isle of Mull *(John Hendy)*

three vessel service again with the *Optima Seaways* but the vessel returned to Baltic after only a month. A trial passenger service started in August 2022 but only on the DFDS owned *Regina Seaways*.

In January 2021 Brittany Ferries established a single weekly sailing between Rosslare and Cherbourg, interworked with a twice weekly Rosslare - Bilbao sailing. Operated initially by the *Cap Finistere*, the following week the *Connemara* took over. In February, the company introduced their St Malo and Roscoff to Rosslare service, operated by the *Armorique* two months earlier than initially planned.

CLdN continued their involvement with The Irish Republic. In April 2021 the Rotterdam - Dublin container vessel *Arx* was sold to Finnish owners and delivered in May. She was replaced by an additional ro-ro sailing from the Dutch port. An additional weekly sailing was also introduced from Zeebrugge.

P&O's *Norbank*, which operates between Liverpool and Dublin, crewed by Dutch officers and Filipino crew was only briefly affected by the mass redundancies in March 2022 but the previously UK crewed *Norbay* took rather longer to resume service with its new crew. The chartered *Clipper Pennant* and *Stena Forecaster* continued to operate as normal. However, the charter of the *Stena Forecaster* was ended in May 2022.

The Isle of Man Steam Packet Company was hard hit by the Covid-19 pandemic in 2020 and 2021. Being a holiday island, tourist traffic collapsed and the Manx TT motorcycle races, which bring many fans to the island from the UK and Ireland, were cancelled. Covdi restrictions on people entering were also very strict. However, the lifeline service by the *Ben My Chree* from Heysham continued, with the crew taking special precautions to avoid bringing the virus to the island. A more normal service started in 2022, with the TT races taking place over Man and June. Meanwhile work continued in South Korea on the new *Manxman* which will replace the *Ben My Chree* in 2023.

SCOTLAND

As in Dover, P&O's Cairnryan - Larne service, was interrupted on 17 March when all staff were made redundant and like Dover it took several weeks to get MCA approval to operate the *European Causeway* and *European Highlander*. Unlike Dover-Calais it was necessary to pay the new crews, whatever their nationality, the UK minimum wage as it is a domestic service. To compensate for the lack of capacity Stena Line brought their spare vessel, the *Stena Nordica* onto their own Cairnryan - Belfast route for five weeks

Caledonian MacBrayne had another difficult summer, trying to cope with increasing traffic, an aging fleet and continuing delays in the two ships being built by Ferguson's at Port Glasgow. The introduction of Road Equivalent Tariff (RET) in 2017 and the increasing popularity of the Scottish Islands for tourists created a situation where island residents could not take their vehicles - cars and trucks - onto the mainland. The higher demand for 'staycation' holidays during 2021 caused by difficulties in foreign travel due to Covid-19 added to these problems.

After her launch in late 2017 very little progress was made on the *Glen Sannox*, as the builders and the owners, Caledonian Maritime Assets argued about the impact of changes made to the design since the contract was awarded. The second hull still remains un-launched and, whilst it is now hoped that the *Glen Sannox* might be delivered in 2023, there is no certainty about this. During 2022 Caledonia Maritime Assets placed an order for two 5861t ferries for the Islay services. To be delivered in 2024 and 3025, they are to be built at the Cemre Shipyard in Turkey.

Caledonian Maritime Assets have been under pressure for several years to buy second hand ferries suitable for updating the fleet - particularly from Norway where a combination of new bridges and tunnels and a drive for electric ferries had lead to a number of modern diesel powered ferries becoming available. A suitable vessel for he Oban - Craignure (Mull) service was at last found in the form of the 2015 built *Utne* of Norled, which was purchased in November 2021. After a major refit at Rosyth she entered service as the *Loch Frisa* in June 2022. This enabled the *Coruisk* to return the Mallaig - Armadale route (which she was built for) in the summer, replacing the combination of 'Loch class' ferries and a larger vessel operating between trips to the outer isles (which often got cancelled due to late running). The *Loch Fyne* continues to share the service.

Argyll and Bute Council's new Lismore ferry, the *Lady of Lismore* was delivered by Mainstay Marine Solutions, Pembroke Dock in January 2022 but they had to wait several weeks for a window in the weather to ensure a safe journey from Wales to Scotland. She eventually entered service in May. The previous vessel, *The Lismore*, was then sold to Highland Ferries for use on the Fort William - Camusnagaul service.

In April 2020 Orkney Ferries acquired the small Norwegian passenger ferry, the *Nordic Sea* to replace the 1973 built *Golden Mariana* on the Westray - Papa Westray route. The latter vessel remains in the fleet as a reserve, since no other units are suitable substitutes.

IRELAND

In 2021 Arranmore Island Ferry Services had their former CalMac 'Island Class' ferry, the *Rhum* lengthened by thee metres to increase capacity. Their second vessel, the *Coll* was similarly lengthened in spring 2022. The company competes head-on with rival operator Arranmore Fast Ferries, trading as 'The Arranmore Ferry'. Both operators operate two 'Island Class' vessels. In July 2022 the latter company announced the building of a new vessel for the route.

Nick Widdows

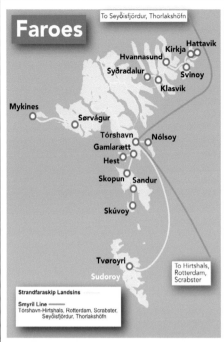

Faroes

To Seyðisfjördur, Thorlakshöfn

Hattavik
Kirkja
Hvannasund
Svinoy
Syðradalur
Klasvik
Mykines
Sørvágur
Tórshavn
Nólsoy
Gamlarætt
Hest
Skopun
Sandur
Skúvoy
Tvøroyri
Sudoroy

To Hirtshals,
Rotterdam,
Scrabster

Strandfaraskip Landsins

Smyril Line
Tórshavn-Hirtshals, Rotterdam, Scrabster,
Seyðisfjördur, Thorlakshöfn

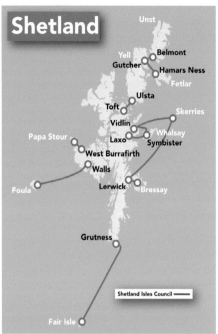

Shetland

Unst
Belmont
Yell
Gutcher
Hamars Ness
Fetlar
Ulsta
Toft
Skerries
Vidlin
Papa Stour
Whalsay
Laxo
Symbister
West Burrafirth
Walls
Foula
Lerwick
Bressay
Grutness

Shetland Isles Council

Fair Isle

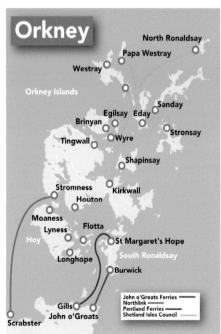

Orkney

North Ronaldsay
Papa Westray
Westray
Orkney Islands
Sanday
Egilsay Eday
Brinyan
Stronsay
Tingwall
Wyre
Shapinsay
Stromness
Kirkwall
Houton
Moaness
Lyness
Flotta
Hoy
St Margaret's Hope
Longhope
South Ronaldsay
Burwick
Gills
Scrabster
John o'Groats

John o'Groats Ferries
Northlink
Pentland Ferries
Shetland Isles Council

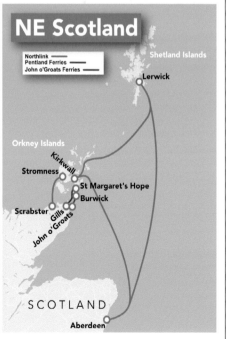

NE Scotland

Northlink
Pentland Ferries
John o'Groats Ferries

Shetland Islands

Lerwick

Orkney Islands
Kirkwall
Stromness
St Margaret's Hope
Scrabster
Burwick
Gills
John o'Groats

SCOTLAND

Aberdeen

A Guide to using this book

Sections Listing is in seven sections. *Section 1* - Services from Great Britain and Ireland to the Continent and between Great Britain and Ireland (including services to/from the Isle of Man and Channel Islands), *Section 2* - Domestic services within Great Britain and Ireland, *Section 3* - Freight-only services from Great Britain and Ireland and domestic routes, *Section 4* - GB & Ireland - RO-RO operators conveying private traffic, *Section 5* - GB & Ireland - Chain, Cable Etc Ferries, Section 6 - Minor vehicle ferries in Great Britain and Ireland (chain and cable ferries etc), *Section 7* - Major passenger-only operators, *Section 8* - Major car ferry operators in Northern Europe, Section 9 - Companies not operating regular services possessing vehicle ferries which may be chartered or sold to other operators.

Order The company order within each section is alphabetical. Note that the definite article and words meaning 'company' or 'shipping company' (eg 'AG', 'Reederei') do not count. However, where this is part of a ship's name it does count. Sorting is by normal English convention eg 'Å' is treated the same as 'A' and comes at the start, not as a separate character which comes at the end of the alphabet as is the Scandinavian convention. Where ships are numbered, order is by number whether the number is expressed in Arabic or Latin digits.

Listing of Ships When a ship owned by a company listed in this book is on charter to another company listed, then she is shown under the company which operates her. When a ship owned by a company listed in this book is on charter to another company not listed, then she is shown under the company which owns her.

IMO Number All ships of 100t or greater (except vessels solely engaged in fishing, ships without mechanical means of propulsion (eg chain ferries), pleasure yachts, ships engaged on special service (eg lightships), hopper barges, hydrofoils, air cushion vehicles, floating docks and structures classified in a similar manner, warships and troopships, wooden ships) are required to be registered by the International Maritime Organisation (IMO), an agency of the United Nations. The seven digit number (the final digit is a check digit) is retained by the ship throughout her life, however much the vessel is rebuilt. This number is now required to be displayed on the ship externally and on top so that it can be read from the air. The scheme is administered by Lloyd's Register-Fairplay, who maintain a database of all ships in excess of 100t (with some exceptions), not just those classified through them. Some vessels which do not qualify for an IMO number have a Lloyd's number in the same series.

Company Information This section gives general information regarding the status of the company. That is, nationality, whether it is public or private sector and whether it is part of a larger group.

Management The Managing Director and Marketing Director or Manager of each company are listed. Where these posts do not exist, other equivalent people are listed. Where only initials are given, that person is, as far as is known, male.

Address This is the address of the company's administrative headquarters. In the case of some international companies, British and overseas addresses are given.

Telephone and Fax Numbers are expressed as follows: + [*number*] (this is the international dialling code which is dialled in combination with the number dialled for international calls (00 in the UK, Ireland and most other European countries); it is not used for calling within the country), ([*number*]) (this is the number which precedes area codes when making long-distance domestic calls - it is not dialled when calling from another country or making local calls (not all countries have this)), [*number*] (this is the rest of the number including, where appropriate, the area dialling code). UK '08' numbers are sometimes not available from overseas and the full number must be dialled in all circumstances.

Internet Email addresses and **Website** URLs are given where these are available; the language(s) used is shown. The language listed first is that which appears on the home page when accessed from a UK based computer; the others follow in alphabetical order. In a few cases Email facility is only available through the Website. To avoid confusion, there is no other punctuation on the Internet line.

Routes operated After each route there are, in brackets, details of **1** normal journey time, **2** regular vessel(s) used on the route (number as in list of vessels) and **3** frequencies (where a number per day is given, this relates to return sailings). In the case of freight-only sailings which operate to a regular schedule, departure times are given where they have been supplied. Please note that times are subject to quite frequent change and cancellation.

Winter and Summer In this book, Winter generally means the period between October and Easter while Summer means Easter to October. The peak Summer period is generally June, July and August. In Scandinavia, the Summer peak ends in mid-August whilst in the UK it starts rather later and generally stretches into the first or second week of September. Dates vary according to operator.

Terms The following words mean *'shipping company'* in various languages: Redereja (Latvian), Rederi (Danish, Norwegian, Swedish), Rederij (Dutch), Reederei (German) and Zegluga (Polish). The following words mean *'limited company'*: AB - Aktiebolaget (Swedish) (Finnish companies who use both the Finnish and Swedish terms sometimes express it as Ab), AG - Aktiengesellschaft (German), AS - Aksjeselskap (Norwegian), A/S - Aktie Selskabet (Danish), BV - Besloten Vennootschap (Dutch), GmbH - Gesellschaft mit beschränkter Haftung (German), NV - Naamloze Vennootschap (Dutch), Oy - (Finnish), Oyj - (Finnish (plc)) and SA - Société Anonyme (French).

Spelling The convention now used in respect of town and country names is that local names are used for towns and areas of countries (eg Göteborg rather than Gothenburg) and English names for countries (eg Germany rather than Deutschland). Many towns in Finland have both Finnish and Swedish names; we have used the Finnish name except in the case of Åland which is an almost 100% Swedish-speaking area. In the case of Danish towns, the alternative use of 'å' or 'aa' follows local convention. The following towns, islands and territories, which have alternative English names, are expressed using their local names - the English name is shown following: Antwerpen/Anvers - Antwerp, Funen - Fyn, Génova - Genoa, Gent - Ghent, Göteborg - Gothenburg, Hoek van Holland - Hook of Holland, Jylland - Jutland, København - Copenhagen, Oostende - Ostend, Porto - Oporto, Sevilla - Seville, Sjælland - Sealand and Venezia - Venice.

Types of Ferry

These distinctions are necessarily general and many ships will have features of more than one category.

Car Ferry Until about 1970, most vehicle ferries were primarily designed for the conveyance of cars and their passengers and foot passengers. Little regard was paid to the conveyance of lorries and trailers, since this sort of traffic had not begun to develop. Few vessels of this type are still in service.

Multi-purpose Ferry From about 1970 onwards vehicle ferries began to make more provision for freight traffic, sharing the same ship with passengers and cars. Features usually include higher vehicle decks, often with retractable mezzanine decks, enabling two levels of cars or one level of freight and coaches, and separate facilities (including cabins on quite short crossings) for freight drivers.

Cruise Ferry In the 1980s the idea of travelling on a ferry, not just to get from A to B but for the pleasure of the travel experience, became more and more popular and ferries were built with increasingly luxurious and varied passenger accommodation. Such vessels also convey cars and freight but the emphasis is on passenger accommodation with a high level of berths (sometimes providing berths for all passengers).

Ro-pax Ferry A vessel designed primarily for the carriage of freight traffic but which also carries a limited number of ordinary passengers. Features generally include a moderate passenger capacity - up to about 500 passengers - and a partly open upper vehicle deck. Modern ro-pax vessels are becoming increasingly luxurious with facilities approaching those of a cruise ferry. The term 'Ro-pax' can also be used for any ferry designed to convey ro-ro traffic and passengers.

Ro-ro Ferry A vessel designed for the conveyance of road freight, unaccompanied trailers and containers on low trailers (known as 'Mafis' although often made by other manufacturers) and new cars. Some such vessels have no passenger accommodation but the majority can accommodate up to 12 passengers (usually drivers of accompanied freight units) – the maximum allowed without a passenger certificate. On routes where there is a low level of driver-accompanied traffic (mainly the longer ones), ordinary passengers, with or without cars, can sometimes be conveyed. On routes with a high level of driver-accompanied traffic, passenger capacity will sometimes be higher but facilities tend to be geared to the needs of freight drivers eg lounge with video, high level of cabins on routes of three hours or more. Technically such vessels are passenger ferries (having a passenger certificate).

Con-ro Many ro-ro vessels are capable of having ISO (International Standards Organisation) containers crane-loaded on the upper 'weather' deck. In this book the term con-ro applies only to vessels whose upper deck can only take containers and other crane loaded traffic and has no vehicle access.

Fast Ferry Streamlined vessel of catamaran or monohull construction, speed in excess of 30 knots, water jet propulsion, generally aluminium-built but some have steel hulls, little or no freight capacity and no cabins.

Timescale Although the book goes to press in September 2022, I have sought to reflect the situation as it will exist in October 2022 with regard to the introduction of new ships or other known changes. Vessels due to enter service after October 2022 are shown as '**Under Construction**'. This term does not necessarily man that physical work has started but an order has been placed with a shipyard. The book is updated at all stages of the production process where this is feasible, although major changes once the text has been paginated are not possible; there is also a 'Late News' section on page 220 for changes which cannot be incorporated into the text.

List of vessels

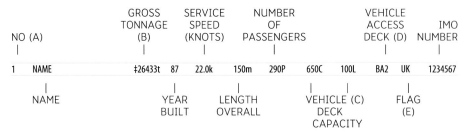

NO (A)	GROSS TONNAGE (B)		SERVICE SPEED (KNOTS)	NUMBER OF PASSENGERS				VEHICLE ACCESS DECK (D)	IMO NUMBER
1 NAME	‡26433t	87	22.0k	150m	290P	650C	100L	BA2 UK	1234567
NAME	YEAR BUILT		LENGTH OVERALL		VEHICLE (C) DECK CAPACITY			FLAG (E)	

(A) >> = fast ferry, • = vessel laid up, F = freight-only vessel (max 12 passengers), F+ = freight-only vessel (with passenger certificate), p = passenger-only vessel.

(B) C = Cars, L = Lorries (**15m**), T = Trailers (**13.5m**), r = can also take rail wagons, - = No figure quoted.

(C) B = Bow, A = Aft, S = Side, Q = Quarterdeck, R = Slewing ramp, 2 = Two decks can be loaded at the same time, C = Vehicles must be crane-loaded aboard, t = turntable ferry.

(D) The following abbreviations are used:

In the notes ships are in CAPITAL LETTERS, shipping lines and other institutions are in *italics*.

Capacity In this book, capacities shown are the maxima. Sometimes vessels operate at less than their maximum passenger capacity due to reduced crewing or to operating on a route on which they are not permitted to operate above a certain level. Car and lorry/trailer capacities are the maximum for either type. The two figures are not directly comparable. Some parts of a vessel may allow cars on two levels to occupy the space that a trailer or lorry occupies on one level, some may not; some parts of a vessel with low headroom may only be accessible to cars. All figures have to be approximate.

AX = Åland Islands	DK = Denmark	IM = Isle of Man	NL = Netherlands
BE = Belgium	EE = Estonia	IE = Republic of	NO = Norway
BM = Bermuda	ES = Spain	Ireland	PA = Panama
BS = Bahamas	FI = Finland	IT = Italy	PT = Portugal
CA = Canada	FO = Faroe Islands	LT = Lithuania	SG = Singapore
CY = Cyprus	FR = France	LV = Latvia	SE = Sweden
DE = Germany	GR = Greece	MT = Malta	UK = United Kingdom

Ownership The ownership of many vessels is very complicated. Some are actually owned by finance companies and banks, some by subsidiary companies of the shipping lines, some by subsidiary companies of a holding company of which the shipping company is also a subsidiary and some by companies which are jointly owned by the shipping company and other interests like a bank, set up specifically to own one ship or a group of ships. In all these cases the vessel is technically chartered to the shipping company. However, in this book, only those vessels chartered from one shipping company to another or from a ship-owning company unconnected with the shipping line are recorded as being on charter. Vessels are listed under the current operator rather than the owner. Charter is 'bareboat' (without crew) unless otherwise stated. If chartered with crew, vessels are 'time-chartered'.

Gross Tonnage This is a measure of enclosed capacity rather than weight, based on a formula of one gross ton = 100 cubic feet. Even small alterations can alter the gross tonnage. Under old measurement systems, the capacity of enclosed car decks was not included but, under the 1969 Convention, all vessels laid down after 1982 have been measured by a new system which includes enclosed vehicle decks as enclosed space, thereby considerably increasing the tonnage of vehicle ferries. Under this Convention, from 1st January 1995 all vessels were due to be re-measured under this system. Tonnages quoted here are, where possible, those given by the shipping companies themselves.

The following people are gratefully thanked for their assistance with this publication, many of them in ferry companies in the UK and abroad: John Bryant, Andrew Cooke, Matthew Davies, Ian Hall, Geoff Hamer, Peter Therkildsen, Bruce Peter, Richard Seville, Kai Ortel, Richard Kirkman, Kenneth Karsten and Ian Smith (The Camrose Organisation), and Forrest Print, Milford Haven.

Whilst every effort has been made to ensure that the facts contained here are correct, neither the publishers nor the writer can accept any responsibility for errors contained herein. We would, however, appreciate comments from readers, which we will endeavour to reflect in the next edition which we plan to publish in Autumn 2023.

erries

BARFLEUR
CHERBOURG

SECTION 1 –
GB AND IRELAND – MAJOR PASSENGER OPERATORS

BRITTANY FERRIES

THE COMPANY *Brittany Ferries* is the trading name of *BAI SA*, a French private sector company and the operating arm of the *Brittany Ferries Group*. The UK operations are run by *BAI (UK) Ltd*, a UK private sector company, wholly owned by the *Brittany Ferries Group*.

MANAGEMENT CEO Christophe Mathieu, **Commercial Directors, Passengers** Simon Johnson, Joëlle Croc, Florence Gourdon, **Commercial Director, Freight** Simon Wagstaff, **Director, UK** John Napton.

ADDRESS Millbay Docks, Plymouth, Devon PL1 3EW.

TELEPHONE Reservations *All Services* +44 (0)330 159 7000, **Freight - Administration & Enquiries** +44 (0)330 159 5000, **Reservations** +44 (0)330 159 5000.

INTERNET Websites *Passenger* www.brittanyferries.com *(English, French, Spanish, German)*, *Freight* www.brittanyferriesfreight.co.uk *(English)*

ROUTES OPERATED *All year* Plymouth - Roscoff (6 hrs (day), 7 hrs - 9 hrs (night); *ARMORIQUE, PONT-AVEN*; up to 2 per day (Summer), 1 per day (Winter)), Poole - Cherbourg (4 hrs 15 mins; *BARFLEUR*; 1 per day), Portsmouth - St Malo (8 hrs 45 mins (day), 10 hrs 45 mins (night); *BRETAGNE*; (1 per day), Portsmouth - Caen (Ouistreham) (6 hrs (day), 6 hrs - 8 hrs (night); *NORMANDIE, MONT ST MICHEL*; 3 per day), Portsmouth - Cherbourg (6-8 hrs); *GALICIA, SALAMANCA;* 2 per week), Portsmouth - Santander (Spain) (24 hrs; *GALICIA*; 2 per week), Portsmouth - Bilbao (Spain) (31-33 hrs; *SALAMANCA*; 2 per week, Plymouth - Santander (20-22 hrs; *PONT AVEN*; 2 per week), Rosslare - Bilbao (27 hrs 45 min; *CONNEMARA*, 2 per week), Rosslare - Cherbourg (15hrs 15 mins; *CONNEMARA*; 1 per week), **Summer only** Plymouth - Santander (Spain) (20-22 hrs; *PONT-AVEN*; 2 per week (April - October)), Cork - Roscoff (14 hrs-16 hrs 30 mins; *ARMORIQUE, PONT-AVEN*; 2 per week), **High Speed service (summer only)**: Portsmouth – Cherbourg (3 hrs; *CONDOR LIBERATION*; 2 per week).

Freight-only service Portsmouth - Le Havre (8 hrs; *COTENTIN*; 5 per week), Le Havre - Rosslare (20 hrs, 30 mins; *COTENTIN*; 1 per week), Poole - Bilbao (31 hrs; *MN PELICAN*; 2 per week).

1	ARMORIQUE	29468t	09	23.0k	167.0m	1500P	470C	65L	BA2	FR	9364980
2	BARFLEUR	20133t	92	19.0k	158.0m	1212P	590C	112T	BA2	FR	9007130
3	BRETAGNE	24534t	89	19.5k	151.0m	1926P	580C	84T	BA	FR	8707329
4	CONNEMARA	26500t	07	24.0k	186.5m	800P	170C	140L	BA	CY	9349760
5F+	COTENTIN	22542t	07	23.0k	167.0m	160P	-	140L	BA2	FR	9364978
6	GALICIA	41671t	20	22.0k	214.5m	1000P	300C	180L	BA2	FR	9856189
7F	MN PELICAN	12076t	99	20.0k	154.5m	12P	-	115T	A2	FR	9170999
8	MONT ST MICHEL	35592t	02	21.2k	173.0m	2200P	880C	166T	BA2	FR	9238337
9	NORMANDIE	27541t	92	20.5k	161.0m	2120P	600C	126T	BA2	FR	9006253
10	PONT-AVEN	41748t	04	26.0k	184.3m	2400P	650C	85L	BA	FR	9268708
11	SALAMANCA	41716t	22	22.0k	214.5m	1000P	300C	165L	BA2	FR	9867592

ARMORIQUE Built by STX Europe, Helsinki, Finland for *Brittany Ferries* to operate between Plymouth and Roscoff.

BARFLEUR Built as the BARFLEUR by Kvaerner Masa-Yards, Helsinki for the *Truckline* (freight division of *Brittany Ferries*) Poole - Cherbourg service to replace two passenger vessels and to inaugurate a year-round passenger service. In 1999 the *Truckline* branding was dropped for passenger services and she was repainted into full *Brittany Ferries* livery. In 2005 operated partly Cherbourg - Poole and partly Cherbourg - Portsmouth but in 2006 returned to operating mainly to Poole. In February 2010, she was laid up. The conventional car ferry service ended the following month. In February 2011 she resumed service on the Poole - Cherbourg route. In

Galicia *(George Holland)*

Salamanca *(Darren Holdaway)*

Barfleur *(Kevin Mitchell)*

Bretagne *(Darren Holdaway)*

September 2011 she was withdrawn again. In April 2012 chartered to *DFDS Seaways* to operate between Dover and Calais and renamed the DEAL SEAWAYS. In November 2012 returned to *Brittany Ferries* and renamed the BARFLEUR. Resumed the Poole - Cherbourg service in March 2013, replacing the COTENTIN but offering a service for both freight and passengers. In 2020 and most of 2021 laid up. Resumed on the Poole - Cherbourg service in 2022.

BRETAGNE Built by Chantiers de l'Atlantique, St Nazaire for the Plymouth - Santander and Cork - Roscoff services (with two sailings per week between Plymouth and Roscoff). In 1993 she was transferred to the Portsmouth - St Malo service. In 2004 also operated between Portsmouth and Cherbourg. In 2005 operated between Plymouth and Roscoff. In 2006 returned to the Portsmouth - St Malo route. In 2020 and most of 2021 laid up. Resumed service in March 2022.

CONNEMARA Built by CN Visentini, Porto Viro, Italy. Whilst under construction, sold to *Stena RoRo* of Sweden and provisionally named the STENA AUSONIA. However, before delivery a charter was arranged with *Balearia* of Spain and she was delivered as the BORJA. Operated between Barcelona and Palma (Majorca). In February 2010 the charter ended and she was laid up at Rotterdam. In April 2010 chartered to *Ave Line* and renamed the BALTIC AMBER. In October 2010 chartered to *DFDS Seaways* to replace the fire-damaged LISCO GLORIA. In March 2011 chartered to *LD Lines* to operate between Marseilles and Rades (Tunisia). In April she was moved to the Saint Nazaire (Nantes) - Gijon route. In June 2011 renamed the NORMAN ASTURIAS. In October 2011 the charter was ended but resumed the following month. Also operated between Poole, Santander and Gijon. In September 2014 chartered to *Intershipping*, Morocco and operated between Algeciras and Tangiers. In February 2016 chartered to *Anek Lines* of Greece, renamed the ASTERION and placed on the Patras - Igoumenitsa - Venezia route. In April 2018 chartered to *Brittany Ferries*, renamed the CONNEMARA and inaugurated a new twice weekly Cork - Santander service, with an additional service to Roscoff. In November 2019 transferred from the Cypriot to the French flag and operated on other routes.

COTENTIN Built as the by STX Finland, Helsinki, Finland for *Brittany Ferries*. Used on a freight service from Poole to Cherbourg and Santander. In March 2013 replaced by the BARFLEUR (operating to Cherbourg only). During summer 2013 operated twice weekly from Poole to Bilbao and Santander. In October 2013 chartered to *Stena RoRo* and renamed the STENA BALTICA. In November 2013 sub-chartered to *Stena Line* and placed on the Karlskrona - Gdynia route. In November 2020 charter ended. Returned to *Brittany Ferries* and renamed the COTENTIN. In January 2021 placed on a freight-only service between Poole and Cherbourg. In April transferred to the Portsmouth - Le Havre route.

GALICIA, SALAMANCA Built by CMI Jinling Weihai Shipyard, Weihai, China for *Stena RoRo*. Before delivery the GALICIA was fitted with scrubbers to run on fuel oil. The SALAMANCA is designed to run on LNG. Upon delivery chartered to *Brittany Ferries* for five years.

MN PELICAN Built as the TRANS BOTNIA for *SeaTrans ANS* of Norway. Hull constructed by Santierul Naval, Galatz, Romania and vessel completed by Fosen Mekaniske Verksteder, Frengen, Norway. Chartered to *Transfennica* for service between Finland and Western Europe. In June 2006 sold to *Maritime Nantaise* of France. In January 2007 renamed the MN PELICAN. Placed on long term charter to the *French MOD*. In 2015 placed on the charter market. In January 2016 time chartered to *Brittany Ferries*.

MONT ST MICHEL Built by Van der Giessen de Noord, Krimpen aan den IJssel, Rotterdam for *Brittany Ferries*. Used on the Portsmouth - Caen route.

NORMANDIE Built by Kvaerner Masa-Yards, Turku, Finland for *Brittany Ferries*. Used on the Portsmouth - Caen route.

PONT-AVEN Built by Jos L Meyer Werft, Papenburg, Germany for *Brittany Ferries* to operate on the Plymouth - Roscoff, Plymouth - Santander and Cork - Roscoff routes.

Under Construction

12	SANTOÑA	42000t	23	22.0k	214.5m	1000P	300C	165L	BA2	FR	9886847
13	SAINT MALO	30000t	24	22.0k	194.0m	1290P	370C	63L	BA2	FR	9946324

| 14 | NEWBUILDING | 30000t | 25 | 22.0k | 194.0m | 1310P | 470C | 120L | BA2 | FR | 9946336 |

SANTOÑA Under construction by CMI Jinling Weihai Shipyard, Weihai, China for *Stena RoRo*. Designed to run on LNG. Upon delivery, to be chartered to *Brittany Ferries* for five years.

SAINT MALO, NEWBUILDING E-Flexers under construction by CMI Jinling Weihai Shipyard, Weihai, China for *Stena RoRo*. Shortened version, designed to run on LNG and battery. Upon delivery, to be chartered to *Brittany Ferries* for five years. To replace the BRETAGNE and NORMANDIE respectively.

CALEDONIAN MACBRAYNE

THE COMPANY *Caledonian MacBrayne* is the trading name of *CalMac Ferries Ltd*, a subsidiary of *David MacBrayne Limited*, a Scottish registered company, wholly owned by the Scottish Ministers. The majority of *CalMac Ferries* vessels are owned by *Caledonian Maritime Assets Limited*, a separate company which is also owned by the Scottish Ministers.

MANAGEMENT Managing Director Robbie Drummond, **Director of Operations** Robert Morrison **Group Director of Communications and Community Engagement** Stuart Wilson.

ADDRESS Ferry Terminal, Gourock PA19 1QP.

TELEPHONE Administration +44 (0)1475 650100, **Vehicle Reservations** *in UK* 0800 066 5000, *International* +44 1475 650397.

FAX Administration +44 (0)1475 650336, **Vehicle Reservations** +44 (0)1475 635235.

INTERNET Email enquiries@calmac.co.uk **Website** www.calmac.co.uk *(English, Scots Gaelic, German)*

ROUTES OPERATED All-year vehicle ferries (frequencies are for Summer – services are listed alphabetically by mainland port or larger island port where service is between two islands). Ardmhor (Barra) - Eriskay (40 mins; *LOCH ALAINN*; up to 5 per day), Ardrossan - Brodick (Arran) (55 mins; *CALEDONIAN ISLES, ISLE OF ARRAN*; up to 6 per day), Colintraive - Rhubodach (Bute) (5 mins; *LOCH DUNVEGAN*; frequent service), Kennacraig - Port Askaig (Islay) (2 hrs 5 mins; *FINLAGGAN, HEBRIDEAN ISLES*; up to 4 per day), Kennacraig - Port Ellen (Islay) (2 hrs 20 mins; *FINLAGGAN, HEBRIDEAN ISLES*; service currently suspended due to harbour works), Largs - Cumbrae Slip (Cumbrae) (10 mins; *LOCH RIDDON, LOCH SHIRA*; every 30 or 15 mins), Leverburgh (Harris) - Berneray (1 hr 10 mins; *LOCH PORTAIN*; 3-4 per day), Lochaline - Fishnish (Mull) (15 mins; *LOCHINVAR*; up to 14 per day), Mallaig - Armadale (Skye) (23 mins; *LOCHNEVIS* (Winter) *CORUISK, LOCH FYNE,* (Summer); up to 9 per day (2 in Winter)), Mallaig - Lochboisdale (South Uist) (3 hrs 30 mins; *LORD OF THE ISLES*; 1 per day), Oban - Castlebay (Barra) (5 hrs; *ISLE OF LEWIS*; 1 per day), Oban - Coll - Tiree (2 hrs 45 min to Coll 3 hrs 50 min to Tiree via Coll; *CLANSMAN*; 1 per day), Oban - Colonsay (2 hrs 15 mins; *CLANSMAN*; 5 per week), Oban - Craignure (Mull) (45 mins; *ISLE OF MULL, LOCH FRISA*; up to 11 per day), Oban - Lismore (50 mins; *LOCH STRIVEN*; up to 5 per day), Sconser (Skye) - Raasay (15 mins; *HALLAIG*; up to 11 per day), Tarbert (Loch Fyne) - Portavadie (25 mins;; up to 12 per day), Tayinloan - Gigha (20 mins; *LOCH RANZA*; up to 10 per day), Tobermory (Mull) - Kilchoan (35 mins; *LOCH TARBERT*; up to 7 per day), Uig (Skye) - Lochmaddy (North Uist) (1 hr 45 mins; *HEBRIDES*; 1 or 2 per day), Uig (Skye) - Tarbert (Harris) (1 hr 40 mins; *HEBRIDES*; 1 or 2 per day), Ullapool - Stornoway (Lewis) (2 hrs 45 mins; *LOCH SEAFORTH*; up to 3 per day (one freight only)), Wemyss Bay - Rothesay (Bute) (35 mins; *BUTE*; hourly). **All-year passenger and restricted vehicle ferries** (frequencies are for Summer) Gallanach (near Oban) - Kerrera (5 mins; *CARVORIA*; up to 12 per day), Fionnphort (Mull) - Iona (5 mins; *LOCH BUIE*; frequent), Mallaig - Eigg - Muck - Rum - Canna - Mallaig (round trip 7 hrs (all islands); *LOCHNEVIS*; at least 1 sailing per day - most islands visited daily). **Note** Although these services are operated by vehicle ferries special permission is required to take a vehicle and tourist cars are not normally conveyed. **Summer-only vehicle ferries** Ardrossan - Campbeltown (2 hrs 30 mins; *ISLE OF ARRAN*; 3 per week), Claonaig - Lochranza (Arran) (30 mins; *CATRIONA*; up to 9 per day), Kennacraig - Port Askaig - Colonsay - Oban (3 hrs 35 mins; *HEBRIDEAN ISLES*; 1 per week). **Winter-only vehicle ferry** Tarbert (Loch Fyne) - Lochranza (Arran) (1 hr; *varies*; 1 per day). **All-year passenger-only ferries** Gourock

Isle of Lewis *(Andrew Cooke)*

Isle of Arran *(Andrew Cooke)*

- Dunoon (20 mins; ***ALI CAT, ARGYLL FLYER, CORUISK (winter only)***; 1 or 2 per hour, Gourock - Kilcreggan (13 mins; ***CHIEFTAIN***; approx hourly).

1p	ALI CAT	78t	99	8.5k	19.8m	250P	0C	0L	-	UK	
2	ARGYLE	2643t	07	14.0k	69.0m	450P	60C	-	BAS	UK	9365178
3p	ARGYLL FLYER	300t	01	19.5k	29.9m	227P	0C	0L	-	UK	9231016
4	BUTE	2612t	05	14.0k	69.0m	450P	60C	-	AS	UK	9319741
5	CALEDONIAN ISLES	5221t	93	15.0k	94.3m	1000P	120C	10L	BA	UK	9051284
6	CARVORIA	9t	17	8.0k	12.0m	12P	1C	0L	B	UK	
7	CATRIONA	499t	16	9.0k	43.5m	150P	23C	2L	BA	UK	9759862
8p	CHIEFTAIN	54t	07	9.5k	19.5m	100P	0C	0L	-	UK	
9	CLANSMAN	5499t	98	16.5k	99.0m	638P	90C	6L	BA	UK	9158953
10	CORUISK	1599t	03	14.0k	65.0m	250P	40C	-	BA	UK	9274836
11	FINLAGGAN	5626t	11	16.5k	89.9m	550P	88C	-	BA	UK	9482902
12	HALLAIG	499t	13	9.0k	43.5m	150P	23C	2L	BA	UK	9652832
13	HEBRIDEAN ISLES	3040t	85	15.0k	85.1m	494P	68C	10L	BAS	UK	8404812
14	HEBRIDES	5506t	00	16.5k	99.0m	612P	110C	6L	BA	UK	9211975
15	ISLE OF ARRAN	3296t	84	15.0k	85.0m	446P	68C	8L	BA	UK	8219554
16	ISLE OF CUMBRAE	201t	77	8.5k	37.7m	139P	18C	-	BA	UK	7521625
17	ISLE OF LEWIS	6753t	95	18.0k	101.2m	680P	123C	10L	BA	UK	9085974
18	ISLE OF MULL	4719t	88	15.0k	90.1m	962P	80C	20L	BA	UK	8608339
19	LOCH ALAINN	396t	98	10.0k	43.0m	150P	24C	-	BA	UK	9147722
20	LOCH BHRUSDA	246t	96	8.0k	35.4m	150P	18C	-	BA	UK	9129483
21	LOCH BUIE	295t	92	9.0k	35.5m	250P	9C	-	BA	UK	9031375
22	LOCH DUNVEGAN	549t	91	9.0k	54.2m	200P	36C	-	BA	UK	9006409
23	LOCH FRISA	1160t	15	12.0k	49.9m	195P	40C	4L	BA	UK	9740720
24	LOCH FYNE	549t	91	9.0k	54.2m	200P	36C	-	BA	UK	9006411
25	LOCH LINNHE	206t	86	9.0k	35.5m	199P	12C	-	BA	UK	8512308
26	LOCH PORTAIN	950t	03	10.5k	50.0m	200P	32C	-	BA	UK	9274824
27	LOCH RANZA	206t	87	9.0k	35.7m	199P	12C	-	BA	UK	8519887
28	LOCH RIDDON	206t	86	9.0k	35.5m	199P	12C	-	BA	UK	8519875
29	LOCH SEAFORTH	8478t	14	19.2k	116.0m	700P	143C	20L	BA	UK	9665437
30	LOCH SHIRA	1024t	07	13.0k	43.0m	250P	24C	-	BA	UK	9376919
31	LOCH STRIVEN	206t	86	9.0k	35.7m	199P	12C	-	BA	UK	8512293
32	LOCH TARBERT	211t	92	9.0k	34.5m	149P	18C	-	BA	UK	9039389
33	LOCHINVAR	523t	14	9.0k	43.5m	150P	23C	2L	BA	UK	9652844
34	LOCHNEVIS	941t	00	13.0k	49.1m	190P	14C	-	A	UK	9209063
35	LORD OF THE ISLES	3504t	89	16.0k	84.6m	506P	56C	16L	BAS	UK	8710869

Note In the following list, Gaelic names are shown in parenthesis.

ALI CAT Catamaran built for *Solent & Wight Line Cruises* of Ryde, Isle of Wight. She operated a passenger service from Cowes to Hamble and Warsash and cruises from Cowes. At times chartered to *Wightlink* to cover for their fast catamarans. In 2002 chartered to *Red Funnel Ferries* who had contracted with *Caledonian MacBrayne* to operate passenger-only services between Gourock and Dunoon in the morning and evening peaks. In June 2011 purchased by and operated by *Argyll Ferries*. In January 2019, operation was transferred to *Caledonian MacBrayne*.

ARGYLE *(EARRA-GHÀIDHEAL)*, BUTE *(EILEAN BHÒID)* Built by Stocznia Remontowa, Gdańsk, Poland to operate on the Wemyss Bay - Rothesay route.

ARGYLL FLYER Built as the QUEEN OF ARAN II by OCEA, Les Sables d'Olonne, France for *Inis Mór Ferries*. In 2007 sold to *Aran Island Ferries* and renamed the BANRION CHONAMARA. In June 2011 sold to *Argyll Ferries*, renamed the ARGYLL FLYER and replaced the car ferry SATURN on the Gourock - Dunoon service. In January 2019, operation was transferred to *Caledonian MacBrayne*.

CALEDONIAN ISLES *(EILEANAN CHALEDONIA)* Built by Richards Shipyard, Lowestoft, UK for the Ardrossan - Brodick (Arran) service.

Loch Shira *(Andrew Cooke)*

Loch Striven *(Andrew Cooke)*

Isle of Lewis *(Andrew Cooke)*

AliCat and Lord of the Isles *(Andrew Cooke)*

Hebridean Isles *(John Hendy)*

Chieftain *(Andrew Cooke)*

Loch Frisa *(Andrew Cooke)*

Clansman *(Miles Cowsill)*

CARVORIA Built by Malakoff Limited, Lerwick, Shetland for *Caledonian Maritime Assets* and chartered to *Caledonian MacBrayne* to replace the chartered GYLEN LADY on the Gallanach - Kerrera service.

CATRIONA Built by Ferguson Marine Engineering, Port Glasgow. Near sister vessel of the HALLAIG and LOCHINVAR. Operates on the Claonaig - Lochranza service during the summer and other routes during the winter.

CHIEFTAIN Built as the SEABUS by Voyager Boatyard, Millbrook, Plymouth for Clyde Marine Services, Scotland and operated on the ferry service between Gourock, Kilgreggan and Helensburgh on behalf of Strathclyde Partnership for Transport. In 2013 the contract to operate this service was awarded to *Clydelink* (Gourock - Kilcreggan only) and she was transferred to private hire and excursion work. In January 2014 she was renamed the CHIEFTAIN. In May 2018 the contract returned to *Clyde Marine Services* and she returned to this route. In June 2020 the service came under auspices of *Transport Scotland* and the contract was transferred to *Caledonian MacBrayne*; the CHIEFTAIN was chartered to them.

CLANSMAN *(FEAR-CINNIDH)* Built by Appledore Shipbuilders Ltd, Appledore, UK to replace the LORD OF THE ISLES on the Oban - Coll and Tiree and Oban - Castlebay and Lochboisdale services in the summer. She also serves as winter relief vessel on the Stornoway, Tarbert, Lochmaddy, Mull/Colonsay and Brodick routes.

CORUISK *(COIR' UISG')* Built by Appledore Shipbuilders Ltd, Appledore, UK to operate on the Mallaig - Armadale route during the summer. During the winter she operates on the Gourock - Dunoon passenger service during peak periods and when the usual vessels cannot sail due to adverse weather. Since summer 2016 she has operated as second vessel on the Oban - Craignure service. In summer 2023 she returned to the Mallaig - Armadale service.

FINLAGGAN *(FIONN LAGAN)* Built by Stocznia Remontowa, Gdańsk, Poland for the Kennacraig - Islay service.

HALLAIG *(HALLAIG)* Built by Ferguson Shipbuilders, Port Glasgow, UK to replace the LOCH STRIVEN on the Sconser - Raasay service. The vessel has both diesel and battery electric propulsion and can be 'plugged in' to a land supply on Raasay overnight.

HEBRIDEAN ISLES *(EILEANAN INNSE GALL)* Built by Cochrane Shipbuilders, Selby UK for the Uig - Tarbert/Lochmaddy service. She was used initially on the Ullapool - Stornoway and Oban - Craignure/Colonsay services pending installation of link-span facilities at Uig, Tarbert and Lochmaddy. She took up her regular role in May 1986. From May 1996 she no longer operated direct services in summer between Tarbert and Lochmaddy, this role being taken on by the new Harris - North Uist services of the LOCH BHRUSDA. In 2001 she was replaced by the HEBRIDES and transferred to the Islay service. In Autumn 2002 she operated between Scrabster and Stromness for *NorthLink Orkney and Shetland Ferries* before port modifications at Scrabster enabled the HAMNAVOE to enter service in Spring 2003. She then returned to the Islay service. She also relieved on the *NorthLink* Pentland Firth service between 2004 and 2007.

HEBRIDES *(INNSE GALL)* Built by Ferguson Shipbuilders Ltd, Port Glasgow, UK for the Uig - Tarbert and Uig - Lochmaddy services.

ISLE OF ARRAN *(EILEAN ARAINN)* Built by Ferguson Ailsa, Port Glasgow, UK for the Ardrossan - Brodick service. In 1993 transferred to the Kennacraig - Port Ellen/Port Askaig service, also undertaking the weekly Port Askaig - Colonsay - Oban summer service. From then until 1997/98 she also relieved on the Brodick, Coll/Tiree, Castlebay/Lochboisdale, Craignure and Tarbert/Lochmaddy routes in winter. In 2001 she was replaced by the HEBRIDEAN ISLES and became a reserve for the larger vessels. She has operated on the two-ship Islay service in summer since 2003; this service is now all-year-round. Following the delivery of the FINLAGGAN in May 2011 she became a spare vessel, and operates extra services between Ardrossan and Brodick and Ardrossan and Campbeltown during the peak summer period.

ISLE OF CUMBRAE *(EILEAN CHUMRAIGH)* Built by Ailsa Shipbuilding Ltd, Troon, UK for the Largs - Cumbrae Slip (Cumbrae) service. In 1986 she was replaced by the LOCH LINNHE and the LOCH STRIVEN and transferred to the Lochaline - Fishnish (Mull) service. She used to spend most of the winter as secondary vessel on the Kyle of Lochalsh - Kyleakin service; however, this ceased following the opening of the Skye Bridge in 1995. In 1997 she was transferred to the Colintraive - Rhubodach service. In Summer 1999 she was transferred to the Tarbert - Portavadie service. In May 2015 replaced by the new LOCHINVAR and laid up. In summer 2016 returned to the Tarbert - Portavadie service.

ISLE OF LEWIS *(EILEAN LEÒDHAIS)* Built by Ferguson Shipbuilders Ltd, Port Glasgow, UK for the Ullapool - Stornoway service. In February 2015 replaced by the new LOCH SEAFORTH. Now operates between Oban and Castlebay (Barra).

ISLE OF MULL *(AN T-EILEAN MUILEACH)* Built by Appledore Ferguson, Port Glasgow, UK for the Oban - Craignure (Mull) service.

LOCH ALAINN *(LOCH ÀLAINN)* Built by Buckie Shipbuilders Ltd, Buckie, UK for the Lochaline - Fishnish service. Launched as the LOCH ALINE but renamed the LOCH ALAINN before entering service. After a brief period on the service for which she was built, she was transferred to the Colintraive - Rhubodach route. In 1998 she was transferred to the Largs - Cumbrae Slip service. In 2007 moved to the Ardmhor (Barra) - Eriskay service. She relieves the larger 'Loch' class vessels in the winter, with her own service covered by the LOCH BHRUSDA.

LOCH BHRUSDA *(LOCH BHRÙSTA)* Built by McTay Marine, Bromborough, Wirral, UK to inaugurate a new Otternish (North Uist) - Leverburgh (Harris) service. In 2001 the service became Berneray - Leverburgh. In 2003 she moved to the Eriskay - Barra service, previously operated by *Comhairle Nan Eilean Siar* vessels. In 2007 she became a spare vessel on the Clyde. In summer 2016 operated between Mallaig and Armadale. Note 'Bhrusda' is pronounced "Vroosta".

LOCH BUIE *(LOCH BUIDHE)* Built by J W Miller & Sons Ltd, St Monans, Fife, UK for the Fionnphort (Mull) - Iona service to replace the MORVERN (see *Arranmore Island Ferry Services*) and obviate the need for a relief vessel in the summer. Due to height restrictions, loading arrangements for vehicles taller than private cars are stern-only. Only islanders' cars and service vehicles (eg mail vans, police) are carried; no tourist vehicles are conveyed.

LOCH DUNVEGAN *(LOCH DÙNBHEAGAN)* Built by Ferguson Shipbuilders Ltd, Port Glasgow, UK for the Kyle of Lochalsh - Kyleakin service. On the opening of the Skye Bridge in October 1995 she was withdrawn from service and offered for sale. In Autumn 1997, she returned to service on the Lochaline - Fishnish route. In 1998 she was due to be transferred to the Colintraive - Rhubodach route but this was delayed because of problems in providing terminal facilities. She operated on the Clyde and between Mallaig and Armadale during the early summer and spent the rest of that summer laid up. In 1999 she was transferred to the Colintraive - Rhubodach route.

LOCH FRISA *(LOCH FRÌOSA)* Built as the UTNE by Sefine Shipyard, Yalova, Turkey for NORLED of Norway. Operated in South Western Norway. In October 2021 sold to CALEDONIAN MARITIME ASSETS and chartered to CALEDONIAN MACBRAYNE to operate between OBAN and Mull. In June 2022 renamed the LOCH FRISA and entered service.

LOCH FYNE *(LOCH FINE)* Built by Ferguson Shipbuilders Ltd, Port Glasgow, UK for the Kyle of Lochalsh - Kyleakin service (see the LOCH DUNVEGAN). In Autumn 1997, she also served on the Lochaline - Fishnish route and was transferred to this route as regular vessel in 1998. In summer 2017 transferred to the Mallaig - Armadale route.

LOCH LINNHE *(AN LINNE DHUBH)* Built by Richard Dunston (Hessle) Ltd, Hessle, UK. Until 1997 she was used mainly on the Largs - Cumbrae Slip (Cumbrae) service and until Winter 1994/95 she was usually used on the Lochaline - Fishnish service during the winter. Since then she has relieved on various routes in winter. In Summer 1998 she operated mainly on the Tarbert - Portavadie route. In 1999 she was transferred to the Tobermory - Kilchoan service in summer.

LOCH PORTAIN *(LOCH PORTAIN)* Built by McTay Marine, Bromborough, Wirral, UK (hull constructed in Poland) to replace the LOCH BHRUSDA on the Berneray - Leverburgh service.

LOCH RANZA *(LOCH RAONASA)* Built by Richard Dunston (Hessle) Ltd, Hessle, UK for the Claonaig - Lochranza (Arran) seasonal service and used a relief vessel in the winter. In 1992 she was replaced by the LOCH TARBERT and transferred to the Tayinloan - Gigha service.

LOCH RIDDON *(LOCH RAODAIN)* Built by Richard Dunston (Hessle) Ltd, Hessle, UK. Until 1997 she was used almost exclusively on the Colintraive - Rhubodach service. In 1997, she was transferred to the Largs - Cumbrae Slip service. In January 2014 she became regular vessel on the Oban - Lismore service. However, after problems with using the slipways, she became the second vessel on the Largs - Cumbrae Slip service.

LOCH SEAFORTH *(LOCH SHIPHOIRT)* Built by Flensburger Schiffbau-Gesellschaft, Flensburg, Germany for the Stornoway - Ullapool service, replacing the ISLE OF LEWIS and freight vessel CLIPPER RANGER.

LOCH SHIRA *(LOCH SIORA)* Built by Ferguson Shipbuilders, Port Glasgow, UK for the Largs – Cumbrae Slip route.

LOCH STRIVEN *(LOCH SROIGHEANN)* Built by Richard Dunston (Hessle) Ltd, Hessle, UK. Used mainly on the Largs - Cumbrae Slip service until 1997. In Winter 1995/96 and 1996/97 she was used on the Tarbert - Portavadie and Claonaig - Lochranza routes. In 1997 she took over the Sconser - Raasay service. In winter 2014 replaced by the HALLAIG. In summer 2014 transferred to the Oban - Lismore route.

LOCH TARBERT *(LOCH AN TAIRBEIRT)* Built by J W Miller & Sons Ltd, St Monans, Fife, UK for the Claonaig - Lochranza service. Now a relief vessel.

LOCHINVAR *(LOCH AN BARR)* As the HALLAIG. Initially operated on the Tarbert - Portavadie route. In summer 2016 transferred to Mallaig - Armadale and in summer 2017 to the Lochaline - Fishnish route.

LOCHNEVIS *(LOCH NIBHEIS)* Built by Ailsa Shipbuilding, Troon, UK to replace the LOCHMOR on the Mallaig - Small Isles service and the winter Mallaig - Armadale service. Although a vehicle ferry, cars are not normally carried to the Small Isles; the ro-ro facility is used for the carriage of agricultural machinery and livestock and it is possible to convey a vehicle on the ferry from which goods can be unloaded directly onto local transport rather than transhipping at Mallaig.

LORD OF THE ISLES *(RIGH NAN EILEAN)* Built by Appledore Ferguson, Port Glasgow, UK to replace the CLAYMORE on the Oban - Castlebay and Lochboisdale services and also the COLUMBA (1420t, 1964) on the Oban - Coll and Tiree service. Now in the winter she operates as a relief vessel. In summer she operates between Mallaig and Lochboisdale and also between Mallaig and Armadale.

Under Construction

36	GLEN SANNOX	5000t	23	16.5k	102.4m	1000P	127C	16L	BA	UK	9794513
37	NEWBUILDING 1	5000t	23	16.5k	102.4m	1000P	127C	16L	BA	UK	9794525
38	NEWBUILDING 2	5861t	24	16.5k	95.0m	450P	100C	10L	BA	UK	9970923
39	NEWBUILDING 3	5861t	25	16.5k	95.0m	450P	100C	10L	BA	UK	9970935

GLEN SANNOX *(GLEANN SHANNAIG)*, NEWBUILDING 1 Under construction by Ferguson Marine Port Glasgow Ltd for *Caledonian Maritime Assets* (CMAL) and to be chartered to *Caledonian MacBrayne*. The GLEN SANNOX is planned to operate on the Ardrossan - Brodick service and the second vessel is likely to operate between Uig and Harris and North Uist. Construction has been heavily delayed and delivery dates are based on latest estimates.

NEWBUILDING 2, NEWBUILDING 3 Under construction by Cemre Shipyard, Cemre, Turkey for *Caledonian Maritime Assets* (CMAL). To be chartered to *Caledonian MacBrayne*. To operate on the service from Kennacraig to Islay. Diesel - electric battery hybrid propulsion.

CONDOR FERRIES

THE COMPANY *Condor Ferries Ltd* is a Channel Islands' private sector company owned by the Condor Group, Guernsey which is owned by *Brittany Ferries* and Columbia Threadneedle Investments.

MANAGEMENT Chief Executive Officer John Napton, **Executive Director – Commercial** Greg Yeoman,

ADDRESS Head Office New Jetty Offices, White Rock, St Peter Port, Guernsey GY1 2LL, **Sales and Marketing** Condor House, New Harbour Road South, Hamworthy, Poole BH15 4AJ.

TELEPHONE Administration *Guernsey* +44 (0)1481 728620, *Poole* +44 (0)1202 207207, **Passenger Reservations** +44 (0)345 609 1024, **Freight Reservations** +44 (0)1481 728620.

INTERNET Email *Passenger* contactcentre@condorferries.co.uk **Freight** freight@condorferries.co.uk **Website** www.condorferries.com *(English)* www.condorferries.fr *(French),*

ROUTES OPERATED *COMMODORE CLIPPER (Conventional Passenger and Freight Ferry)* Portsmouth to Guernsey (from 7 hrs) and Jersey (from 9 hrs) daily except Sun. *Fast Ferries CONDOR LIBERATION*; Poole - Guernsey (3 hrs) and Jersey (4 hrs 30 min); 1 per day (operates on a seasonal basis; less frequent during off-peak seasons), *CONDOR VOYAGER*; Guernsey (1 hr 55 min) and Jersey (1 hr 25 mins) to St Malo (1 per day). *Freight Ferry COMMODORE GOODWILL*; Portsmouth - Guernsey - Jersey (10 hrs 30 min; 1 per day), Guernsey - Jersey - St Malo (13 hrs; 1 per week).

1	COMMODORE CLIPPER	14000t	99	18.0k	129.1m	500P	100C	92T	A	BS	9201750
2F	COMMODORE GOODWILL	11166t	96	17.3k	126.4m	12P	-	92T	A	BS	9117985
3»	CONDOR LIBERATION	6307t	10	39.0k	102.0m	873P	245C	12L	A	BS	9551363
4»	CONDOR VOYAGER	6581t	00	40.0k	97.2m	900P	260C	-	A	BS	9221358

COMMODORE CLIPPER Ro-pax vessel built by Van der Giessen de Noord, Krimpen aan den IJssel, Rotterdam for *Commodore Ferries* to operate between Portsmouth and the Channel Islands. She replaced the ISLAND COMMODORE, a freight-only vessel. Her passenger capacity is normally restricted to 300 between the Channel Islands and the UK but is increased to 500 between Jersey and Guernsey.

COMMODORE GOODWILL Built by Koninklijke Scheldegroep BV, Vlissingen, The Netherlands for *Commodore Ferries.*

CONDOR LIBERATION Austal 102-metre Trimaran built speculatively by Austal Ships Pty, Fremantle, Australia as AUSTAL HULL 270. Laid up. In August 2014 sold to *Condor Ferries.* During autumn and early winter 2014/15 she was modified by Austal Ships in their shipyard at Balamban, Cebu, Philippines and in March 2015 renamed the CONDOR LIBERATION and placed on the Poole - Channel Islands service.

CONDOR VOYAGER Incat Evolution 10 catamaran built as the INCAT TASMANIA. In November 2000 chartered to *TranzRail* of New Zealand and renamed THE LYNX. Placed on the Wellington – Picton service. In July 2003 replaced by 1997-built Incat 86m craft INCAT 046, given the marketing name 'The Lynx' and laid up. In Spring 2005 chartered to *Brittany Ferries* to operate on their Cherbourg – Portsmouth and Caen – Portsmouth services and renamed the NORMANDIE EXPRESS. In 2007 purchased by *Brittany Ferries.* In 2015 operated to Cherbourg and Le Havre but since then has only operated to Cherbourg. She did not operate in 2020 and in May 2021 chartered to *Condor Ferries* and renamed the CONDOR VOYAGER.

Commodore Clipper *(Darren Holdaway)*

Condor Liberation *(Darren Holdaway)*

DFDS FERRY

THE COMPANY *DFDS Ferry* is a division within *DFDS A/S*, a Danish Private sector company. DFDS provides ferry and logistics services in Europe and Turkey. DFDS' 8,000 employees are located on ferries and in offices across 20 countries. DFDS was founded in 1866, is headquartered in Copenhagen, and listed on Nasdaq Copenhagen. It operates one of the largest networks of ferry routes in and around Europe, including owns terminals in key locations. The Newhaven - Dieppe route is branded as *Transmanche Ferries*, operating under a franchise awarded by *Syndicat Mixte de L'Activité Transmanche* in Dieppe. In June 2018 *DFDS* acquired *UN RoRo* of Turkey. The Mediterranean fleet is outside the scope of this book.

MANAGEMENT President and CEO DFDS A/S Torben Carlsen, **Executive Vice President, Head of Ferry Division** Mathieu Girardin **Managing Director, Immingham Ferry** Andrew Byrne, **Senior Vice President North Sea South** Kell Robdrup, **Head of Business Unit Channel** Filip Hermann, **Vice President, Head of Business Unit Passenger** Kasper Moos.

ADDRESSES (UK) Dover DFDS A/S, Whitfield Court, White Cliffs Business Park Whitfield, Dover CT16 3PX, **Immingham** DFDS Seaways Plc, Nordic House, Immingham Dock, Immingham DN40 2LZ.

TELEPHONE Administration +44 (0)1304 874001. **Passenger Reservations** *Dover-Calais* 0871 574 7235, +44 (0)208 127 8303, *Newcastle - Ijmuiden* 0871 522 9955, +44 330 333 0245, *Newhaven - Dieppe* 0800 917 1201, +33 232 144 729[Mg3], **Freight Reservations** See Website.

INTERNET Websites *Passenger* www.dfds.com/en-gb/passenger-ferries *(various)* **Freight** www.dfds.com/en/freight-shipping *(English)* **Corporate** www.dfds.com *(English)*

ROUTES OPERATED *Passenger ferries* Newcastle (North Shields) - IJmuiden (near Amsterdam, The Netherlands) (15 hrs; *KING SEAWAYS, PRINCESS SEAWAYS*; daily). Dover - Dunkerque (2 hrs; *DELFT SEAWAYS, DOVER SEAWAYS, DUNKERQUE SEAWAYS*; 12 per day), Dover - Calais (1 hr 30 mins; *CÔTE D'OPALE, CÔTE DES DUNES, CÔTE DES FLANDRES*; 15 per day), Newhaven - Dieppe (4 hrs; *CÔTE D'ALBÂTRE, SEVEN SISTERS*; up to 3 per day). **Freight Ferries (with higher passenger capacity)**. Rosslare (Irish Republic) - Dunkerque (23-24 hrs; *REGINA SEAWAYS, VISBORG*; 5 per week). *Freight ferries (12 passengers)* Esbjerg - Immingham (18 hrs; ; 6 per week), Cuxhaven - Immingham (19 hrs; 5 per week), Göteborg - Immingham (26 hrs (direct), *45 hrs (via Brevik (Fri)) 5 per week), Brevik - Immingham (25 hrs (direct), 42 hrs (via Göteborg); 2 per week), Göteborg - Brevik (Norway) - Gent (Belgium) (Göteborg 32 hrs, Brevik 32 hrs; 6 per week (1 per week via Brevik), Göteborg - Zeebrugge (34 hrs; 6 per week) (joint timetable with *CLdN*), Vlaardingen - Immingham (14 hrs; 8 per week), Vlaardingen - Felixstowe (7 hrs; ; 3 per day), Zeebrugge - Immingham - Halden (Norway) - Fredrikstad - Zeebrugge (; weekly circuit), Calais - Sheerness (5 hrs; 1 per day). Note because vessels are moved between services it is not possible to be specific as to which vessels operate on which routes. At the time of going to press passengers with cars are being carried experimentally between Rosslare and Dunkerque on the REGINA SEAWAYS but not the VISBORG.

DFDS also operates services in the Baltic (see section 7) and Mediterranean (which are outside the scope of this book).

1F	ACACIA SEAWAYS	32770t	17	21.0k	209.8m	12P	-	262T	A2	LT	9809112
2F	ARK DANIA	33313t	14	20.0k	195.2m	12P	-	206T	A	DK	9609964
3F	BEGONIA SEAWAYS	37722t	04	22.5k	230.0m	12P	-	340T	AS	DK	9262089
4F	BOTNIA SEAWAYS	11530t	00	20.0k	162.2m	12P	-	140T	A	LT	9192129
5F	BRITANNIA SEAWAYS	24196t	00	21.1k	197.5m	12P	-	200T	AS	DK	9153032
6	CÔTE D'ALBÂTRE	18425t	06	22.0k	112.0m	600P	300C	62L	BA	FR	9320128
8	CÔTE D'OPALE	40331t	21	22.0k	214.5m	1000P	300C	180L	BA2	FR	9858321
8	CÔTE DES DUNES	33796t	01	25.0k	186.0m	1500P	700C	120L	BA2	FR	9232527
9	CÔTE DES FLANDRES	33940t	05	25.0k	186.0m	1500P	700C	120L	BA2	FR	9305843
10	DELFT SEAWAYS	35923t	06	25.5k	187.0m	780P	200C	120L	BA2	UK	9293088
11	DOVER SEAWAYS	35923t	06	25.8k	187.0m	780P	200C	120L	BA2	UK	9318345

Connecting Europe
through knowledge.

Delft Seaways and Pride of Canterbury (George Holland)

Princess Seaways (Richard Seville)

12	DUNKERQUE SEAWAYS	35923t	05	25.8k	187.0m	780P	200C	120L	BA2	UK	9293076
13F	FICARIA SEAWAYS	37939t	04	22.5k	230.0m	12P	-	340T	AS	DK	9320568
14F	FLANDRIA SEAWAYS	60465t	20	21.0k	237.4m	12P	-	480T	A2	DK	9860142
15F	FREESIA SEAWAYS	37722t	04	22.5k	230.0m	12P	-	340T	AS	DK	9274848
16F	GARDENIA SEAWAYS	32336t	17	21.0k	209.6m	12P	-	262T	A2	LT	9809095
17F	HOLLANDIA SEAWAYS	60465t	19	21.0k	237.4m	12P	-	480T	A2	DK	9832585
18F	HUMBRIA SEAWAYS	60465t	20	21.0k	237.4m	12P	-	480T	A2	DK	9832597
19	KING SEAWAYS	31788t	87	20.0k	161.6m	1400P	600C	104T	BA	DK	8502406
20F	MAGNOLIA SEAWAYS	32289t	03	22.5k	199.8m	12P	-	280T	AS	DK	9259496
21F	PETUNIA SEAWAYS	32289t	04	22.5k	199.8m	12P	-	280T	AS	DK	9259501
22F	PRIMULA SEAWAYS	37985t	04	22.5k	229.8m	12P	-	340T	AS	DK	9259513
23	PRINCESS SEAWAYS	31356t	86	18.5k	161.0m	1600P	600C	100T	BA	DK	8502391
24	REGINA SEAWAYS	25518t	10	24.0k	199.1m	600P	-	190T	A	LT	9458535
25F	SCANDIA SEAWAYS	60465t	21	21.0k	237.4m	12P	-	480T	A2	DK	9864681
26F	SELANDIA SEAWAYS	24196t	98	21.0k	197.5m	12P	-	206T	A	DK	9157284
27	SEVEN SISTERS	18425t	06	22.0k	112.0m	600P	300C	62L	BA	FR	9320130
28F	SUECIA SEAWAYS	24196t	99	21.0k	197.5m	12P	-	206T	AS	DK	9153020
29F	TRANSPORTER	6620t	91	16.5k	122.0m	0P	-	90T	A	FI	8820858
30F	TULIPA SEAWAYS	32336t	17	21.0k	209.6m	12P	-	262T	A2	LT	9809100
31	VISBORG	29746t	03	28.5k	195.8m	1500P	500C	118T	BAS2	MT	9223784

ACACIA SEAWAYS Built as the MELEQ by Flensburger Schiffbau-Gesellschaft, Flensburg, Germany for *Alternative Transport (Ekol)* of Turkey. In January 2019 chartered to *CLdN*. In January 2019 purchased by *CLdN* and re-flagged, initially to Malta and then to Belgium. In April 2021, purchased by *DFDS*, renamed the ACACIA SEAWAYS and chartered back to *CLdN*. In December charter ended and delivered to *DFDS*.

ARK DANIA, ARK GERMANIA Built by P+S Werften GmbH, Stralsund, Germany. They are used for the German/Danish joint ARK Project providing NATO transport but are also available for *DFDS* use and charter when not required. They have a crane for loading containers on the weather deck. In December 2012 the order for these vessels was cancelled due to late delivery. Following negotiations with the shipyard it was agreed that they would be completed under a new contract which was signed in February 2013. Both vessels were delivered to *DFDS* in April 2014, the ARK GERMANIA almost complete, the ARK DANIA still incomplete. The latter vessel was towed to the Fayard shipyard, Odense, to be completed. The ARK GERMANIA entered service a few days after delivery, the ARK DANIA in November 2014.

BEGONIA SEAWAYS Built as the TOR BEGONIA by Flensburger Schiffbau-Gesellschaft, Flensburg, Germany for *DFDS Tor Line*. Operates on the Göteborg - Immingham/Brevik route. In Summer 2009 lengthened by 30m by MWB Motorenwerke Bremerhaven AG, Germany. In July 2012 renamed the BEGONIA SEAWAYS.

BOTNIA SEAWAYS Built as the FINNMASTER by Jinling Shipyard, Nanjing, China for the *Macoma Shipping Group* and chartered to *Finncarriers*. In 2008 sold to *DFDS Lisco* and in January 2009 delivered, chartered to *DFDS Tor Line* and renamed the TOR BOTNIA. Operated on the Immingham - Rotterdam route until December 2010. In January 2011 moved to the Kiel - St Petersburg route. In January 2013 renamed the BOTNIA SEAWAYS. After operating on a number of routes, in March 2022 she was transferred to the Calais-Sheerness service.

BRITANNIA SEAWAYS Built as the TOR BRITANNIA by Fincantieri-Cantieri Navali Italiani SpA, Ancona, Italy for *DFDS Tor Line*. Operated on the Göteborg - Immingham route until 2004 when she was transferred to the Esbjerg - Immingham route. In January 2010 chartered to *Norfolkline* to operate between Vlaardingen and Felixstowe. In May 2011 renamed the BRITANNIA SEAWAYS.

CÔTE D'ALBÂTRE Built by Astilleros Barreras SA, Vigo, Spain for *Transmanche Ferries* to operate between Newhaven and Dieppe. In February 2009 she was moved to the Boulogne - Dover and Dieppe - Dover routes for *LD Lines*. In September 2009 moved to the Le Havre - Portsmouth route. The vessel has had periods laid up when not required on the Newhaven – Dieppe route.

CÔTE D'OPALE Built by CMI Jinling Weihai Shipyard, Weihai, China for *Stena RoRo*. Designed to run on either methanol or LNG but before delivery fitted with scrubbers to run on fuel oil. Upon delivery chartered to *DFDS Seaways* for ten years to operate between Dover and Calais.

CÔTE DES DUNES Built as the SEAFRANCE RODIN by Aker Finnyards, Rauma, Finland for *SeaFrance*. Launched in November 2001. In November 2011 laid up. In June 2012 sold to *Eurotransmanche*. In July 2012 renamed the RODIN. In August 2012 chartered to *MyFerryLink* and resumed operation between Calais and Dover. In July 2015 chartered to *DFDS Seaways* after *MyFerryLink* operations ceased. After a prolonged occupation by former *MyFerryLink* workers. *DFDS Seaways* took possession in early September and in November 2015 she was renamed the CÔTE DES DUNES. She re-entered service on the Dover - Calais route in February 2016. In June 2017 purchased by *DFDS Seaways*.

CÔTE DES FLANDRES Built as the SEAFRANCE BERLIOZ by Chantiers de l'Atlantique, St Nazaire for *SeaFrance*. Launched in March 2005. In November 2011 laid up. In June 2012 sold to *Eurotransmanche*, a *Groupe Eurotunnel* company. In July 2012 renamed the BERLIOZ. In August 2012 chartered to *MyFerryLink* and resumed operation between Calais and Dover. In July 2015 chartered to *DFDS Seaways* after *MyFerryLink* operations ceased. After a prolonged occupation by former *MyFerryLink* workers, *DFDS Seaways* took possession in early September and, in November 2015, she was renamed the CÔTE DES FLANDRES. She re-entered service on the Dover - Calais route in February 2016. In June 2017 purchased by *DFDS Seaways*.

DELFT SEAWAYS, DOVER SEAWAYS, DUNKERQUE SEAWAYS Built as the MAERSK DELFT, MAERSK DOVER and MAERSK DUNKERQUE by Samsung Heavy Industries, Koje (Geoje) Island, South Korea for *Norfolkline* to operate between Dover and Dunkerque. In July and August 2010 renamed the DELFT SEAWAYS, DOVER SEAWAYS and DUNKERQUE SEAWAYS.

FICARIA SEAWAYS Built as the TOR FICARIA by Flensburger Schiffbau-Gesellschaft, Flensburg, Germany for *DFDS Tor Line*. Operated on the Göteborg - Immingham/Brevik service. In Summer 2009 lengthened by 30m by MWB Motorenwerke Bremerhaven AG, Germany. In July 2011 renamed the FICARIA SEAWAYS. In March 2015 placed on the Vlaardingen - Immingham service.

FREESIA SEAWAYS Built as the TOR FREESIA by Flensburger Schiffbau-Gesellschaft, Flensburg, Germany for *DFDS Tor Line*. Operates on the Göteborg - Immingham/Brevik service. In Summer 2009 lengthened by 30m by MWB Motorenwerke Bremerhaven AG, Germany. In August 2012 renamed the FREESIA SEAWAYS.

GARDENIA SEAWAYS, TULIPA SEAWAYS Built by Flensburger Schiffbau-Gesellschaft, Flensburg, Germany for the Siem Industries Inc (owners of FSG). They are bareboat chartered to *DFDS Seaways* for five years with an option to purchase at the end of the charter period.

FLANDRIA SEAWAYS, HOLLANDIA SEAWAYS, HUMBRIA SEAWAYS, SCANDIA SEAWAYS Built by Jinling Shipyard, Nanjing, China.

KING SEAWAYS Built as the NILS HOLGERSSON by Schichau Seebeckwerft AG, Bremerhaven, Germany for *Rederi AB Swedcarrier* of Sweden for their service between Trelleborg and Travemünde, joint with *TT-Line* of Germany (trading as *TT-Line*). In 1992 purchased by *Brittany Ferries* for entry into service in Spring 1993. After a major rebuild, she was renamed the VAL DE LOIRE and introduced onto the Plymouth - Roscoff, Plymouth - Santander and Cork - Roscoff routes. In 2004 transferred to the Portsmouth - St Malo and Portsmouth – Cherbourg services. In 2005 operated mainly Portsmouth - St Malo. In 2006 sold to *DFDS*, renamed the KING OF SCANDINAVIA and placed on the Newcastle – IJmuiden route. In January 2011 renamed the KING SEAWAYS.

MAGNOLIA SEAWAYS Built as the TOR MAGNOLIA by Flensburger Schiffbau-Gesellschaft, Flensburg, Germany for *DFDS Tor Line*. In July 2011 renamed the MAGNOLIA SEAWAYS.

PETUNIA SEAWAYS Built as the TOR PETUNIA by Flensburger Schiffbau-Gesellschaft, Flensburg, Germany for *DFDS Tor Line*. In July 2011 renamed the PETUNIA SEAWAYS.

Dunkerque Seaways *(Miles Cowsill)*

Botnia Seaways *(George Holland)*

Côte d'Opale (Frank Lose)

Côte d'Albatre (John Bryant)

PRIMULA SEAWAYS Built as the TOR PRIMULA by Flensburger Schiffbau-Gesellschaft, Flensburg, Germany for *DFDS Tor Line*. In July 2010 renamed the PRIMULA SEAWAYS. In July 2016 lengthened by 30m by MWB Motorenwerke Bremerhaven AG, Germany.

PRINCESS SEAWAYS Built by Schichau Seebeckwerft AG, Bremerhaven, Germany as the PETER PAN for *TT-Line* for the service between Travemünde and Trelleborg. In 1992 sold to *TT Line* of Australia (no connection) for use on their service between Port Melbourne (Victoria) and Devonport (Tasmania) and renamed the SPIRIT OF TASMANIA. In 2002 sold to *Nordsjøferger K/S* of Norway and renamed the SPIR. After modification work she was, in 2003, renamed the FJORD NORWAY and chartered to *Fjord Line*. Placed on the Bergen - Egersund - Hanstholm route. In 2005 placed on the Bergen - Stavanger - Newcastle route, but operated once a week to Hanstholm. In October 2006 sold to *DFDS* and renamed the PRINCESS OF NORWAY, remaining on the Newcastle - Norway service but no longer serving Hanstholm. In May 2007 moved to the Newcastle - IJmuiden route. In February 2011 renamed the PRINCESS SEAWAYS.

REGINA SEAWAYS Built as the ENERGIA by Nuovi Cantieri Apuani, Marina di Carrara, Italy for *Grimaldi Holdings* of Italy. In August 2011 chartered to *DFDS* and moved to Klaipėda for modifications. In September 2011 renamed the REGINA SEAWAYS and placed on the Klaipėda - Kiel service. In May 2022 moved to the Dunkerque-Rosslare service.

SELANDIA SEAWAYS Built as the TOR SELANDIA by Fincantieri-Cantieri Navali Italiani SpA, Ancona, Italy for *DFDS Tor Line*. Operated on the Göteborg - Immingham route until 2004 when she was moved to the Göteborg – Gent route. In 2005 she moved to the Göteborg – Harwich route. In July the UK terminal moved to Tilbury. In August 2010 renamed the SELANDIA SEAWAYS. Currently operates on the Rotterdam - Felixstowe route.

SEVEN SISTERS Built by Astilleros Barreras SA, Vigo, Spain for *Transmanche Ferries* to operate between Newhaven and Dieppe. In recent years generally held as a reserve vessel. In March 2014 transferred to the *DFDS* Portsmouth - Le Havre service. She continues to carry *Transmanche Ferries* branding. In 2015 returned to the Newhaven - Dieppe service as second vessel, continuing to operate for *DFDS*. The vessel has had periods laid up when not required on the Newhaven – Dieppe route.

SUECIA SEAWAYS Built as the TOR SUECIA by Fincantieri-Cantieri Navali Italiani SpA, Ancona, Italy for *DFDS Tor Line*. Operated on the Göteborg - Immingham route until 2004 when she was transferred to the Esbjerg - Immingham route. Later transferred to the Danish flag. In March 2010 chartered to *Norfolkline* to operate between Vlaardingen and Felixstowe and continued on the route when it was taken over by *DFDS*. In June 2011 renamed the SUECIA SEAWAYS.

TRANSPORTER Built as the HAMNÖ by Brodogradiliste "Sava", Macvanska Mitrovica, Yugoslavia (fitted out by Fosen Mekaniske Verksteder of Rissa, Norway) for *Rederi AB Gustav Erikson* of Finland and chartered to *Transfennica* for service between Finland and Germany. In 1995 the owning company became *United Shipping* and in 2002 *Birka Cargo AB*. In 2000 she was chartered to the *Korsnäs Paper Group* to carry their traffic from Gävle (Sweden) to Chatham and Terneuzen (The Netherlands). In 2002 she was renamed the BIRKA TRANSPORTER. In April 2004 chartered to *Grimaldi Lines* of Italy to operate between Marseille and Tunis and in 2010 to *Holmen Paper Ab* of Sweden. In April 2013 ownership was transferred to *Eckerö Shipping Ab* of Finland and in June she was renamed the TRANSPORTER. In January 2016 she was sold to *Naviera Benzu Sl* of Spain. In March 2019 she was sold back to *Eckerö Shipping* and in April she was chartered to *DFDS Seaways* to operate on the Zeebrugge - Immingham - Halden - Fredrikstad service.

VISBORG Built as the VISBY by Guangzhou Shipyard International, Guangzhou, China for *Rederi AB Gotland* for use on *Destination Gotland* services. In December 2020 chartered to *DFDS Seaways* to operate between Dunkerque and Rosslare. In February 2022 renamed the VISBORG.

IRISH FERRIES

THE COMPANY *Irish Ferries* is a Republic of Ireland private sector company, part of the *Irish Continental Group*. It was originally mainly owned by the state-owned *Irish Shipping* and partly by *Lion Ferry AB* of Sweden. *Lion Ferry* participation ceased in 1977 and the company was sold into the private sector in 1987. Formerly state-owned *B&I Line* was taken over in 1991 and from 1995 all operations were marketed as *Irish Ferries*.

MANAGEMENT Irish Continental Group Chief Executive Officer Eamonn Rothwell, **Irish Ferries Limited Managing Director** Andrew Sheen.

ADDRESS PO Box 19, Ferryport, Alexandra Road, Dublin 1, D01 W2F5, Republic of Ireland.

TELEPHONE Administration +353 (0)1 607 5700, **Reservations** *Ireland* +353 (0)818300 400, *Rosslare Harbour* +353 (0)53 913 3158, *Holyhead* +44 (0)3717 300 200, *Pembroke Dock* +44 (0)3717 300 500, *National* +44 (0)3717 300 400, *24 hour information* +353 (0)8 18 300 400 (Ireland) or +44 (0)3717 300 400).

FAX Administration & Reservations *Dublin* +353 (0)1 607 5660, *Rosslare* +353 (0)53 913 3544.

INTERNET Email info@irishferries.com **Website** www.irishferries.com *(English, French, German, Italian and Dutch)*

ROUTES OPERATED Conventional Ferries Dublin - Holyhead (3 hrs 15 mins; *EPSILON, ULYSSES, W. B. YEATS*; 2-4 per day), Rosslare - Pembroke Dock (4 hrs; *BLUE STAR 1*; 2 per day), Dublin - Cherbourg (17-19 hrs; *EPSILON, W. B. YEATS*; up to 4 per week), Dover-Calais (1 hr 30 mins; *ISLE OF INISHMORE, ISLE OF INNISFREE*; *ISLE OF INISHEER*; 15 per day).
Fast Ferry Dublin - Holyhead (2 hr 15 min; *DUBLIN SWIFT*; 2 per day).

1	BLUE STAR 1	29415t	00	27.0k	176.1m	830P	640C	100L	BA	GR	9197105
2»	DUBLIN SWIFT	8403t	01	35.0k	101.0m	900P	200C	16T	BA	CY	9243227
3	EPSILON	26375t	11	24.0k	177.5m	500P	500C	190T	A	CY	9539054
4	ISLE OF INISHEER	22152t	00	22.5k	179.9m	450P	-	125L	BA2	CY	9181091
5	ISLE OF INISHMORE	34031t	97	21.3k	182.5m	2200P	802C	130L	BA2	CY	9142605
6	ISLE OF INNISFREE	28833t	91	21.0k	163.6m	1850P	600C	100L	BA2	CY	8908466
7	ULYSSES	50938t	01	22.0k	209.0m	1875P	1342C	241L	BA2	CY	9214991
8	W. B. YEATS	51388t	18	22.5k	194.8m	1800P	1550C	165L	BA2	CY	9809679

BLUE STAR 1 Built as SUPERFERRY ATLANTIC by Van der Gissen de Noord, Krimpen aan den Ijssel, Netherlands for *Strintzis Line* of Greece. By the time she was delivered the company had been rebranded as *Blue Star Ferries*, following the acquisition of 48% holding by *Attica Enterprises* (owners of *Superfast Ferries*). She was renamed the BLUE STAR 1 and used on services between Greece and Italy and from the Greek mainland to the Greek islands. Between January and September 2007 she was chartered to *Superfast Ferries* to operate between Zeebrugge and Rosyth (Scotland). She then returned to the Mediterranean. In March 2021 chartered to *Irish Ferries* and placed on the Rosslare-Pembroke Dock route.

DUBLIN SWIFT Austal Auto-Express 101 catamaran built by Austal Ships Pty, Fremantle, Australia as the WESTPAC EXPRESS. Chartered through a number of third-party companies to the *US Marine Corps* as a support vessel. In 2015 returned to *Austal Ships*. In May 2016 sold to the *Irish Continental Group*. Chartered to *Sealift Inc* of the USA and continued to be operated for the *US Marine Corps*. In November 2017 charter ended; laid up in Belfast. In March 2018 renamed the DUBLIN SWIFT and in April replaced the JONATHAN SWIFT on the Holyhead - Dublin route.

EPSILON Built as the CARTOUR EPSILON by CN Visentini, Porto Viro, Italy. Chartered to *Caronte & Tourist SPA* of Italy. In November 2013 chartered to *Irish Ferries*. In February 2014 renamed the EPSILON. In March 2019 purchased by *Caronte & Tourist SPA* of Italy. The charter to *Irish Ferries* continued. In March 2022 purchased by *EuroAfrica Shipping* of Poland for delivery in November 2022. The charter to *Irish Ferries* continued.

Sea travel differently

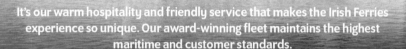

It's our warm hospitality and friendly service that makes the Irish Ferries experience so unique. Our award-winning fleet maintains the highest maritime and customer standards.

Along with Club Class, cabins, restaurants, and extensive duty free shopping, we offer the best value fares for car drivers, passengers and freight customers alike.

And now with a full schedule of 3 ships and operating on Dover - Calais. offering even more choice, we're embarking on another exciting chapter.

Irish Ferries. Sea Travel Differently.

ISLE OF INISHEER Built as the NORTHERN MERCHANT by Astilleros Espanoles SA (AESA), Spain for Cenargo (owners of *NorseMerchant Ferries*). On delivery, chartered to *Norfolkline* to inaugurate a Dover - Dunkerque (Ouest) service in March 2000. In April 2006, chartered to *Acciona Trasmediterranea* of Spain and in July renamed the ZURBARAN and, in April 2019, renamed the CIUDAD DE MAHON. In July 2021 sold to *Trasmed* of Spain. In November 2021 sold to *Irish Continental Group* of the Irish Republic for delivery in January 2022. In January 2022 renamed the ISLE OF INISHEER. Introduced onto the Dover - Calais service in March 2022.

ISLE OF INISHMORE Built by Van der Giessen de Noord, Krimpen aan den IJssel, Rotterdam for *Irish Ferries* to operate on the Holyhead - Dublin service. In 2001 replaced by the ULYSSES and moved to the Rosslare - Pembroke Dock route. In June 2021 moved to a new Dover - Calais service.

ISLE OF INNISFREE Built as the PRINS FILIP by NV Boelwerf SA, Temse, Belgium for *Regie voor Maritiem Transport (RMT)* of Belgium for the Oostende - Dover service. Although completed in 1991, she did not enter service until May 1992. In 1994 the British port became Ramsgate. Withdrawn in 1997 and laid up for sale. In 1998 she was sold to *Stena RoRo* and renamed the STENA ROYAL. In November 1998 she was chartered to *P&O Ferries* to operate as a freight-only vessel on the Dover - Zeebrugge route. In Spring 1999 it was decided to charter the vessel on a long-term basis and she was repainted into *P&O Stena Line* (later *P&O Ferries*) colours and renamed the P&OSL AQUITAINE. In Autumn 1999 she was modified to make her suitable to operate between Dover and Calais and was transferred to that route, becoming a passenger vessel again. In August 2002 renamed the PO AQUITAINE and in 2003 the PRIDE OF AQUITAINE. In September 2005 sold to *LD Lines* and renamed the NORMAN SPIRIT. In October, inaugurated a Le Havre - Portsmouth service, replacing that previously operated by *P&O Ferries*. In November 2009 moved to the Dover - Boulogne route. In March 2010 chartered to *TransEuropa Ferries*, placed on the Oostende - Ramsgate service (as part of a joint venture) and renamed the OSTEND SPIRIT. In May 2011 returned to the Portsmouth - Le Havre route and renamed the NORMAN SPIRIT. In November 2011 chartered to *DFDS Seaways* to add extra capacity to their Dover - Dunkerque route. In February 2012 transferred to the new Dover - Calais route, joint with *DFDS Seaways*. Ownership transferred to *DFDS Seaways* in late 2012. In March 2013 refurbished, repainted into *DFDS Seaways* colours and renamed the CALAIS SEAWAYS. In July 2021 replaced by the new CÔTE D'OPALE and laid up. In November 2021 sold to *Irish Ferries* and renamed the ISLE OF INNISFREE.

ULYSSES Built by Aker Finnyards, Rauma, Finland for *Irish Ferries* for the Dublin - Holyhead service.

W. B. YEATS Built by Flensburger Schiffbau-Gesellschaft, Flensburg, Germany. Operates between Dublin and Cherbourg in the summer and Dublin and Holyhead in the winter.

ISLE OF MAN STEAM PACKET COMPANY

THE COMPANY The *Isle of Man Steam Packet Company Limited* is an Isle of Man-registered company owned by the Isle of Man Government.

MANAGEMENT Managing Director **Brian Thomson.**

ADDRESS Imperial Buildings, Douglas, Isle of Man IM1 2BY.

TELEPHONE Administration +44 (0)1624 645645, **Reservations *UK*** 08722 992 992, *International* +44 8722 992 992 (Outside UK).

INTERNET Email iom.reservations@steam-packet.com **Website** www.steam-packet.com *(English),*

ROUTES OPERATED Conventional Ferry *All year* Douglas (Isle of Man) - Heysham (3 hrs 45 mins; ***BEN-MY-CHREE***; up to 2 per day), Douglas – Belfast (5 hours; ***BEN-MY-CHREE***; occasional). **Fast Ferry** *March-October* Douglas - Liverpool (2 hrs 45 mins; ***MANANNAN***; up to 2 per day), Douglas - Belfast (3 hrs; ***MANANNAN***; up to 2 per week), Douglas - Dublin (3

Isle of Inisheer *(Darren Holdaway)*

Ulysses *(Miles Cowsill)*

Manannan *(Miles Cowsill)*

Hamnavoe *(Northlink)*

hrs; **MANANNAN**; up to 2 per week), Douglas - Heysham (2 hrs 15 mins; **MANANNAN**; occasional), **Freight Ferry** Douglas - Heysham (4 hrs 30 mins; **ARROW**; as required).

1F	ARROW	7606t	98	15.0k	122.3m	12P	-	84T	A	IM	9119414
2	BEN-MY-CHREE	12747t	98	18.0k	124.9m	630P	275C	90T	A	IM	9170705
3»	MANANNAN	5743t	98	43.0k	96.0m	865P	200C	-	A	IM	9176072

ARROW Built as the VARBOLA by Astilleros de Huelva SA, Huelva, Spain for the *Estonian Shipping Company*. On completion, chartered to *Dart Line* and placed on the Dartford - Vlissingen route. In 1999 she was renamed the DART 6. At the end of August 1999, the charter was terminated and she was renamed the VARBOLA. She undertook a number of short-term charters, including *Merchant Ferries*. In 2000 long-term chartered to *Merchant Ferries* to operate between Heysham and Dublin. In 2003 the charter ended and she was chartered to *Dart Line* to replace the DART 9; she was placed initially on the Dartford - Vlissingen route but later transferred to the Dartford - Dunkerque route. Later sub-chartered to *NorseMerchant Ferries* and placed on the Heysham – Dublin route. In 2004 the charter transferred to *NorseMerchant Ferries*. In 2005 sold to *Elmira Shipping* of Greece and renamed the RR ARROW. In October 2007 sold to *Seatruck Ferries* but the charter to *Norfolkline* continued. Renamed the ARROW. In June 2009 returned to *Seatruck Ferries*. In April 2014 long term chartered to *IOMSP*. When not required she is sub-chartered to other operators.

BEN-MY-CHREE Built by Van der Giessen de Noord, Krimpen aan den IJssel, Rotterdam for the *IOMSP Co* and operates between Douglas and Heysham. Additional passenger accommodation was added at her spring 2004 refit. In 2005 her passenger certificate was increased from 500 to 630. She operates some sailings between Douglas and Belfast in the summer.

MANANNAN Incat 96m catamaran built as the INCAT 050 at Hobart, Tasmania. Initially chartered to *Transport Tasmania* of Australia and operated between Port Melbourne (Victoria) and Georgetown (Tasmania). In 1999 chartered to *Fast Cat Ferries* of New Zealand and operated between Wellington (North Island) and Picton (South Island) under the marketing name 'Top Cat'. In 2000 she was laid up. In 2001 she was chartered to the *US Navy* and renamed the USS JOINT VENTURE (HSV-X1). In 2008 the charter was terminated and she was renamed the INCAT 050. Later purchased by *IOMSP*. Following conversion back to civilian use, in May 2009 she was renamed the MANANNAN.

Under Construction

| 4 | MANXMAN | 14000t | 23 | 19.3k | 133.0m | 949P | 250C | 89L | BA | IM | 9917244 |

MANXMAN Under construction by Hyundai Mipo Dockyard, Ulsan, South Korea. She will replace the BEN MY CHREE on the Douglas - Heysham service, which will become a back-up vessel.

NORTHLINK FERRIES

THE COMPANY NorthLink Ferries is a UK based company, wholly owned by *Serco Group plc*. The service is operated on behalf of Scottish Ministers.

MANAGEMENT Managing Director Stuart Garrett, **Customer Service Director** Billy Robb.

ADDRESS Ferry Terminal, Ferry Road, Stromness, Orkney KW16 3BH.

TELEPHONE Customer Services *UK* 0800 1114422, ***International*** +44 (0)1856 885500), **Freight Reservations** 0800 1114434.

INTERNET Email info@northlinkferries.co.uk **Website** www.northlinkferries.co.uk *(English)*

ROUTES OPERATED *Passenger Ferries* Scrabster - Stromness (Orkney) (1 hr 30 min; **HAMNAVOE**; up to 3 per day), Aberdeen - Lerwick (Shetland) (direct) (12 hrs; **HJALTLAND, HROSSEY**; 3 northbound/4 southbound per week), Aberdeen - Kirkwall, Hatston New Pier (Orkney) (5 hrs 45 mins) - Lerwick (14 hrs; **HJALTLAND, HROSSEY**; 4 northbound/3 southbound per week). ***Freight Ferries*** Aberdeen - Kirkwall (Orkney) (12 hrs; **HELLIAR, HILDASAY**; 4 per week), Aberdeen - Lerwick (Shetland) (**HELLIAR, HILDASAY**; 4 per week).

| 1 | HAMNAVOE | 8780t | 02 | 19.3k | 112.0m | 600P | 95C | 20L | BA | UK | 9246061 |

2F	HELLIAR	7800t	98	17.0k	122.3m	12P	-	86T	A	IM	9119397
3F	HILDASAY	7606t	99	17.0k	122.3m	12P	-	84T	A	IM	9119426
4	HJALTLAND	11720t	02	24.0k	125.0m	600P	150C	30L	BA	UK	9244958
5	HROSSEY	11720t	02	24.0k	125.0m	600P	150C	30L	BA	UK	9244960

HAMNAVOE Built by Aker Finnyards, Rauma, Finland for *NorthLink Orkney and Shetland Ferries Ltd* to operate on the Scrabster - Stromness route. Did not enter service until Spring 2003 due to late completion of work at Scrabster to accommodate the ship. *Caledonian MacBrayne's* HEBRIDEAN ISLES covered between October 2002 and Spring 2003. Initially owned by the *Royal Bank of Scotland*, she was acquired by *Caledonian Maritime Assets Ltd* (owned by *Transport Scotland*) in May 2018.

HELLIAR Built as the LEHOLA by Astilleros de Huelva SA, Huelva, Spain for the *Estonian Shipping Company*. Initially used on *ESCO* Baltic services. In 1998 chartered to *Czar Peter Line* to operate between Moerdijk (The Netherlands) and Kronstadt (Russia). In 1999 chartered to *Delom* of France to operate between Marseilles and Sete and Tunis. In 2000 she returned to *ESCO*, operating between Kiel and Tallinn. In 2003 chartered to *Scandlines AG* and transferred to subsidiary *Scandlines Estonia AS*. Operated Rostock - Helsinki – Muuga initially and later Rostock – Helsinki. Service finished at the end of 2004 and in 2005 she was chartered to *P&O Ferries* to operate between Hull and Rotterdam and Hull and Zeebrugge. In 2005 sold to *Elmira Shipping* of Greece. Later renamed the RR TRIUMPH. In 2006 transferred to *P&O Irish Sea* to operate between Liverpool and Dublin. In 2007 chartered to *Balearia* of Spain and operated from Barcelona. In December 2007 purchased by *Seatruck Ferries* and renamed the TRIUMPH. In Spring 2008 she was sub-chartered to *Condor Ferries* to cover for the refit period of the COMMODORE GOODWILL. In June 2008 placed on the Liverpool - Dublin route and in July renamed the CLIPPER RACER. In February 2009 replaced by the new CLIPPER PACE. In April 2009 again chartered to *Balearia*. In January 2011 chartered to *NorthLink Ferries* and renamed the HELLIAR. In June 2017 sold to *CF Clip Helliar LLC*; the charter continued. In March 2019 purchased by *Caledonian Maritime Assets Ltd* (owned by *Transport Scotland*).

HILDASAY Built as the LEILI by Astilleros de Huelva SA, Huelva, Spain for the *Estonian Shipping Company*. Used on Baltic services. In 2002 chartered to *Crowley Maritime* of the USA and renamed the PORT EVERGLADES EXPRESS. In 2004 resumed the name LEILI and chartered to *NorseMerchant Ferries* to operate between Birkenhead and Dublin. In July 2005 moved to the Heysham - Belfast route and at the same time sold to *Elmira Shipping* of Greece and renamed the RR SHIELD. In 2007 sold to *Attica Group* of Greece and renamed the SHIELD. In January 2008 sold to *Seatruck Ferries* but continued to be chartered to *Norfolkline*. In June 2009 returned to *Seatruck Ferries*. In January 2009 chartered to *NorthLink Orkney and Shetland Ferries* and renamed the HILDASAY. In June 2017 sold to *CF Clip Hildasay LLC*; the charter continued. In March 2019 purchased by *Caledonian Maritime Assets Ltd* (owned by *Transport Scotland*).

HJALTLAND, HROSSEY Built by Aker Finnyards, Rauma, Finland for *NorthLink Orkney and Shetland Ferries* to operate on the Aberdeen - Kirkwall - Lerwick route when services started in 2002. Initially owned by the *Royal Bank of Scotland*, they were acquired by *Caledonian Maritime Assets Ltd* (owned by *Transport Scotland*) in May 2018.

ORKNEY FERRIES

THE COMPANY *Orkney Ferries Ltd* (previously the *Orkney Islands Shipping Company*) is a British company, an arms-length organisation of *Orkney Islands Council*.

MANAGEMENT Ferry Services Manager Andrew Blake.

ADDRESS Shore Street, Kirkwall, Orkney KW15 1LG.

TELEPHONE Administration +44 (0)1856 872044, **Reservations** +44 (0)1856 872044.

FAX Administration & Reservations +44 (0)1856 872921.

INTERNET Email info@orkneyferries.co.uk **Website** www.orkneyferries.co.uk *(English)*,

Eynhallow *(Miles Cowsill)*

Earl Sigurd *(Miles Cowsill)*

ROUTES OPERATED Kirkwall (Mainland) to Eday (1 hr 15 mins), Rapness (Westray) (1 hr 25 mins), Sanday (1 hr 25 mins), Stronsay (1 hr 35 mins), Papa Westray (1 hr 50 mins), North Ronaldsay (2 hrs 30 mins) ('North Isles service') (timings are direct from Kirkwall - sailings via other islands take longer; *EARL SIGURD, EARL THORFINN, VARAGEN*; 1/2 per day except Papa Westray which is twice weekly and North Ronaldsay which is weekly), Pierowall (Westray) - Papa Westray (25 mins; *NORDIC SEA*; up to six per day (Summer service - passenger-only)), Kirkwall - Shapinsay (25 mins; *SHAPINSAY*; 6 per day), Houton (Mainland) to Lyness (Hoy) (35 mins; *HOY HEAD*; 5 per day), and Flotta (35 mins; *HOY HEAD*; 4 per day) ('South Isles service') (timings are direct from Houton - sailings via other islands take longer), Tingwall (Mainland) to Rousay (20 mins; *EYNHALLOW*; 6 per day), Egilsay (30 mins; *EYNHALLOW*; 5 per day) and Wyre (20 mins; *EYNHALLOW*; 5 per day) (timings are direct from Tingwall - sailings via other islands take longer), Stromness (Mainland) to Moaness (Hoy) (25 mins; *GRAEMSAY*; 2/3 per day) and Graemsay (25 mins; *GRAEMSAY*; 2/3 per day) (passenger/cargo service - cars not normally conveyed).

1	EARL SIGURD	771t	90	12.5k	45.0m	190P	26C	-	BA	UK	8902711
2	EARL THORFINN	771t	90	12.5k	45.0m	190P	26C	-	BA	UK	8902723
3	EYNHALLOW	104t	87	10.5k	28.8m	95P	11C	-	BA	UK	8960880
4p•	GOLDEN MARIANA	33t	73	9.5k	15.2m	40P	0C	-	-	UK	
5	GRAEMSAY	90t	96	10.0k	20.6m	73P	2C	-	C	UK	
6	HOY HEAD	358t	94	11.0k	53.5m	125P	24C	3L	BA	UK	9081722
7p	NORDIC SEA	69t	12	10.0k	21.5m	40P	0C	0L	C	UK	
8	SHAPINSAY	199t	89	10.0k	32.6m	91P	16C	-	B	UK	8814184
9	THORSVOE	385t	91	10.6k	35.0m	122P	16C	-	BA	UK	9014743
10	VARAGEN	928t	88	14.5k	49.9m	144P	33C	5L	BA	UK	8818154

EARL SIGURD, EARL THORFINN Built by McTay Marine, Bromborough, Wirral, UK to inaugurate ro-ro working on the 'North Isles service'.

EYNHALLOW Built by David Abels Boat Builders, Bristol, UK to inaugurate ro-ro services from Tingwall (Mainland) to Rousay, Egilsay and Wyre. In 1991 she was lengthened by 5 metres, to increase car capacity.

GOLDEN MARIANA Built by Bideford Shipyard Ltd, Bideford, UK for *A J G England* of Padstow as a dual-purpose passenger and fishing vessel. In 1975 sold to *M MacKenzie* of Ullapool, then to *Pentland Ferries*, *Wide Firth Ferry* in 1982, and *Orkney Islands Council* in 1986. Passenger-only vessel. Generally operates summer-only feeder service between Pierowall (Westray) and Papa Westray.

GRAEMSAY Built by Ailsa Shipbuilding, Troon UK to operate between Stromness (Mainland), Moaness (Hoy) and Graemsay. Designed to offer an all-year-round service to these islands, primarily for passengers and cargo. Between October 2009 and January 2010 lengthened by 4.4 metres.

HOY HEAD Built by Appledore Shipbuilders Ltd, Appledore, UK to replace the THORSVOE on the 'South Isles service'. During winter 2012/13 extended by 14 metres at Cammell Laird Shiprepairers & Shipbuilders, Birkenhead, England.

NORDIC SEA Built by GS Marine Produktion AS, Haugsbygda, Norway for *Salten Cruise AS* of Bodø, Norway. Later operated for *Nordland County*. In April 2020 sold to *Orkney Ferries* to replace the GOLDEN MARIANA on the Westray - Papa Westray service.

SHAPINSAY Built by Yorkshire Drydock Ltd, Hull, UK for the service from Kirkwall (Mainland) to Shapinsay. In April 2011 lengthened by 6 metres at the Macduff Shipyards, Macduff, Scotland to increase car capacity from 12 to 16 and re-engined.

THORSVOE Built by Campbeltown Shipyard, Campbeltown, UK for the 'South Isles service'. In 1994 replaced by the new HOY HEAD and became the main reserve vessel for the fleet.

VARAGEN Built by Cochrane Shipbuilders, Selby, UK for *Orkney Ferries*, a private company established to start a new route between Gills Bay (Caithness, Scotland) and Burwick (South Ronaldsay, Orkney). However, due to problems with the terminals it was not possible to maintain regular services. In 1991, the company was taken over by *Orkney Islands Shipping Company* and the VARAGEN became part of their fleet, sharing the 'North Isles service' with the EARL SIGURD and the EARL THORFINN and replacing the freight vessel ISLANDER (494t, 1969).

P&O FERRIES

THE COMPANY *P&O Ferries Holdings Ltd* is a private sector company, a subsidiary of *Dubai World*, owned by the Government of Dubai. In Autumn 2002 *P&O North Sea Ferries*, P&O Irish Sea, *P&O Portsmouth* and *P&O Stena Line* (*Stena Line* involvement having ceased) were merged into a single operation.

MANAGEMENT Chief Executive Peter Hebblethwaite, **Chief Financial Officer** Karl Howarth, **Managing Director Short Routes** Vacant, **Business Unit Director Overnight Routes**.Vacant.

ADDRESSES *Head Office and Dover Services* Channel House, Channel View Road, Dover, Kent CT17 9TJ, ***Hull*** King George Dock, Hedon Road, Hull HU9 5QA, ***Larne*** P&O Irish Sea, Larne Harbour, Larne, Co Antrim BT40 1AW ***Rotterdam*** Beneluxhaven, Rotterdam (Europoort), Postbus 1123, 3180 Rozenburg, Netherlands, ***Zeebrugge*** Leopold II Dam 13, Havendam, 8380 Zeebrugge, Belgium.

TELEPHONE Administration *UK* +44 (0)1304 863000, **Passenger Reservations *UK*** +44 (0)1304 448 888, ***France*** +33 (0)825 12 01 56, ***Belgium*** +32 (0)70 70 77 71, ***The Netherlands*** +31 (0)20 20 08333, ***Spain*** +34 (0)902 02 04 61, ***Luxembourg*** +34 (0)20 80 82 94. **Freight Reservations** See freight website.

INTERNET Email customer.services@poferries.com **Websites** www.poferries.com *(English, French, Dutch, German)* www.poferriesfreight.com *(English, French, German)*

ROUTES OPERATED Passenger Dover - Calais (1 hr 30 mins; ***PRIDE OF BURGUNDY, PRIDE OF CANTERBURY, PRIDE OF KENT, SPIRIT OF BRITAIN, SPIRIT OF FRANCE***; up to 22 per day), Hull - Rotterdam (Beneluxhaven, Europoort) (The Netherlands) (from 10 hrs; ***PRIDE OF HULL, PRIDE OF ROTTERDAM***; 1 per day), Cairnryan - Larne (1 hr 45 min; ***EUROPEAN CAUSEWAY, EUROPEAN HIGHLANDER***; 7 per day), Liverpool - Dublin (8 hrs; ***NORBANK, NORBAY***; up to 2 per day. **Freight-only** Tilbury - Zeebrugge (8 hrs; ***NORSKY, NORSTREAM***; 10 per week), Middlesbrough (Teesport) - Rotterdam (Beneluxhaven, Europoort) **(16 hrs; *BORE SONG, ESTRADEN*; 3 per week),** Middlesbrough (Teesport) - Zeebrugge **(15 hrs 30** mins; ***BORE SONG, ESTRADEN***; 6 per week), Liverpool - Dublin (8 hrs; ***CLIPPER PENNANT***; 1 per day (plus services on passenger ferries)). **Container service** Hull - Zeebrugge (Belgium) (from 12 hrs 30 mins; ***FREYA***; 3 per week).

1F	BORE SONG	25586t	11	18.5k	195.0m	12P	-	210T	A2	NL	9443566
2F	CLIPPER PENNANT	14759t	09	22.0k	142.0m	12P	-	120T	A	CY	9372688
4F	ESTRADEN	18205t	99	19.0k	162.7m	12P	130C	170T	A	FI	9181077
5	EUROPEAN CAUSEWAY	20646t	00	22.7k	159.5m	410P	315C	84T	BA2	BS	9208394
6	EUROPEAN HIGHLANDER	21128t	02	22.6k	162.7m	410P	315C	84T	BA2	BS	9244116
7F	FREYA	5067t	00	-	118.3m	0P		648teu	C	NL	9219874
8	NORBANK	17464t	93	22.5k	166.7m	114P	-	125T	A	NL	9056583
9	NORBAY	17464t	92	21.5k	166.7m	114P	-	125T	A	BM	9056595
10F	NORSKY	19992t	99	20.0k	180.0m	12P	-	194T	A	FI	9186182
11F	NORSTREAM	19992t	99	20.0k	180.0m	12P	-	194T	A	FI	9186194
12	PRIDE OF BURGUNDY	28138t	92	21.0k	179.7m	1420P	465C	120L	BA2	CY	9015254
13	PRIDE OF CANTERBURY	30635t	91	21.0k	179.7m	2000P	537C	120L	BA2	CY	9007295
14	PRIDE OF HULL	59925t	01	22.0k	215.4m	1360P	205C	263T	AS	BS	9208629
15	PRIDE OF KENT	30635t	92	21.0k	179.7m	2000P	537C	120L	BA2	CY	9015266
16	PRIDE OF ROTTERDAM	59925t	00	22.0k	215.4m	1360P	205C	263T	AS	NL	9208617
17	SPIRIT OF BRITAIN	47592t	11	22.0k-	212.0m	2000P	194C	180L	BA2	CY	9524231
18	SPIRIT OF FRANCE	47592t	12	22.0k-	212.0m	2000P	194C	180L	BA2	CY	9533816

BORE SONG Built by Flensburger Schiffbau-Gesellschaft, Flensburg, Germany for *Bore Shipowners (Rettig Group Bore)* of Finland. In July 2011 chartered to *Mann Lines* to cover for the ESTRADEN'S refit. In September 2011 chartered to *P&O Ferries* and placed on the Middlesbrough - Zeebrugge route.

CLIPPER PENNANT Built by Astilleros Sevilla SA, Sevilla, Spain for *Seatruck Ferries*. In November 2018 chartered to *Canary Bridge Seaways,* a joint venture between *Fred. Olsen Express* and *Balearia* to operate between the Spanish mainland and the Canary Islands. In December 2019 chartered to *P&O Ferries* to operate between Liverpool and Dublin.

ESTRADEN Built as the ESTRADEN by Aker Finnyards, Rauma, Finland for *Rederi Ab Engship* (later *Bore Shipowners*) of Finland and chartered to *ArgoMann*. Later in 1999 renamed the AMAZON. In 2001 the charter was taken over by *Mann Lines* and in August she resumed the name ESTRADEN. In 2006 *Rederi AB Engship* was taken over by *Rettig Group Bore*; she remained on charter to *Mann Lines*. In January 2015 chartered to *P&O Ferries*.

EUROPEAN CAUSEWAY Built by Mitsubishi Heavy Industries, Shimonoseki, Japan for *P&O Irish Sea* for the Cairnryan - Larne service.

EUROPEAN HIGHLANDER Built by Mitsubishi Heavy Industries, Shimonoseki, Japan for *P&O Irish Sea* for the Cairnryan - Larne service.

FREYA Container ship built by J.J. Sietas KG Schiffswerft GmbH & Co for *Holwerda Shipmanagement BV* of The Netherlands. In June 2021 introduced as a second vessel on the Hull - Zeebrugge container service.

NORBANK Built by Van der Giessen de Noord, Krimpen aan den IJssel, Rotterdam, The Netherlands for *North Sea Ferries* for the Hull - Rotterdam service. She was originally built for and chartered to *Nedlloyd* but the charter was taken over by *P&O* in 1996 and she was bought by *P&O* in 2003. She retains Dutch crew and registry. In May 2001 moved to the Felixstowe - Europoort route. In January 2002 transferred to *P&O Irish Sea* and operated on the Liverpool – Dublin route.

NORBAY Built by Van der Giessen de Noord, Krimpen aan den IJssel, Rotterdam, The Netherlands for *North Sea Ferries* for the Hull - Rotterdam service. Owned by *P&O*. In January 2002 transferred to *P&O Irish Sea* and operated on the Liverpool – Dublin route.

NORSKY, NORSTREAM Built by Aker Finnyards, Rauma, Finland for *Bore Line* of Finland and chartered to *P&O North Sea Ferries*. They generally operated on the Teesport - Zeebrugge service. In September 2011, the NORSTREAM was moved to the Tilbury - Zeebrugge route. In January 2013, the NORSKY was also moved to the Tilbury - Zeebrugge route. However, they are sometimes transferred to Teesport services.

PRIDE OF BURGUNDY Built by Schichau Seebeckwerft AG, Bremerhaven, Germany for *P&O European Ferries* for the Dover - Calais service. When construction started she was due to be a freighter called the EUROPEAN CAUSEWAY and operate on the Zeebrugge freight route like PRIDE OF CANTERBURY and PRIDE OF KENT before their rebuild. However, it was decided that she should be completed as a passenger/freight vessel (the design allowed for conversion) and she was launched as the PRIDE OF BURGUNDY. In 1998, transferred to *P&O Stena Line* and renamed the P&OSL BURGUNDY. In 2002 renamed the PO BURGUNDY and in 2003 renamed the PRIDE OF BURGUNDY. In 2004 she operated mainly in freight-only mode. In 2005 returned to full passenger service. In March 2020 laid up. Resumed service between Dover and Calais in freight-only mode in June 2021 but laid up again in December.

PRIDE OF CANTERBURY Built as the EUROPEAN PATHWAY by Schichau Seebeckwerft AG, Bremerhaven, Germany for *P&O European Ferries* for the Dover - Zeebrugge freight service. In 1998 transferred to *P&O Stena Line*. In 2001 car/foot passengers were again conveyed on the route. In 2002/03 rebuilt as a full passenger vessel and renamed the PRIDE OF CANTERBURY; now operates between Dover and Calais.

PRIDE OF HULL Built by Fincantieri-Cantieri Navali Italiani SpA, Venezia, Italy for *P&O North Sea Ferries* to replace (with the PRIDE OF ROTTERDAM) the NORSEA and NORSUN plus the freight vessels NORBAY and NORBANK on the Hull - Rotterdam service.

Norbay (Miles Cowsill)

Pride of Kent (Darren Holdaway)

P&O Liberté *(Builders photo)*

Red Jet 7 *(Andrew Cooke)*

PRIDE OF KENT Built as the EUROPEAN HIGHWAY by Schichau Seebeckwerft AG, Bremerhaven, Germany for *P&O European Ferries* for the Dover - Zeebrugge freight service. In 1998 transferred to *P&O Stena Line*. In Summer 1999 she operated full-time between Dover and Calais. She returned to the Dover - Zeebrugge route in the autumn when the P&OSL AQUITAINE was transferred to the Dover - Calais service. In 2001 car/foot passengers were again conveyed on the route. In 2002/03 rebuilt as a full passenger vessel and renamed the PRIDE OF KENT; now operates between Dover and Calais.

PRIDE OF ROTTERDAM Built by Fincantieri-Cantieri Navali Italiani SpA, Venezia, Italy. Keel laid as the PRIDE OF HULL but launched as the PRIDE OF ROTTERDAM. Owned by Dutch interests until 2006 when she was sold to *P&O Ferries*. Further details as the PRIDE OF HULL.

SPIRIT OF BRITAIN, SPIRIT OF FRANCE Built by STX Europe, Rauma, Finland for the Dover - Calais service. Car capacity relates to dedicated car deck only; additional cars can be accommodated on the freight decks as necessary.

Under Construction

19	P&O PIONEER	47394t	23	22.0k-	230.0m	1500P	200C	170L	BA2	CY	9895161
20	P&O LIBERTÉ	47394t	23	22.0k-	230.0m	1500P	200C	170L	BA2	CY	9895173

P&O PIONEER, P&O LIBERTÉ Under construction by Guangzhou Shipyard International, Guangzhou, China for the Dover - Calais service. Double ended. The car capacity quoted is on the dedicated upper car deck only.

PENTLAND FERRIES

THE COMPANY *Pentland Ferries* is a UK private sector company.

MANAGEMENT Managing Director Helen Inkster, **Designated Person Ashore** Douglas Bain.

ADDRESS Pier Road, St Margaret's Hope, South Ronaldsay, Orkney KW17 2SW.

TELEPHONE Administration +44 (0)1856 831226.

INTERNET Email sales@pentlandferries.co.uk **Website** www.pentlandferries.co.uk *(English)*

ROUTE OPERATED Gills Bay (Caithness) - St Margaret's Hope (South Ronaldsay, Orkney) (1 hour; *ALFRED*; up to 3 per day).

1	ALFRED	2963t	19	16.0k	84.5m	430P	98C	12L	A	UK	9823467
2	PENTALINA	2382t	08	17.1k	59.0m	247P	70C	9L	A	UK	9437969

ALFRED Built by Strategic Marine Shipyard, Vũng Tàu, Vietnam.

PENTALINA Catamaran built by FBMA Marine, Cebu, Philippines for *Pentland Ferries*. In November 2019 replaced by the ALFRED and laid up. In July 2021 chartered to *Caledonian MacBrayne* to operate initially between Ardrossan and Brodick and later between Oban and Craignure.

RED FUNNEL FERRIES

THE COMPANY *Red Funnel Ferries* is the trading name of the *Southampton, Isle of Wight and South of England Royal Mail Steam Packet Company Limited*, a British private sector company owned by a consortium of British and Canadian pension funds led by the West Midland Pensions Fund of the UK and the Workplace Safety and Insurance Board of the Province of Ontario, Canada.

MANAGEMENT CEO Fran Collins, **Commercial Director** Colin Hetherington.

ADDRESS 12 Bugle Street, Southampton SO14 2JY.

TELEPHONE Administration +44 (0)2380 019192**, Reservations** +44 (0)2380 248500.

FAX Administration & Reservations +44 (0)2380 24 8501.

INTERNET Email post@redfunnel.co.uk **Website** www.redfunnel.co.uk *(English),*

ROUTES OPERATED Conventional Ferries Southampton - East Cowes (55 mins; **RED EAGLE, RED FALCON, RED OSPREY**; hourly). **Fast Passenger Ferries** Southampton - Cowes (22 mins; **RED JET 4, RED JET 6, RED JET 7**; every hour or half hour). **Freight Ferry** (1 hour, 10 mins; **RED KESTREL**; as required).

1	RED EAGLE	3953t	96	13.0k	93.2m	895P	200C	18L	BA	UK	9117337
2	RED FALCON	3953t	94	13.0k	93.2m	895P	200C	18L	BA	UK	9064047
3»p	RED JET 4	342t	03	35.0k	39.8m	277P	0C	0L	-	UK	9295854
4»p	RED JET 6	363t	16	35.0k	41.1m	275P	0C	0L	-	UK	9788083
5»p	RED JET 7	363t	18	35.0k	41.1m	275P	0C	0L	-	UK	9847645
6F	RED KESTREL	1070t	19	12.5k	74.3m	12P	-	12L	BA	UK	9847645
7	RED OSPREY	3953t	94	13.0k	93.2m	895P	200C	18L	BA	UK	9064059

RED EAGLE Built by Ferguson Shipbuilders, Port Glasgow, UK for the Southampton - East Cowes service. During Winter 2004/05 stretched by 10 metres and height raised by 3 metres at Gdansk, Poland. In spring 2018 she received an upgrade (as RED FALCON in 2014).

RED FALCON Built by Ferguson Shipbuilders, Port Glasgow, UK for the Southampton - East Cowes service. In 2004 stretched by 10 metres and height raised by 3 metres at Gdansk, Poland. In spring 2014 she received a £2m upgrade.

RED JET 4 Catamaran built North West Bay Ships Pty Ltd Hobart, Tasmania, Australia.

RED JET 6, RED JET 7 Catamaran built by Wight Shipyard, Cowes, Isle of Wight, UK.

RED KESTREL Built by Cammell Laird, Birkenhead. She is designed to provide additional year-round freight capacity for the Southampton - East Cowes route.

RED OSPREY Built by Ferguson Shipbuilders, Port Glasgow, UK for the Southampton - East Cowes service. In 2003 stretched by 10 metres and height raised by 3 metres at Gdansk, Poland. In spring 2015 she received an upgrade (as RED FALCON in 2014).

SHETLAND ISLANDS COUNCIL

THE COMPANY *Shetland Islands Council* is a British local government authority.

MANAGEMENT Ferry Operations Manager Kevin Main, **Marine Superintendent** Ian Pearson.

ADDRESS Port Administration Building, Sella Ness, Mossbank, Shetland ZE2 9QR.

TELEPHONE Administration +44 (0)1806 244200 **Reservations** *Yell Sound, Bluemull*, *Whalsay*, *Skerries & Papa Stour*, *Fair Isle* +44 (0)1595 760363.

INTERNET Email ferries@shetland.gov.uk **Website:** www.shetland.gov.uk/ferries *(English)*

ROUTES OPERATED Yell Sound Service Toft (Mainland) - Ulsta (Yell) (20 mins; **DAGALIEN, DAGGRI**; up to 26 per day), **Bluemull Sound Service** (Gutcher (Yell) - Belmont (Unst) (10 mins; **BIGGA, GEIRA**; up to 28 per day), Gutcher – Hamars Ness (Fetlar) (25 mins; **BIGGA, GEIRA**; up to 8 per day), **Bressay** Lerwick (Mainland) - Maryfield (Bressay) (5 mins; **LEIRNA**; up to 23 per day), **Whalsay** Laxo/Vidlin (Mainland) - Symbister (Whalsay) (30-45 mins; **HENDRA, LINGA**; up to 18 per day), **Skerries** Vidlin (Mainland) – Out Skerries (1 hr 30 mins; **FILLA**; up to 10 per week), Out Skerries – Lerwick (3 hours; **FILLA**; 2 per week), **Fair Isle** (Grutness (Mainland) - Fair Isle (3 hrs; **GOOD SHEPHERD IV**; 2 per week), **Papa Stour** West Burrafirth (Mainland) – Papa Stour (40 mins; **SNOLDA**; up to 7 per week). The **FIVLA** is used to cover while vessels other than **GOOD SHEPHERD IV** are at annual refit.

1	BIGGA	274t	91	11.0k	33.5m	96P	21C	2L	BA	UK	9000821
2	DAGALIEN	1861t	04	12.0k	65.4m	144P	30C	4L	BA	UK	9291626
3	DAGGRI	1861t	04	12.0k	65.4m	144P	30C	4L	BA	UK	9291614
4	FILLA	356t	03	12.0k	35.5m	30P	10C	2L	A	UK	9269192
5	FIVLA	230t	85	11.0k	29.9m	95P	10C	2L	BA	UK	8410237
6	GEIRA	226t	88	10.8k	29.9m	95P	10C	2L	BA	UK	8712489

Red Osprey (Andrew Cooke)

Leirna (Miles Cowsill)

Hendra *(Miles Cowsill)*

Stena Britannica *(Rob de Visser)*

7	GOOD SHEPHERD IV	76t	86	10.0k	18.3m	12P	2C	0L	C	UK	
8	HENDRA	248t	82	11.0k	30.2m	95P	12C	2L	BA	UK	8200254
9	LEIRNA	420t	92	9.0k	35.1m	124P	20C	2L	BA	UK	9050199
10	LINGA	658t	01	11.0k	36.2m	100P	16C	2L	BA	UK	9242170
11	SNOLDA	130t	83	9.0k	24.4m	12P	6C	1L	A	UK	8302090

BIGGA Built by JW Miller & Sons Ltd, St Monans, Fife, UK. Used on the Toft - Ulsta service. In 2005 moved to the Bluemull Sound service.

DAGALIEN, DAGGRI Built by Stocznia Polnócna, Gdansk, Poland to replace the BIGGA and HENDRA on Toft - Ulsta service.

FILLA Built by Stocznia Polnócna, Gdansk, Poland for the Lerwick /Vidlin - Out Skerries service. She looks like an oil rig supply vessel and is capable of transporting fresh water for replenishing the tanks on the Skerries in case of drought. Additional to deck space vessel has 2 holds with capacity for 90 tons.

FIVLA Built by Ailsa Shipbuilding, Troon, UK. Now a spare vessel, though often used on the Bluemull service.

GEIRA Built by Richard Dunston (Hessle), Hessle, UK. Formerly used on the Laxo - Symbister route. Replaced by the HENDRA in 2005 and moved to the Bluemull Sound service.

GOOD SHEPHERD IV Built by JW Miller & Sons Ltd, St Monans, Fife, UK. Used on the service between Grutness (Mainland) and Fair Isle. This vessel is not roll-on roll-off; vehicles are conveyed by Lift on Lift off with a weight restriction of 1.5 tons. She is pulled up on the marine slip on Fair Isle at the conclusion of each voyage.

HENDRA Built by McTay Marine, Bromborough, Wirral, UK for the Laxo - Symbister service. In 2002 transferred to the Toft - Ulsta service. In 2004 replaced by new vessels DAGGRI and DAGALIEN and moved to the Bluemull Sound service. In May 2005 returned to the Laxo - Symbister service as second vessel.

LEIRNA Built by Ferguson Shipbuilders, Port Glasgow, UK. Used on the Lerwick - Maryfield (Bressay) service.

LINGA Built by Stocznia Polnócna, Gdansk, Poland. Used on the Laxo - Symbister service.

SNOLDA Built as the FILLA by Sigbjorn Iversen, Flekkefjord, Norway. Used on the Lerwick (Mainland) - Out Skerries and Vidlin (Mainland) - Out Skerries services. At other times she operated freight and charter services around the Shetland Archipelago. Passenger capacity was originally 20 from 1st April to 31st October inclusive but is now 12 all year. In 2003 renamed the SNOLDA; replaced by the new FILLA and, in 2004, transferred to the West Burrafirth - Papa Stour route which is now Roll on Roll off with hold space available.

STENA LINE

MANAGEMENT Chief Executive Niclas Mårtensson, **Trade Director North Sea** Annika Hult, **Trade Director Irish Sea** Paul Grant.

ADDRESS UK Stena House, Station Approach, Holyhead, Anglesey LL65 1DQ, **The Netherlands** PO Box 2, 3150 AA, Hoek van Holland, The Netherlands.

TELEPHONE Administration UK +44 (0)1407 606618, **The Netherlands** +31 (0)174 389 333, **Reservations UK** 03447 707070 (from UK only), **The Netherlands** +31 (0)174 315811. **Freight - Commercial Vehicles over 6.0m 08450 704 000 / 08708 503 535.**

INTERNET Email info@stenaline.com **Website** www.stenaline.co.uk (English),

ROUTES OPERATED Conventional Ferries Cairnryan - Belfast (2 hrs 15 mins; **STENA SUPERFAST VII, STENA SUPERFAST VIII**; up to 6 per day, Port of Liverpool (Twelve Quays River Terminal, Birkenhead) - Belfast (8 hrs; **STENA EDDA, STENA EMBLA**; up to 2 per day), Holyhead - Dublin (3 hrs 15 mins; **STENA ADVENTURER, STENA ESTRID**; 4 per day), Fishguard - Rosslare (3 hrs 15 mins on day sailings; **STENA EUROPE**; 2 per day), Rosslare - Cherbourg (18 hrs; **STENA HORIZON**; 3 per week), Harwich - Hoek van Holland (The

Netherlands) (7 hrs 30 mins; **STENA BRITANNICA, STENA HOLLANDICA**; 2 per day).
Freight Ferries Heysham - Belfast (7 hrs; **STENA HIBERNIA, STENA SCOTIA**; 2 per day),
Port of Liverpool (Twelve Quays River Terminal, Birkenhead) - Belfast (8 hrs; **SEATRUCK
PANORAMA**; 1 per day), Rosslare - Cherbourg (18 hrs; **STENA FORETELLER**; 3 per week),
Harwich - Rotterdam (8 hrs; **SOMERSET, STENA FORERUNNER**; 11 per week), Killingholme -
Hoek van Holland (11 hrs; **STENA TRANSIT, STENA TRANSPORTER**; 1 per day), Immingham
- Rotterdam (13 hrs; **FIONIA SEA, JUTLANDIA SEA**; 6 per week).

1F	FIONIA SEA	25609t	09	20.0k	184.8m	12P	-	250T	AS	UK	9395343
2F	JUTLANDIA SEA	25609t	10	20.0k	184.8m	12P	-	250T	AS	SE	9395355
3	SEATRUCK PANORAMA	14759t	09	22.0k	142.0m	12P	-	120T	A	CY	9372676
4F	SOMERSET	21005t	00	18.0k	183.4m	12P	-	180T	A	NL	9188221
5	STENA ADVENTURER	43532t	03	22.0k	210.8m	1500P	-	210L	BA2	UK	9235529
6	STENA BRITANNICA	63600t	10	22.0k	240.0m	1200P	-	300T	BA2	UK	9419175
7	STENA EDDA	41671t	20	22k	214.5m	927P	300C	180L	BA2	CY	9807308
8	STENA EMBLA	41671t	20	22k	214.5m	927P	300C	180L	BA2	CY	9807322
9	STENA ESTRID	41671t	19	22k	214.5m	927P	300C	180L	BA2	CY	9807293
10	STENA EUROPE	24828t	81	20.5k	149.0m	2076P	456C	60T	BA	UK	7901760
11F	STENA FORERUNNER	24688t	02	22.0k	195.3m	12P	-	210T	A2	NL	9227259
12F	STENA FORETELLER	24688t	02	22.0k	195.3m	12P	-	210T	A2	DK	9214666
13F	STENA HIBERNIA	13017t	96	18.6k	142.5m	12P	-	114T	A	UK	9121637
14	STENA HOLLANDICA	63600t	10	22.5k	240.0m	1200P	-	300T	BA2	NL	9419163
15	STENA HORIZON	26500t	06	23.5k	186.5m	720P	160C	135L	A	IT	9332559
16F	STENA SCOTIA	13017t	96	18.6k	142.5m	12P	-	114T	A	UK	9121625
17	STENA SUPERFAST VII	30285t	01	22.0k	203.3m	1200P	660C	110L	BA2	UK	9198941
18	STENA SUPERFAST VIII	30285t	01	22.0k	203.3m	1200P	660C	110L	BA2	UK	9198953
19F+	STENA TRANSIT	34700t	11	22.2k	212.0m	300P	-	290T	A2	NL	9469388
20F+	STENA TRANSPORTER	34700t	11	22.2k	212.0m	300P	-	290T	A2	NL	9469376

FIONIA SEA Built as the TOR FIONIA by Jinling Shipyard, Nanjing, China for *Macoma Shipping
Ltd* of the UK. Launched as the JINGLING 3. She was time-chartered to *DFDS Tor Line* for ten
years (with an option on a further three). Delivered in May 2009 and initially replaced the TOR
BEGONIA, TOR FICARIA and TOR FREESIA while they were being lengthened. In October 2011
renamed the FIONIA SEAWAYS. In December 2018 sold to *Leomar RoRo* of Sweden. The
charter ended at the end of January 2020. In February 2020 renamed the FIONIA SEA and
chartered to *Finnlines*. In August charter ended. In January 2021 chartered to *Wallenius SOL*.
In February 2022 chartered to *Stena Line*.

JUTLANDIA SEA Built as the TOR JUTLANDIA by Jinling Shipyard, Nanjing, China for *Macoma
Shipping Ltd* of the UK and time-chartered to *DFDS Tor Line* for ten years. In July 2011 renamed
the JUTLANDIA SEAWAYS. In December 2018 sold to *Leomar RoRo* of Sweden. In March 2020
the charter ended and laid up. In April renamed the JUTLANDIA SEA and in January 2021
chartered to *Wallenius SOL*. In January 2022 chartered to *Stena Line*.

SEATRUCK PANORAMA Built by Astilleros de Huelva SA, Huelva Spain for *Seatruck Ferries*.
Launched as the CLIPPER PENNANT and renamed the CLIPPER PANORAMA before delivery. In
December 2011 renamed the SEATRUCK PANORAMA. In September 2020 chartered to *Stena
Line*.

SOMERSET Built as the SPAARNEBORG by Flender Werft AG, Lübeck, Germany for *Wagenborg*
of The Netherlands and time-chartered to *Stora-Enso* to operate between Zeebrugge and
Göteborg in conjunction with *Cobelfret Ferries*. She also operated between Tilbury and
Göteborg during 2010. In August 2011 chartered to the *Canadian MoD* to operate between
Montreal and Cyprus in connection with the Libyan 'no fly zone'. On return in November she
was laid up in Zeebrugge and in January 2012 moved to Göteborg. In August 2012 chartered
to *LD Lines* to operate between Marseilles and Tunis. In March 2013 returned to the *Stora
Enso/Cobelfret Ferries* Zeebrugge - Göteborg service. In November 2014 the arrangement
between *Stora Enso* and *Cobelfret Ferries* ended and she was chartered to *SOL Continent Line*
who took over the operation of the service, operating between Finland, Germany, Belgium and
the UK. In January 2015 sold to *CLdN* and renamed the SOMERSET. Generally operated

Stena Hibernia *(Darren Holdaway)*

Stena Superfast VII *(Darren Holdaway)*

between Zeebrugge and Göteborg. In August 2018 chartered to *Stena Line* to operate between Rotterdam and Harwich.

STENA ADVENTURER Ro-pax vessel built by Hyundai Heavy Industries, Ulsan, South Korea, for *Stena RoRo* and chartered to *Stena Line* to operate between Holyhead and Dublin.

STENA BRITANNICA Built by Waden Yards in Wismar and Warnemünde, Germany, for *Stena Rederi* (bow sections constructed at Warnemünde and stern and final assembly at Wismar). Replaced the 2003 built STENA BRITANNICA on the Harwich - Hoek van Holland service.

STENA EDDA, STENA EMBLA, STENA ESTRID Built by CMI Jinling Weihai Shipyard. They are known as 'E-Flexers' being of flexible construction so that their internal layout can be tailored to the needs of the routes they will operate on. They are designed to run traditional fuel but are under the class notation "gas ready" and can be converted to run on natural gas.

STENA EUROPE Built as the KRONPRINSESSAN VICTORIA by Götaverken Arendal AB, Göteborg, Sweden for *Göteborg-Frederikshavn Linjen* of Sweden (trading as *Sessan Linjen*) for their Göteborg - Frederikshavn service. Shortly after delivery, the company was taken over by *Stena Line* and services were marketed as *Stena-Sessan Line* for a period. In 1982 she was converted to an overnight ferry by changing one vehicle deck into two additional decks of cabins and she was switched to the Göteborg - Kiel route (with, during the summer, daytime runs from Göteborg to Frederikshavn and Kiel to Korsør (Denmark)). In 1989 she was transferred to the Oslo - Frederikshavn route and renamed the STENA SAGA. In 1994, transferred to *Stena Line BV*, renamed the STENA EUROPE and operated between Hoek van Holland and Harwich. She was withdrawn in June 1997, transferred to the *Lion Ferry* (a *Stena Line* subsidiary) Karlskrona - Gdynia service and renamed the LION EUROPE. In 1998 she was transferred back to *Stena Line* (remaining on the same route) and renamed the STENA EUROPE. In early 2002 the cabins installed in 1982 were removed and other modifications made and she was transferred to the Fishguard - Rosslare route.

STENA FORERUNNER Built by Dalian Shipyard Co Ltd, Dalian, China for *Stena RoRo* and chartered to *Transfennica*. In January 2018 chartered to *Stena Line* and placed on the Rotterdam - Harwich service. In August 2018 transferred to the Birkenhead - Belfast service. In February 2019 transferred to the Rotterdam - Killingholme service. In March 2020 transferred to the Rotterdam - Harwich route.

STENA FORETELLER Built as the STENA FORETELLER by Dalian Shipyard Co Ltd, Dalian, China for *Stena RoRo*. Initially chartered to *Cetam* of France to operate between Marseilles and Tunis and renamed the CETAM MASSILIA. In November 2003 the charter ended and she resumed her original name. A number of short-term commercial and military charters followed until June 2006 when she was chartered to *StoraEnso* paper group to operate between Göteborg and Finnish ports. In September 2009 she was chartered to *Rederi AB Transatlantic* who took over responsibility to operate all *StoraEnso's* Baltic services. In February 2012 she was chartered to *Transfennica*. In January 2015 chartered to *Mann Lines*. In December 2017 chartered to *DFDS Seaways*. In December 2019 charter ended. Chartered to *Irish Ferries* to cover during the overhaul of the ULYSSES operating Dublin - Holyhead and Dublin - Cherbourg. Charter ended April 2020, then laid up. In December 2020 chartered to *Stena Line* and used on the Rosslare - Cherbourg service to enhance capacity.

STENA HIBERNIA Built as the MAERSK IMPORTER by Miho Shipyard, Shimizu, Japan for *Norfolkline*. Used on the Scheveningen (from 2007 Vlaardingen) - Felixstowe service. In October 2009 moved to the Heysham-Belfast service. In July 2010 renamed the HIBERNIA SEAWAYS. In July 2011 renamed the STENA HIBERNIA. In September 2012 transferred to *Stena RoRo*. In November chartered to *Stena Line* and placed on the Birkenhead - Belfast service. In September 2015 moved to the Heysham - Belfast route.

STENA HOLLANDICA Built by Nordic Yards in Wismar and Warnemünde, Germany, for *Stena Rederi* (bow sections constructed at Warnemünde and stern and final assembly at Wismar) to replace the previous STENA HOLLANDICA on the Harwich - Hoek van Holland service. Entered service May 2010.

Stena Europe *(Miles Cowsill)*

Stena Adventurer *(Miles Cowsill)*

Stena Edda *(Darren Holdaway)*

Sound of Shuna *(Miles Cowsill)*

STENA HORIZON Built as the CARTOUR BETA by CN Visentini, Porto Viro, Italy for Levantina Trasporti of Italy. Chartered to *Caronte & Tourist* of Italy and operated between Messina and Salerno (Sicily). In October 2011 chartered to *Celtic Link Ferries*, renamed the CELTIC HORIZON and placed on the Rosslare - Cherbourg route. In March 2014 service and charter taken over by *Stena Line*. Renamed the STENA HORIZON.

STENA SCOTIA Built as the MAERSK EXPORTER by Miho Shipyard, Shimizu, Japan for *Norfolkline*. Used on the Scheveningen (from 2007 Vlaardingen) - Felixstowe service until March 2009 when she was moved to the Heysham - Belfast route. In July 2010 renamed the SCOTIA SEAWAYS. In July 2011 renamed the STENA SCOTIA. In September 2013 transferred to *Stena RoRo* and placed on the charter market. In September 2014 chartered to *Stena Line* and inaugurated a new service between Rotterdam and Killingholme. In January 2018 transferred to Rotterdam - Harwich service. In August 2018 transferred to the Heysham - Belfast service.

STENA SUPERFAST VII, STENA SUPERFAST VIII Built as the SUPERFAST VII and SUPERFAST VIII by Howaldtswerke Deutsche Werft AG, Kiel, Germany for *Attica Enterprises* (now *Attica Group*) for use by *Superfast Ferries* between Rostock and Hanko. In 2006 sold to *Tallink*. The Finnish terminal was transferred to Helsinki and daily return trips between Helsinki and Tallinn were introduced. These ceased in September 2008. The operation was ceased for the winter season in December 2009 and 2010. Service resumed at the end of April 2010 and 2011. In August 2011 chartered to *Stena Line* and renamed the STENA SUPERFAST VII, STENA SUPERFAST VIII. In November 2011, after a major refit, they were placed on a service between Cairnryan and Belfast (replacing the Stranraer - Belfast service). In December 2017 purchased by *Stena Ropax*.

STENA TRANSIT, STENA TRANSPORTER Built by Samsung Heavy Industries, Koje, South Korea. Used on the Hoek van Holland - Killingholme service.

WESTERN FERRIES

THE COMPANY *Western Ferries (Clyde) Ltd* is a British private sector company.

MANAGEMENT Managing Director Gordon Ross.

ADDRESS Hunter's Quay, Dunoon, Argyll PA23 8HJ.

TELEPHONE Administration +44 (0)1369 704452, **Reservations** Not applicable.

INTERNET Email enquiries@western-ferries.co.uk **Website** www.western-ferries.co.uk (English)

ROUTE OPERATED McInroy's Point (Gourock) - Hunter's Quay (Dunoon) (20 mins; **SOUND OF SCARBA, SOUND OF SEIL, SOUND OF SHUNA, SOUND OF SOAY**; every 20 mins (15 mins in peaks)).

1	SOUND OF SCARBA	489t	01	11.0k	49.95m	220P	40C	4/5L	BA	UK	9237424
2	SOUND OF SEIL	497t	13	11.0k	49.95m	220P	40C	4/5L	BA	UK	9665217
3	SOUND OF SHUNA	489t	03	11.0k	49.95m	220P	40C	4/5L	BA	UK	9289441
4	SOUND OF SOAY	497t	13	11.0k	49.95m	220P	40C	4/5L	BA	UK	9665229

SOUND OF SCARBA, SOUND OF SHUNA Built by Ferguson Shipbuilders, Port Glasgow, UK for *Western Ferries*.

SOUND OF SEIL, SOUND OF SOAY Built by Cammell Laird Shiprepairers & Shipbuilders, Birkenhead, UK for *Western Ferries*.

WIGHTLINK

THE COMPANY *Wightlink* is a British private sector company, 50% owned by *Basalt Infrastructure Partners LLP of the UK* (formerly known as *Balfour Beatty Infrastructure Partners (BBIP)*) and 50% by *Fiera Infrastructure Inc* of Canada.

MANAGEMENT Chief Executive Keith Greenfield, **Finance Director** Paul Winter, **Fleet & Operations Director** John Burrows, **Marketing and Innovation Director** Stuart James, **Commercial Director** Phillip Delaney, **Human Resources Director** Karen Wellman.

ADDRESS Gunwharf Road, Portsmouth PO1 2LA.

TELEPHONE Administration and Reservations +44 (0)333 999 7333.

INTERNET Email bookings@wightlink.co.uk **Website** www.wightlink.co.uk *(English)*

ROUTES OPERATED Conventional Ferries Lymington - Yarmouth (Isle of Wight) (approx 40 mins; *WIGHT LIGHT, WIGHT SKY*; *WIGHT SUN*; hourly), Portsmouth - Fishbourne (Isle of Wight) (45 mins; *ST. CLARE, ST. FAITH, VICTORIA OF WIGHT*; hourly with extras during morning peak). **Fast Cats** Portsmouth - Ryde (Isle of Wight) (passenger-only) (22 mins; *WIGHT RYDER I, WIGHT RYDER II*; up to 2 per hour).

1	ST. CLARE	5359t	01	13.0k	86.0m	878P	186C	-	BA2	UK	9236949
2	ST. FAITH	3009t	89	12.5k	77.0m	771P	142C	12L	BA	UK	8907228
3	VICTORIA OF WIGHT	8200t	18	13.0k	89.7m	1208P	178C	-	BA2	UK	9791028
4	WIGHT LIGHT	2546t	08	11.0k	62.4m	360P	65C	-	BA	UK	9446972
5»p	WIGHT RYDER I	520t	09	20.0k	40.9m	260P	0C	-	-	UK	9512537
6»p	WIGHT RYDER II	520t	09	20.0k	40.9m	260P	0C	-	-	UK	9512549
7	WIGHT SKY	2546t	08	11.0k	62.4m	360P	65C	-	BA	UK	9446984
8	WIGHT SUN	2546t	09	11.0k	62.4m	360P	65C	-	BA	UK	9490416

ST. CLARE Built by Stocznia Remontowa, Gdansk, Poland for the Portsmouth - Fishbourne service. She is a double-ended ferry with a central bridge. During winter 2015/16 modified for double deck loading.

ST. FAITH Built by Cochrane Shipbuilders, Selby, UK for *Sealink British Ferries* for the Portsmouth - Fishbourne service.

VICTORIA OF WIGHT Built by the Cemre Shipyard, Yalova, Turkey for the Portsmouth - Fishbourne service. She is a hybrid diesel/battery electric vessel.

WIGHT LIGHT, WIGHT SKY, WIGHT SUN Built by Brodogradilište Kraljevica, Croatia for the Lymington - Yarmouth route.

WIGHT RYDER I, WIGHT RYDER II Catamarans built by FBMA Marine, Balamban, Cebu, Philippines. Operate on the Portsmouth - Ryde service.

Wight Ryder II *(Richard Seville)*

St. Clare (Andrew Cooke)

St. Faith (Darren Holdaway)

Eilean Dhiura *(John Hendy)*

111

SECTION 2 - GB & IRELAND - MINOR FERRY OPERATORS

ARGYLL AND BUTE COUNCIL

THE COMPANY *Argyll and Bute Council* is a British local government authority.

MANAGEMENT Head of Roads and Amenity Services Jim Smith.

Marine Operations Manager Stewart Clark.

ADDRESS 1A Manse Brae, Lochgilphead, Argyll PA31 8RD.

TELEPHONE Administration +44 (0)1546 605522.

INTERNET Email info@argyll-bute.gov.uk **Website** www.argyll-bute.gov.uk/transport-and-streets/ferry-travel

ROUTES OPERATED Vehicle ferries Seil - Luing (5 mins; ***BELNAHUA***; approx half-hourly), Port Askaig (Islay) - Feolin (Jura) (5 mins; ***EILEAN DHIURA***; approx half-hourly). **Passenger-only ferries** Port Appin – Lismore (10 mins; ***LADY OF LISMORE***; approx hourly), Ellenabeich – Easdale (5 mins; ***EASDALE***; approx quarter-hourly).

1	BELNAHUA	35t	72	8.0k	17.1m	40P	5C	1L	BA	UK
2p	EASDALE	-	93	6.5k	6.4m	10P	0C	0L	-	UK
3	EILEAN DHIURA	86t	98	9.0k	25.6m	50P	13C	1L	BA	UK
4p	LADY OF LISMORE	-	22	8.0k	12.0m	23P	0C	0L	-	UK

BELNAHUA Built by Campbeltown Shipyard, Campbeltown, UK for *Argyll County Council* for the Seil - Luing service. In 1975, following local government reorganisation, transferred to *Strathclyde Regional Council*. In 1996, transferred to *Argyll and Bute Council*.

EASDALE Built for *Strathclyde Regional Council* for the Ellenabeich - Easdale passenger-only service. In 1996, following local government reorganisation, transferred to *Argyll and Bute Council*.

EILEAN DHIURA Built by McTay Marine, Bromborough, Wirral, UK for *Argyll and Bute Council* to replace the *Western Ferries (Argyll)* SOUND OF GIGHA on the Islay - Jura route. Now operated by the council.

LADY OF LISMORE Built by Mainstay Marine Solutions, Pembroke Dock to replace THE LISMORE on the Port Appin – Lismore route.

ARRANMORE FAST FERRIES

THE COMPANY *Arranmore Fast Ferries (Realt Na Maidne Teoranta Ferry Company)*, trading as *The Arranmore Ferry* and *Tory Ferry*, is a Republic of Ireland private sector company.

MANAGEMENT Managing Director Seamus Boyle.

ADDRESS Blue Ferry Office, Burtonport Pier, Co. Donegal, F94 C449, Republic of Ireland.

TELEPHONE Administration & Reservations +353 (0)87 3171810.

INTERNET Email: info.fastferry@gmail.com **Websites** thearranmoreferry.com *(English)*. toryferry.com *(English)*

ROUTES OPERATED The Arranmore Ferry Burtonport (County Donegal) - Leabgarrow (Arranmore Island) (20 mins; ***CANNA, MORVERN***; up to 8 per day), **Tory Ferry** Magheroarty (County Donegal) - Tory Island (45 mins; ***QUEEN OF ARAN***; up to 4 per day).

1	CANNA	69t	76	8.0k	24.3m	140P	6C	1L	B	IE	7340423
2	MORVERN	83t	73	8.0k	26.6m	96P	10C	1L	B	IE	7235501
3p	OCEAN WARRIOR	18t	89	18.0k	14.3m	12P	0C	-	-	IE	
4p	QUEEN OF ARAN	113t	76	-	20.1m	96P	0C	-	-	IE	7527928

CANNA Built by James Lamont & Co Ltd, Port Glasgow, UK for *Caledonian MacBrayne*. She was the regular vessel on the Lochaline - Fishnish (Mull) service. In 1986 she was replaced by the ISLE OF CUMBRAE and until 1990 she served in a relief capacity in the north, often assisting on the Iona service. In 1990 she was placed on the Kyles Scalpay (Harris) - Scalpay service (replaced by a bridge in Autumn 1997). In Spring 1997 *Caledonian MacBrayne* was contracted to operate the Ballycastle - Rathlin Island route and she was transferred to this service. In June 2008 she was chartered by *Caledonian Maritime Assets Limited* to *Rathlin Island Ferry Ltd* who took over the operation of the service. In June 2017 replaced by the SPIRIT OF RATHLIN and withdrawn. In autumn 2017 sold to *Humphrey O'Leary,* Clare Island and, in 2020, chartered to *Arranmore Fast Ferries.*

MORVERN Built by James Lamont & Co Ltd, Port Glasgow, UK for *Caledonian MacBrayne*. After service on a number of routes she was, after 1979, the main vessel on the Fionnphort (Mull) - Iona service. In 1992 she was replaced by the LOCH BUIE and became a spare vessel. In 1995 sold to *Arranmore Island Ferry Services*. In 2001 sold to *Bere Island Ferries*. In February 2010 refurbished by Bere Island Boatyard and sold to *Arranmore Charters* (now *Arranmore Fast Ferries*). Extended in June 2012.

OCEAN WARRIOR Built by FBM Marine, Cowes, Isle of Wight as an RNLI Tyne class lifeboat ALEXANDER COUTANACHE (No1157) and operated at St Helier, Channel Islands until June 2009 when she became a relief vessel. Bought by *Arranmore Fast Ferries* in December 2014 and renamed the OCEAN WARRIOR. Not in regular service.

QUEEN OF ARAN built in 1976 as the SHONAG OF KISHORN to work at the oil rig construction site in Loch Kishorn in Scotland. Moved to Ireland in 1985 and eventually became the QUEEN OF ARAN. In 2017 sold to *Arranmore Fast Ferries* and, after a major refit, placed on the Tory Island service.

Under Construction

| 5 | NEWBUILDING | - | 23 | 8.0k | 23.0m | - | 10C | 4L | B | IE | - |

NEWBUILDING Under construction by Ardmaleish Boatbuilding Company, Isle of Bute.

Arranmore Island Ferry Services (Bád Farrantoireacht Arainn Mhór), trading as *Arranmore Red Ferry*, is a Republic of Ireland company, supported by *Roinn na Gaeltachta (The Gaeltacht Authority)*, a semi-state-owned body responsible for tourism and development in the Irish-speaking areas of The Republic of Ireland. They also operate the summer only Lough Swilly service.

ARRANMORE ISLAND FERRY SERVICES

THE COMPANY *Arranmore Island Ferry Services (Bád Farrantoireacht Arainn Mhór)*, trading as *Arranmore Red Ferry*, is a Republic of Ireland company, supported by *Roinn na Gaeltachta (The Gaeltacht Authority)*, a semi-state-owned body responsible for tourism and development in the Irish-speaking areas of The Republic of Ireland. They also operate the summer only Lough Swilly service.

MANAGEMENT Managing Director Dominic Sweeney.

ADDRESS Burtonport Pier, Letterkenny, Co. Donegal, F94 AP89, Republic of Ireland.

TELEPHONE Administration & Reservations +353 (0)7495 42233.

INTERNET   Email   info@arranmoreferry.com   loughswillyferry@gmail.com   **Websites** arranmoreferry.com swillyferry.com *(English)*

ROUTES OPERATED *Arranmore Island Service* Burtonport (County Donegal) - Leabgarrow (Arranmore Island) (15 mins; **COLL, RHUM**; up to 8 per day (Summer), 6 per day (Winter)), **Lough Swilly Service (summer only)** Buncrana (County Donegal) - Rathmullan (County Donegal) (20 mins; **SPIRIT OF LOUGH SWILLY**; up to 8 per day).

| 1 | COLL | 80t | 74 | 8.0k | 28.3m | 96P | 9C | - | B | IE | 7327990 |
| 2 | RHUM | 80t | 73 | 8.0k | 28.3m | 96P | 9C | - | B | IE | 7319589 |

3	SPIRIT OF LOUGH SWILLY	110t	59	-	32.0m	130P	80C	-	BA	IE

COLL Built by James Lamont & Co Ltd, Port Glasgow, UK for *Caledonian MacBrayne*. For several years she was employed mainly in a relief capacity. In 1986 she took over the Tobermory (Mull) - Kilchoan service from a passenger-only vessel; the conveyance of vehicles was not inaugurated until 1991. In 1996 she was transferred to the Oban - Lismore route. In 1998 she was sold to *Arranmore Island Ferry Services*. Operates as spare vessel and is available for charter. In 2022 lengthened by 3 metres.

RHUM Built by James Lamont & Co Ltd, Port Glasgow, UK for *Caledonian MacBrayne*. Until 1987, she was used primarily on the Claonaig - Lochranza (Arran) service. After that time she served on various routes. In 1994 she inaugurated a new service between Tarbert (Loch Fyne) and Portavadie. In 1997 she operated between Kyles Scalpay and Scalpay until the opening of the new bridge on 16th December 1997. In 1998 she was sold to *Arranmore Island Ferry Services*. In spring 2021 lengthened by 3 metres at Mevagh Boatyard in County Donegal.

SPIRIT OF LOUGH SWILLY Built as the LORELEY V by Ruthof, Mainz, Germany to operate between St Goarshausen and St Goar on the River Rhine. In 2004 replaced by a new vessel (the LORELEY VI) and became a reserve vessel. In 2007, sold to the *Waterford Castle Hotel* and renamed the LORELEY and, in 2008, replaced the previous ferry. She was modified for cable guidance. In August 2014 replaced by the MARY FITZGERALD and laid up. In July 2017 sold to sold to *Arranmore Island Ferry Services*, changed back to self-steering and renamed the SPIRIT OF LOUGH SWILLY. Placed on the Lough Swilly service.

BERE ISLAND FERRIES

THE COMPANY *Bere Island Ferries Ltd* is a Republic of Ireland private sector company.

MANAGEMENT Operator Colum Harrington.

ADDRESS Ferry Lodge, West End, Bere Island, Beara, County Cork, Republic of Ireland.

TELEPHONE Administration +353 (0)27 75009, **Reservations** Not applicable, **Mobile** +353 (0)86 2423140.

ROUTE OPERATED Castletown Bere (Co Cork) - Bere Island (10 mins; *HOUTON LASS, OILEAN NA H-OIGE, SANCTA MARIA*; up to 8 per day).

INTERNET Email biferry@eircom.net **Website** bereislandferries.com *(English)*

1	HOUTON LASS	58t	60	9.0k	22.9m	12P	10C	1L	B	IR
2	OILEAN NA H-OIGE	69t	80	7.0k	18.6m	75P	4C	-	B	IR
3	SANCTA MARIA	67t	83	7.0k	18.6m	75P	4C	-	B	IR

HOUTON LASS Built by Magnaport Marine Ltd, Poole, UK for Flotta Oil Terminals, Stromness, Orkney Islands. Later sold for use as an antipollution vessel on the Black Isle, near Inverness. In November 2013 delivered to *Bere Island Ferries Ltd*. During 2014-2016 refurbished and lengthened in Galway. Mainly in use for transporting lorries but is also used for taking (up to) 10 cars during busy times.

OILEAN NA H-OIGE Built as the EILEAN NA H-OIGE by Lewis Offshore Ltd, Stornoway, UK for *Western Isles Islands Council* (from 1st April 1996 the *Western Isles Council* and from 1st January 1998 *Comhairle Nan Eilean Siar*) for their Ludaig (South Uist) - Eriskay service. From 2000 operated from a temporary slipway at the Eriskay causeway. This route ceased in July 2001 following the full opening of the causeway and she was laid up. In 2002 she was moved to the Eriskay - Barra service. In 2003 replaced by the LOCH BHRUSDA of *Caledonian MacBrayne* and laid up. Later sold to *Bere Island Ferries* and renamed the OILEAN NA H-OIGE (same name - "The Island of Youth" - in Irish rather than Scots Gaelic).

SANCTA MARIA Built as the EILEAN BHEARNARAIGH by George Brown & Company, Greenock, UK for *Western Isles Islands Council* for their Otternish (North Uist) - Berneray service. From 1996 until 1999 she was operated by *Caledonian MacBrayne* in conjunction with the LOCH BHRUSDA on the service between Otternish and Berneray and during the winter she was laid up. Following the opening of a causeway between North Uist and Berneray in early 1999, the

Shannon Dolphin *(Miles Cowsill)*

Corran *(Andrew Cooke)*

ferry service ceased and she became reserve vessel for the Eriskay route. This route ceased in July 2001 following the opening of a causeway and she was laid up. In 2002 operated between Eriskay and Barra as reserve vessel. In 2003 sold to *Transalpine Redemptorists Inc*, a community of monks who live on Papa Stronsay, Orkney. Used for conveying supplies to the island - not a public service. In 2008 sold to *Bere Island Ferries*. Entered service in May 2009.

BK MARINE

THE COMPANY *BK Marine* is a UK company.

MANAGEMENT Managing Director Gordon Williamson.

ADDRESS Herrislea House Hotel, Veensgarth, Tingwall, Shetland ZE2 9SB.

TELEPHONE Administration & Reservations +44 (0)1595 840208.

INTERNET Email boats@bkmarine.co.uk **Website** bkmarine.co.uk *(English)*

ROUTE OPERATED *All year* Foula - Walls (Mainland) (2 Hrs 15mins; *NEW ADVANCE*; 2 per week (Winter), 3 per week (Summer)).

1	NEW ADVANCE	25t	96	8.7k	9.8m	12P	1C	0L	C	UK	

NEW ADVANCE Built by Richardson's, Stromness, Orkney, UK for *Shetland Islands Council* for the Foula service. Although built at Penryn, Cornwall, she was completed at Stromness. She has a Cygnus Marine GM38 hull and is based on the island where she can be lifted out of the water. Vehicle capacity is to take residents' vehicles to the island - not for tourist vehicles. In 2004 it was announced that the vessel and service would be transferred to the *Foula Community*. However, it was then found that under EU rules the route needed to be offered for competitive tender. In July 2006 the contract was awarded to *Atlantic Ferries Ltd* which began operations in October 2006. In August 2011 replaced by *BK Marine*.

CLARE ISLAND FERRY COMPANY

THE COMPANY *Clare Island Ferry Company* is owned and operated by the O'Grady family, natives of Clare Island, Republic of Ireland, who have been operating the Clare Island Mail Boat Ferry service since 1880.

MANAGEMENT Joint owners Brian & Alan O'Grady.

ADDRESS Clare Island Ferry Co Ltd, Clare Island, Co Mayo, F28 XV50, Republic Of Ireland.

TELEPHONE +353 (0)98 23737, +353 (0)86 8515003, **+353 (0)87 9004115.**

INTERNET Email bookings@clareislandferry.com **Website** www.clareislandferry.com *(English)*

ROUTE OPERATED Roonagh (Co Mayo) - Clare Island (15 mins; *CLEW BAY QUEEN, EIGG, PIRATE QUEEN, SEA SPRINTER*; *Winter* 1 to 2 trips per day, *Summer* up to 5 per day, Roonagh - Inishturk (50 mins; *CLEW BAY QUEEN, EIGG, SEA SPRINTER*; *Winter* 1 per day *Summer* up to 2 per day. Tourist vehicles are not normally carried on either service.

1	CLEW BAY QUEEN	64t	72	10.0k	21.9m	96P	6C	-	B	IE	7217872
2	EIGG	91t	75	8.0k	24.2m	75P	6C	-	B	IE	7340411
3p	PIRATE QUEEN	73t	96	10.5k	19.8m	96P	0C	-	-	IR	
4p	SEA SPRINTER	16t	93	22.0k	11.6m	35P	0C		-	IR	

CLEW BAY QUEEN Built as the KILBRANNAN by James Lamont & Co Ltd, Port Glasgow, UK for *Caledonian Steam Packet* (later *Caledonian MacBrayne*). Used on a variety of routes until 1977, she was then transferred to the Scalpay (Harris) - Kyles Scalpay service. In 1990 she was replaced by the CANNA and, in turn, replaced the CANNA in her reserve/relief role. In 1992 sold to *Arranmore Island Ferry Services* and renamed the ÁRAINN MHÓR. She was subsequently sold to *Údarás na Gaeltachta* and leased back to *Arranmore Island Ferry Services*. In 2008 she was sold to *Clare Island Ferry Company* and renamed the CLEW BAY QUEEN. She operates a passenger and heavy freight service to both Clare Island and Inishturk all year round. In winter passenger capacity is reduced to 47 with 3 crew. Fitted with crane for loading and unloading cargo. Number is Lloyd's Number, not IMO.

EIGG Built by James Lamont & Co, Port Glasgow, UK for *Caledonia MacBrayne*. Since 1976 she was employed mainly on the Oban - Lismore service. In 1996 she was transferred to the Tobermory (Mull) - Kilchoan route, very occasionally making sailings to the Small Isles (Canna, Eigg, Muck and Rum) for special cargoes. In 1999 her wheelhouse was raised to make it easier to see over taller lorries and she returned to the Oban - Lismore route. In June 2018 sold to *Clare Island Ferry Company*. She is a reserve ferry and also available for charter as a workboat. Number is Lloyd's Number, not IMO.

PIRATE QUEEN Built by Arklow Marine Services in 1996 for *Clare Island Ferry Company*. She operated a daily passenger and light cargo service to Clare Island and Inishturk all year round. In winter passenger capacity was reduced to 47 with 3 crew. Fitted with crane for loading and unloading cargo.

SEA SPRINTER Built by Lochin Marine, East Sussex, UK for *Island Ferries* (now *Aran Island Ferries*) of the Irish Republic. In June 2015 sold to *Clare Island Ferries*.

CROSS RIVER FERRIES

THE COMPANY *Cross River Ferries Ltd* is a Republic of Ireland company, part of the *Doyle Shipping Group*.

MANAGEMENT Operations Manager Eoin O'Sullivan.

ADDRESS Westlands House, Rushbrooke, Cobh, County Cork, P24 H940, Republic of Ireland.

TELEPHONE Administration +353 (0)21 481 1485 **Reservations** Not applicable.

INTERNET Email cork@dsg.ie **Website** crossriverferries.ie *(English)*

ROUTE OPERATED Carrigaloe (near Cobh, on Great Island) - Glenbrook (Co Cork) (4 mins; **CARRIGALOE, GLENBROOK**; frequent service 07.00 - 00.15 (one or two vessels used according to demand)).

1	CARRIGALOE	225t	70	8.0k	49.1m	200P	27C	-	BA	IE	7028386
2	GLENBROOK	225t	71	8.0k	49.1m	200P	27C	-	BA	IE	7101607

CARRIGALOE Built as the KYLEAKIN by Newport Shipbuilding and Engineering Company, Newport (Gwent), UK for the *Caledonian Steam Packet Company* (later *Caledonian MacBrayne*) for the Kyle of Lochalsh - Kyleakin service. In 1991 sold to *Marine Transport Services Ltd* and renamed the CARRIGALOE. She entered service in March 1993. In Summer 2002 chartered to the *Lough Foyle Ferry Company*, returning in Spring 2003.

GLENBROOK Built as the LOCHALSH by Newport Shipbuilding and Engineering Company, Newport (Gwent), UK for the *Caledonian Steam Packet Company* (later *Caledonian MacBrayne*) for the Kyle of Lochalsh - Kyleakin service. In 1991 sold to *Marine Transport Services Ltd* and renamed the GLENBROOK. She entered service in March 1993.

FRAZER FERRIES

THE COMPANY *Frazer Ferries Ltd*, is a Republic of Ireland company. In June 2016 it took over *Passage East Ferries* and *Lough Foyle Ferry Service*. The *Carlingford Ferry* started in June 2017.

MANAGEMENT Director John Driscol, **Chief Executive** Paul O'Sullivan **Manager, Passage East Ferry** Peter Hayes.

ADDRESSES Head Office Riverfront, Howley's, Limerick, V94 WTK7, Republic of Ireland, **Lough Foyle Ferry** The Pier, Greencastle, Co Donegal, Republic of Ireland, **Carlingford Ferry** Greenore Port, The Harbour, Greenore, Co. Louth, A91 A0V1, Republic of Ireland. **Passage East Ferry** Barrack Street, Passage East, Co Waterford, X91 C52E, Republic of Ireland.

TELEPHONE Head Office +353 (0)61 316390 **Passage East Ferry** +353 (0)51 382480.

INTERNET Carlingford Lough Ferry Website carlingfordferry.com *(English)*, **Lough Foyle Ferry** www.loughfoyleferry.com *(English)*, **Passage East Ferry Email** passageferry@eircom.net **Website** www.passageferry.ie *(English)*

ROUTES OPERATED Carlingford Lough Ferry Greenore, Co Louth, Republic of Ireland - Greencastle, Co Down, Northern Ireland (20 minutes; *FRAZER AISLING GABRIELLE*; hourly), **Passage East Ferry** Passage East (County Waterford) - Ballyhack (County Wexford) (7 mins; *FRAZER TINTERN*; frequent service), **Summer Service Lough Foyle Ferry July – September** Greencastle (Inishowen, Co Donegal, Republic of Ireland) – Magilligan (Co Londonderry, Northern Ireland) (15 mins; *FRAZER MARINER*; frequent service).

1	FRAZER AISLING GABRIELLE	324t	78	10.0k	47.9m	300P	44C	-	BA	IE	7800033
2	FRAZER MARINER	-	83	7.2k	43.0m	100P	20C	-	BA	IE	
3	FRAZER STRANGFORD	186t	69	10.0k	32.9m	263P	20C	-	BA	IE	6926311
4	FRAZER TINTERN	236t	71	9.0k	54.8m	130P	30C	-	BA	IE	

FRAZER AISLING GABRIELLE Built as the SHANNON WILLOW by Scott & Sons (Bowling) Ltd, Bowling, Glasgow, UK for *Shannon Ferry Ltd*. In 2000 replaced by the SHANNON BREEZE and laid up for sale. In 2003 sold to the *Lough Foyle Ferry Company Ltd* and renamed the FOYLE VENTURE. In November 2015 sold to *Frazer Ferries*. In July 2016 re-opened the *Lough Foyle Ferry;* this ceased in October. In February 2017 renamed the FRAZER AISLING GABRIELLE. In July 2017 inaugurated a new Carlingford Lough service.

FRAZER MARINER Built as the BERNE-FARGE for *Schnellastfähre Berne-Farge GmbH* (from 1993 *Fähren Bremen-Stedingen GmbH*) to operate across the River Weser (Vegesack - Lemwerder and Berne - Farge). In January 2017 sold to *Frazer Ferries*. In July 2017 renamed the FRAZER MARINER and began operating between Greencastle and Magilligan.

FRAZER TINTERN Built as the STADT LINZ by Schiffswerft Oberwinter, Oberwinter, Rhein, Germany for *Rheinfähre Linz - Remagen GmbH* of Germany and operated on the Rhine between Linz and Remagen. In 1990 renamed the ST JOHANNES. In 1997 sold to *Fähren Bremen-Stedingen GmbH*, renamed the VEGESACK and operated across the Weser between Lemwerder and Vegesack. In 2003 she became a reserve vessel and in 2004 was renamed the STEDINGEN. Later sold to *Schraven BV* of The Netherlands and refurbished. In Autumn 2005 sold to *Passage East Ferry* and renamed the FBD TINTERN. During 2017 renamed the FRAZER TINTERN.

FRAZER STRANGFORD Built as the STRANGFORD FERRY by Verolme Dockyard Ltd, Cork, Republic of Ireland for *Down County Council*. Subsequently transferred to the *DOE (Northern Ireland)* and then the *DRD (Northern Ireland)*. Following entry into service of the STRANGFORD II in February 2016, she was withdrawn. In December 2017 sold to *Arranmore Island Ferry Services* (Red Boats) and renamed the STRANGFORD 1. In June 2018 sold to *Frazer Ferries*. In March 2019 renamed the FRAZER STRANGFORD. Used as a reserve vessel.

THE HIGHLAND COUNCIL

THE COMPANY *The Highland Council* is a Scottish local authority.

MANAGEMENT Area Roads Operations Manager Richard Porteous, **Ferry Foremen** Allan McCowan and Donald Dixon.

ADDRESS *Area Office* Lochybridge Depot, Carr's Corner Industrial Estate, Fort William PH33 6TQ, ***Ferry Office*** Ferry Cottage, Ardgour, Fort William PH33 7AA.

TELEPHONE Administration *Area Office* +44 (0)1349 781083, ***Corran*** +44 (0)1855 841243.

INTERNET Email communityservices@highland.gov.uk

Website www.highland.gov.uk/info/1526/public_and_community_transport/812/ corran_ferry_timetable_and_fares *(English)*

ROUTES OPERATED Vehicle Ferries Corran - Ardgour (5 mins; **CORRAN, MAID OF GLENCOUL**; half-hourly).

1	CORRAN	351t	01	10.0k	42.0m	150P	30C	2L	BA	UK	9225990
2	MAID OF GLENCOUL	166t	75	8.0k	32.0m	116P	16C	1L	BA	UK	7521613

CORRAN Built by George Prior Engineering Ltd, Hull, UK for *The Highland Council* to replace the MAID OF GLENCOUL as main vessel.

MAID OF GLENCOUL Built by William McCrindle Ltd, Shipbuilders, Ardrossan, UK for *Highland Regional Council* for the service between Kylesku and Kylestrome. In 1984 the ferry service was replaced by a bridge and she was transferred to the Corran - Ardgour service. In April 1996, ownership transferred to *The Highland Council*. In 2001 she became the reserve vessel.

The *Highland Council* also supports both services operated by *Highland Ferries*.

HIGHLAND FERRIES

THE COMPANY *Highland Ferries* is a UK private sector operation. Services are operated under contract to *The Highland Council*.

MANAGEMENT Operator Dougie Robertson.

TELEPHONE Administration +44(0)7468 417137 **Reservations** Not applicable.

INTERNET Email southuist24@hotmail.co.uk **Website** highlandferries.co.uk *(English)*

1p	BHOY TAYLOR	15t	80	7.5k	9.8m	12P	0C	0L	-	UK
2	RENFREW ROSE	65t	84	7.6k	17.5m	12P	3C	0L	B	UK
3p	THE LISMORE	12t	88	8.0k	9.7m	20P	0C	0L	-	UK

ROUTES OPERATED Vehicle Ferry *1st June - 30th September* Cromarty - Nigg (Ross-shire) (10 mins; **RENFREW ROSE**; half-hourly), **Passenger-only Ferry** Fort William - Camusnagaul (10 mins; **BHOY TAYLOR**, **THE LISMORE** up to 5 per day).

BHOY TAYLOR Built as the CAILIN AN AISEAG by Buckie Shipbuilders Ltd, Buckie, UK for *Highland Regional Council* and used on the Fort William - Camusnagaul passenger-only service. In 2006 the service transferred to *Geoff Ward* under contract with a different vessel. In 2013 the CAILIN AN AISEAG resumed service with *Highland Ferries* as contractor. In April 2013 she was renamed the BHOY TAYLOR.

THE LISMORE Built for *Strathclyde Regional Council* for the Port Appin – Lismore passenger-only service. In 1996, following local government reorganisation, transferred to *Argyll and Bute Council*. In June 2022 sold to *Highland Ferries* to operate the Fort William - Camusnagaul service.

RENFREW ROSE Built by MacCrindle Shipbuilding Ltd, Ardrossan for *Strathclyde PTE* (later *Strathclyde Partnership for Transport*). Built as a small car ferry but operated passenger only between Renfrew and Yoker (apart from occasionally carrying ambulances in earlier days before they became too heavy). In March 2010 laid up. In June 2012 sold to *Arranmore Fast Ferries* of the Irish Republic for use as a passenger/car ferry. In June 2016 sold to *Highland Ferries* to reopen the Cromarty - Nigg service.

INISHBOFIN ISLAND DISCOVERY

THE COMPANY *Inishbofin Island Discovery Ltd* is an Irish Republic private sector Company.

MANAGEMENT Managing Director Pat Concannon.

ADDRESS Cloonamore, Inishbofin Island, Co Galway, Republic of Ireland.

TELEPHONE Administration and Reservations +353 (0)86 171 8829.

INTERNET Email info@inishbofinferry.ie **Website** inishbofinislanddiscovery.com *(English)*

Frazer Tintern *(Nick Widdows)*

Raasay *(Gordon Hislip)*

ROUTE OPERATED *Passenger Service* Cleggan, Co Galway - Inishbofin Island (30 mins, *ISLAND ADVENTURE, ISLAND DISCOVERY*, *ISLAND EXPLORER*; up to 3 per day. **Cargo Service** Cleggan, Co Galway - Inishbofin Island (30 mins, *RAASAY*, 2 per week).

1p	ISLAND ADVENTURE	130t	94	10.9k	27.1m	250P	0C	0L	-	IE	8346553
2p	ISLAND DISCOVERY	107t	91	10.9k	25.0m	99P	0C	0L	-	IE	8650851
3p	ISLAND EXPLORER	-	99	10.9k	15.0m	72P	0C	0L	-	IE	-
4	RAASAY	69t	76	8.0k	24.3m	12P	6C	1L	B	IE	7340435

ISLAND ADVENTURE Built by Société des Ets Merré, Nort-sur-Erdre, France. Previously the JOLIE FRANCE II of Vedettes Jolie France, France. Acquired by Inishbofin Island Discovery Ltd in 2018 and renamed the ISLAND ADVENTURE.

ISLAND DISCOVERY Built by Arklow Marine Service, Arklow, Republic of Ireland.

ISLAND EXPLORER Built by Kingfisher Boats Previously the DINGLE BAY Acquired by *Inishbofin Island Discovery Ltd* and renamed the ISLAND EXPLORER.

RAASAY Built by James Lamont & Co Ltd, Port Glasgow, UK for and used primarily on the Sconser (Skye) - Raasay service. In 1997 she was replaced by the LOCH STRIVEN, became a spare/relief vessel and inaugurated in October 2003 the winter service between Tobermory (Mull) and Kilchoan (Ardnamurchan). From summer 2016 operated as second vessel on Oban - Lismore route. In March 2018 withdrawn and sold to *Humphrey O'Leary* of Clare Island, Co Mayo. In August sold to *Inishbofin Island Discovery* to operate the cargo service. Number is Lloyds Number, not IMO.

ISLES OF SCILLY STEAMSHIP COMPANY

THE COMPANY *Isles of Scilly Steamship Company* is a British private sector company.

MANAGEMENT Chief Executive Officer Stuart Reid, **Marketing & Communications Manager** Sharon Sandercock.

ADDRESS *Scilly* PO Box 10, Hugh Town, St Mary's, Isles of Scilly TR21 0LJ, *Penzance* Steamship House, Quay Street, Penzance, Cornwall, TR18 4BZ.

TELEPHONE Administration & Reservations +44 (0)1736 334220.

INTERNET Email sales@islesofscilly-travel.co.uk **Website** www.islesofscilly-travel.co.uk *(English),*

ROUTES OPERATED *Passenger services:* Penzance - St Mary's (Isles of Scilly) (2 hrs 50 mins; *SCILLONIAN III*; 1 per day), St Mary's - Tresco/St Martin's/St Agnes/Bryher; *LYONESSE LADY, SWIFT LADY (inter-island boats)*; irregular), *Freight service*: *GRY MARITHA*; Freight from Penzance Monday, Wednesday and Fridays (weather dependant, all year round).

>01F	GRY MARITHA	590t	81	10.5k	40.3m	6P	5C	1L	C	UK	8008462
>2	LYONESSE LADY	40t	91	9.0k	15.5m	4P	1C	0L	AC	UK	
>3	SCILLONIAN III	1346t	77	15.5k	67.7m	485P	5C	1L	C	UK	7527796
>4F	SWIFT LADY	-	04	30.0k	8.4m	0P	0C	0L	-	UK	

GRY MARITHA Built by Moen Slip AS, Kolvereid, Norway for *Gjofor* of Norway. In design she is a coaster rather than a ferry. In 1990 she was sold to the *Isles of Scilly Steamship Company*. She operates a freight and passenger service all year (conveying most goods to and from the Islands). During the winter she provides the only sea service to the islands, the SCILLONIAN III being laid up.

LYONESSE LADY Built Lochaber Marine Ltd of Corpach, Fort William, Scotland, for inter-island ferry work.

SCILLONIAN III Built by Appledore Shipbuilders Ltd, Appledore, UK for the Penzance - St Mary's service. She operates from late March to November and is laid up in the winter. She is the last major conventional passenger/cargo ferry built for UK waters and probably Western Europe. Extensively refurbished during Winter 1998/99 and 2012/13. She can carry cars in her hold and on deck, as well as general cargo/perishables, boats, trailer tents and passenger luggage.

SWIFT LADY Stormforce 8.4 RIB (Rigid Inflatable Boat) built by Redbay Boats of Cushendall, Co Antrim, Northern Ireland for inter-island ferry work conveying mail and as back-up to the LYONESSE LADY.

MURPHY'S FERRY SERVICE

THE COMPANY *Murphy's Ferry Service is privately operated.*

MANAGEMENT Operator Brendan Murphy.

ADDRESS Lawrence Cove, Bere Island, Co Cork, Republic of Ireland.

TELEPHONE Landline + 353 (0)27 75988**, Mobile** +353 (0)87 2386095.

INTERNET Email info@murphysferry.com **Website** www.murphysferry.com *(English),*

ROUTE OPERATED Castletownbere (Pontoon - 3 miles to east of town centre) - Bere Island (Lawrence Cove, near Rerrin) (20 mins; *IKOM K*; up to 8 per day).

| 1 | IKOM K | | 55t | 99 | 10.0k | 16.0m | 60P | 4C | 1L | B | IR | |

IKOM K Built by Arklow Marine Services, Arklow, Republic of Ireland for *Murphy's Ferry Service.*

RATHLIN ISLAND FERRY

THE COMPANY *Rathlin Island Ferry Ltd* is a UK private sector company owned by Ciarán and Mary O'Driscoll of County Cork, Republic of Ireland.

MANAGEMENT Managing Director Ciarán O'Driscoll.

ADDRESS Ballycastle Ferry Terminal, 18 Bayview Road, Ballycastle, County Antrim BT54 6BT.

TELEPHONE Administration & Reservations +44 (0)28 2076 9299.

INTERNET Email info@rathlinballycastleferry.com

Website www.rathlinballycastleferry.com *(English),*

ROUTE OPERATED Vehicle Ferry Ballycastle - Rathlin Island (45 min; *SPIRIT OF RATHLIN*; up to 4 per day). **Passenger-only Fast Ferry** (20 min; *RATHLIN EXPRESS*; up to 6 per day). The service is operated on behalf of the *Northern Ireland Department of Regional Development*.

| 1»p | RATHLIN EXPRESS | | 31t | 09 | 18.0k | 17.7m | 98P | 0C | 0L | - | UK | |
| 2 | SPIRIT OF RATHLIN | | 105t | 17 | 8.3k | 25.0m | 125P | 5C | 1L | B | UK | 9780122 |

RATHLIN EXPRESS Built by Arklow Marine Services, Arklow, Republic of Ireland for *Rathlin Island Ferry Ltd.*

SPIRIT OF RATHLIN Built by Arklow Marine Services, Arklow, Irish Republic for *DRD (Northern Ireland)*, UK to replace the CANNA. Chartered to *Rathlin Island Ferry Ltd.*

SHANNON FERRY

THE COMPANY *Shannon Ferry Group Ltd* is a Republic of Ireland private company owned by eighteen shareholders on both sides of the Shannon Estuary.

MANAGEMENT Managing Director Eugene Maher.

ADDRESS Ferry Terminal, Killimer, County Clare, V15 FK09, Republic of Ireland.

TELEPHONE Administration +353 (0)65 9053124, **Reservations** Phone bookings not available; Online booking available at www.shannonferries.com

FAX Administration +353 (0)65 9053125, **Reservations** Fax bookings not available; Online booking available at www.shannonferries.com

INTERNET Email enquiries@shannonferries.com **Website** www.shannonferries.com *(English),*

ROUTE OPERATED Killimer (County Clare) - Tarbert (County Kerry) (20 mins; **SHANNON BREEZE, SHANNON DOLPHIN**; hourly (half-hourly during June, July, August and September)).

1	SHANNON BREEZE	611t	00	10.0k	80.8m	350P	60C	-	BA	IE	9224910
2	SHANNON DOLPHIN	501t	95	10.0k	71.9m	350P	52C	-	BA	IE	9114933

SHANNON BREEZE, SHANNON DOLPHIN Built by Appledore Shipbuilders, Appledore, UK for *Shannon Ferry Group Ltd.*

SHERKIN ISLAND FERRY

THE COMPANY The *Sherkin Island Ferry* is privately operated in the Republic of Ireland.

MANAGEMENT Operator: Vincent O'Driscoll.

ADDRESS Sherkin Ferry, The Cove, Baltimore, Skibbereen, Co Cork, P81 RW71, Republic of Ireland.

TELEPHONE Administration +353 (0)87 244 7828.

INTERNET Email info@sherkinferry.com **Website** www.sherkinferry.ie *(English)*

ROUTE OPERATED Passenger only Baltimore (Co Cork) - Sherkin Island (10 minutes; **MYSTIC WATERS**; **YOKER SWAN**; up to 10 per day). **Note:** No vehicle service advertised.

1p•	MYSTIC WATERS	100t	72		19.8m	99P	0C	0L	-		IE	8943038
2	YOKER SWAN	65t	84		21.9m	50P	3C	0L	B		IE	

MYSTIC WATERS Built by Ryton Marine Ltd, Wallsend, UK as the FREDA CUNNINGHAM for *Tyne & Wear PTE* and operated between North Shields and South Shields. Withdrawn in 1993 and sold to *Tyne Towage Ltd*, Newcastle and renamed the ANYA DEV. Later sold and renamed the LADY LAURA. In 2006 sold to *Sherkin Island Ferry* and renamed the MYSTIC WATERS. Currently laid up.

YOKER SWAN Built by MacCrindle Shipbuilding Ltd, Ardrossan for *Strathclyde PTE* (later *Strathclyde Partnership for Transport*). Built as a small car ferry but operated passenger only between Renfrew and Yoker (apart from carrying ambulances in earlier days before they became too heavy). In March 2010 laid up. Later sold to *Sherkin Island Ferry* for use as a passenger/car ferry. She is used as required to convey vehicles and freight to and from the island, and sometimes conveys passengers. No public vehicle service is advertised.

SKYE FERRY

THE COMPANY The *Skye Ferry* is owned by the *Isle of Skye Ferry Community Interest Company*, a company limited by guarantee.

MANAGEMENT General Manager Jo Crawford.

ADDRESS Shore Station, Glenelg, Kyle, Ross-shire, IV40 8JZ.

TELEPHONE Administration +44 (0)1599 522700. **Reservations** Not applicable.

INTERNET Email info@skyeferry.co.uk **Website** skyeferry.co.uk *(English),*

ROUTE OPERATED *April – mid-October only* Glenelg - Kylerhea (Skye) (10 mins; **GLENACHULISH**; frequent service).

1	GLENACHULISH	44t	69	9.0k	20.0m	12P	6C	-	BSt	UK

GLENACHULISH Built by Ailsa Shipbuilding Company, Troon, UK for the *Ballachulish Ferry Company* for the service between North Ballachulish and South Ballachulish, across the mouth of Loch Leven. In 1975 the ferry was replaced by a bridge and she was sold to *Highland Regional Council* and used on a relief basis on the North Kessock - South Kessock and Kylesku - Kylestrome routes. In 1983 she was sold to *Murdo MacKenzie*, who had operated the Glenelg – Skye route as ferryman since 1959. The vessel was eventually bought by *Roddy MacLeod* and the service resumed in September 1990. The *Isle of Skye Ferry Community Interest Company* reached agreement with *Mr MacLeod* that he would operate the ferry in 2006. In 2007 she was sold to the Company. During winter 2012 she was chartered to *The Highland Council* to operate between North and South Strome following a road closure due to a rock fall. She is the last manually operated turntable ferry in existence.

STRANGFORD LOUGH FERRY SERVICE

THE COMPANY The *Strangford Lough Ferry Service* is operated by the *Department for Infrastructure (DfI)*, a Northern Ireland Government Department.

ADDRESS Strangford Lough Ferry Service, The Slip, Strangford, Co Down BT30 7NE.

TELEPHONE Administration +44 (0)300 200 7898, **Reservations** Not applicable.

INTERNET **Email** Strangfordferry@infrastructure-ni.gov.uk **Website** www.nidirect.gov.uk/strangford-ferry-timetable *(English)*,

ROUTE OPERATED Strangford - Portaferry (County Down) (10 mins; *PORTAFERRY II, STRANGFORD II*; half-hourly).

1	PORTAFERRY II	312t	01	12.0k	38.2m	260P	28C	-	BA	UK	9237436
2	STRANGFORD II	405t	16	12.0k	64.0m	260P	28C	-	BA	UK	9771561

PORTAFERRY II Built by McTay Marine, Bromborough, Wirral, UK for *DRD (Northern Ireland)*.

STRANGFORD II Built by Cammell Laird, Birkenhead for *DRD (Northern Ireland)*, UK to replace the STRANGFORD FERRY. Entered service February 2017.

C TOMS & SON LTD

THE COMPANY *C Toms & Son Ltd* is a British private sector company.

MANAGEMENT Managing Director Allen Toms.

ADDRESS East Street, Polruan-by-Fowey, Cornwall PL23 1PB.

TELEPHONE Administration +44 (0)1726 870232, **Reservations** Not applicable.

INTERNET Email enquiries@ctomsandson.co.uk **Website** www.ctomsandson.co.uk *(English)*

ROUTE OPERATED *Car Ferry* Fowey - Bodinnick (Cornwall) (5 mins; *GELLAN*, *JENACK*; frequent), *Passenger Ferry* Fowey - Polruan (Cornwall) (5 mins; *KALEY*, *LADY DIANA*, *LADY JEAN*, *THREE COUSINS*; frequent).

1	GELLAN	50t	03	4.5k	36.0m	50P	10C	-	BA	UK
2	JENACK	60t	00	4.5k	36.0m	50P	15C	-	BA	UK
3p	KALEY	7.6t	03	-	9.5m	48P	0C	-	-	UK
4p	LADY DIANA	-	81	-	8.2m	36P	0C	-	-	UK
5p	LADY JEAN	-	-	-	-	12P	0C	-	-	UK
6p	THREE COUSINS	-	14	-	-	12P	0C	-	-	UK

GELLAN, JENACK Built by C Toms & Sons Ltd, Fowey, UK.

KALEY, LADY DIANA, LADY JEAN, THREE COUSINS Built by C Toms & Sons Ltd, Fowey, UK.

VALENTIA ISLAND CAR FERRY

THE COMPANY *Valentia Island Car Ferry* is the trading name of *Valentia Island Ferries Ltd*, an Republic of Ireland private sector company.

MANAGEMENT Manager Richard Foran.

ADDRESS Valentia Island, County Kerry, Republic of Ireland.

TELEPHONE Administration +353 (0)87 168 3373, **Reservations** Not applicable.

INTERNET Facebook facebook.com/valentiaferry

ROUTE OPERATED Reenard (Co Kerry) - Knightstown (Valentia Island) (5 minutes; *GOD MET ONS III*; frequent service, 1st April - 30th September).

Glenachulish *(John Hendy)*

Yoker Swan *(Nick Widdows)*

Scillonian III *(Andrew Cooke)*

Dame Vera Lynn *(Ferry Publications Library)*

| 1 | GOD MET ONS III | 95t | 63 | - | 43.0m | 95P | 18C | - | BA | IR | |

GOD MET ONS III Built by BV Scheepswerven Vh HH Bodewes, Millingen, The Netherlands for *FMHE Res* of The Netherlands for a service across the River Maas between Cuijk and Middelaar. In 1987 a new bridge was opened and the service ceased. She was latterly used on contract work in the Elbe and then laid up. In 1996 acquired by *Valentia Island Ferries* and inaugurated a car ferry service to the island. **Note** This island never had a car ferry service before. A bridge was opened at the south end of the island in 1970; before that a passenger/cargo service operated between Reenard Point and Knightstown.

WOOLWICH FREE FERRY

THE COMPANY The *Woolwich Free Ferry* is operated by *London River Services*, part of *Transport for London*, a UK public sector body under the authority of the Mayor of London.

ADDRESS New Ferry Approach, Woolwich, London SE18 6DX.

TELEPHONE Administration +44 (0)343 222 1234 (TfL Switchboard)**, Reservations** Not applicable.

INTERNET Website www.tfl.gov.uk/modes/river/woolwich-ferry *(English)*

ROUTE OPERATED Woolwich - North Woolwich (free ferry) (5 mins; *BEN WOOLLACOTT*, *DAME VERA LYNN*; every 10 mins (weekdays - two ferries in operation), every 15 mins (weekends - one ferry in operation)).

| 1 | BEN WOOLLACOTT | 1538t | 18 | 8.0k | 62.2m | 150P | 42C | 12L | BA | UK | 9822011 |
| 2 | DAME VERA LYNN | 1539t | 18 | 8.0k | 62.2m | 150P | 42C | 12L | BA | UK | 9822023 |

BEN WOOLLACOTT, DAME VERA LYNN Built by Remontowa Shipbuilding, Gdansk, Poland. They are diesel electric battery hybrid vessels.

SECTION 2 – MINOR FERRY OPERATORS

SECTION 3 – GB & IRELAND – FREIGHT ONLY FERRIES

CLDN

THE COMPANY *CLdN RoRo SA* is a Luxembourg private sector company. There are a number of subsidiary companies. *CLdN* stands for *Compagnie Luxembourgouise de Navigation*.

MANAGEMENT CLdN Ro-Ro SA (Luxembourg) Caroline Dubois, **CLdN ro-ro Agencies Ltd (UK)** Karla Fairway.

ADDRESSES *Luxembourg* CLdN CLdN ro-ro SA, 3-7 rue Schiller, 2519 Luxembourg, *UK* CLdN ro-ro UK Ltd, Long Reach House, London Road, Purfleet, Essex RM19 1RP. *Irish Republic* CLdN ro-ro SA, Port Centre, 2nd Floor, Alexandra Road, Dublin Port, Dublin 1, D01 H4C6, Republic of Ireland.

TELEPHONE *Luxembourg* +352 (0)26 44 661 *UK* +44 (0)1708 865522, *Irish Republic* +353 (0)1 856 1608.

INTERNET Email admin.roro@cldn.com **Website** www.cldn.com *(English)*

ROUTES OPERATED Zeebrugge - Purfleet (9 hrs; 2 per day), Zeebrugge - Killingholme (13 hrs; 6 per week), Rotterdam - Purfleet (14 hrs 30 mins); 6 per week), Rotterdam - Killingholme (14 hrs; 12 per week), Zeebrugge - Esbjerg (24hrs; 1 per week), Zeebrugge - Dublin (35-41 hrs; 4 per week), Rotterdam - Dublin (41-47 hrs; 4 per week), Zeebrugge - Cork (35 hrs; 2 per week), Rotterdam - Leixoes (Portugal) (64-69 hrs; 3 per week), Zeebrugge - Santander (50 hrs; 3 per week), Zeebrugge - Göteborg (32-33 hrs; 2 per week (joint service with *DFDS* providing 4 services per week; commercially they operate independently and buy capacity on each other's ships), Dublin - Liverpool - Santander (Dublin - Santander 65 hrs, Liverpool - Santander 47 hrs; 2 per week). NOTE: Because vessels are so often moved between routes it is impossible to say which ro-ro vessels will be on which routes.

Contract Services for Ford Motor Company Vlissingen - Dagenham (11 hrs; 2 per day).

1	ADELINE	21020t	12	15.8k	150.0m	12P	-	170T	A		MT	9539092
2	ALF POLLAK	32887t	18	20.6k	209.6m	12P	-	262T	A2	IT	9848467
3	AMANDINE	33960t	11	18.5k	195.4m	12P	-	270T	A		MT	9424871
4	CADENA 3	23235t	03	17.1k	193.0m	12P	-	180T	A		MT	9234094
5	CAPUCINE	16342t	11	16.0k	150.0m	12P	-	140T	A		MT	9539066
6	CATHERINE	21287t	02	18.0k	182.2m	12P	-	200T	A2	MT	9209453
7	CELANDINE	23987t	00	17.9k	162.5m	12P	630C	157T	A		MT	9183984
8	CELESTINE	23986t	96	17.8k	162.5m	12P	630C	157T	A		MT	9125372
9	CELINE	74273t	17	17.9k	235.0m	12P	1600C	580T	A2	MT	9789233
10	CLEMENTINE	23986t	97	17.8k	162.5m	12P	630C	157T	A		BE	9125384
11	DELPHINE	74273t	18	17.9k	235.0m	12P	1600C	580T	A2	MT	9789245
12	FAUSTINE	50455t	21	18.0k	212.0m	12P	-	360T	A		MT	9889708
13	GIUSEPPE LUCCHESI	29429t	12	21.5k	193.0m	12P	-	270T	A		IT	9503639
14	HERMINE	50443t	19	17.6k	211.6m	12P	-	400T	A2	MT	9831177
15	LAURELINE	50443t	19	18.0k	212.0m	12P	-	400T	A		MT	9823352
16	MARIA GRAZIA ONORATO	32887t	19	20.6k	209.8m	12P	-	262T	A2	IT	9848479
17	MAXINE	21005t	00	18.0k	183.4m	12P	-	180T	A		IM	9188245
18	MAZARINE	31340t	09	18.5k	195.4m	12P	-	250T	A		MT	9376696
19	MELUSINE	23987t	99	17.8k	162.5m	12P	630C	157T	A		BE	9166637
20	OPALINE	33960t	10	18.5k	195.4m	12P	-	270T	A		MT	9424869
21	PALATINE	31340t	09	18.5k	195.4m	12P	-	250T	A		MT	9376701
22	PAULINE	49166t	06	21.7k	200.0m	12P	656C	258T	A		MT	9324473
23	PEREGRINE	25593t	10	18.5k	195.4m	12P	-	180T	A		MT	9376725
24	SERAPHINE	50455t	22	18.0k	212.0m	12P	-	360T	A		MT	9889710
25	SEVERINE	16342t	12	16.0k	150.0m	12P	-	140T	A		MT	9539078
26	SIXTINE	50443t	19	17.6k	211.6m	12P	-	400T	A2	MT	9831165
27	VESPERTINE	31340t	10	18.5k	195.4m	12P	-	250T	A		MT	9376713
29	VICTORINE	23987t	00	17.8k	162.5m	12P	630C	157T	A		BE	9184029

Clementine *(Rob de Visser)*

Seraphine *(Nick Widdows)*

29	WILHELMINE	21020t	12	15.8k	150.0m	12P	-	170T	A	MT	9539080
30	YASMINE	49166t	07	21.7k	200.0m	12P	656C	258T	A	MT	9337353
31	YSALINE	50443t	19	18.0k	212.0m	12P	-	400T	A	MT	9823364

ALF POLLAK Built by Flensburger Schiffbau-Gesellschaft for *Seven Yield Holding Pte. Ltd* of Singapore, an associated company of the yard's then owners, *Seim Industries* of Norway. In December 2018 chartered to *Compagnia Italiana Di Navigazione SPA, (Tirrenia)*. In January 2019 sub-chartered to *DFDS (Turkey)* and operated between Istanbul and Trieste. In May 2021 sub-chartered to *CLdN*.

ADELINE Built by the Kyokuyo Shipyard, Shimonoseki, Japan. After competition, an additional deck and sponsons were retro-fitted at the Chengxi Shipyard, Jiangyin, China.

AMANDINE Built by Flensburger Schiffbau-Gesellschaft, Flensburg, Germany. Operates mainly between Rotterdam and Killingholme and Rotterdam/Zeebrugge and Dublin.

CADENA 3 Built as the BEACHY HEAD by Flensburger Schiffbau-Gesellschaft, Flensburg, Germany for *AWSR Shipping*. On delivery, chartered to *Transfennica* and operated between Hanko (Finland) and Lübeck (Germany). In July 2006 chartered to *Stora Enso* and placed on the Kotka - Gothenburg route. In late August transferred to the Antwerp - Gothenburg service. In 2007 chartered to *Transfennica*. In January 2009 chartered to *Finnlines* and normally used on the Helsinki - Aarhus route. In January 2012 chartered to *North Sea RoRo*. In March 2013 the service ceased and she was chartered to *DFDS* . In April 2014 sold to *C Bulk NV* of Belgium, an associated company of *CLdN/Cobelfret Ferries* and renamed the WILLIAMSBORG. In July she was chartered to *Nordana Line A/S* of Denmark operating from Mediterranean ports to the USA and Latin America. In January 2016 chartered to *Tirrenia* of Italy for five years with a purchase option. She was renamed the MASSIMO MURA. In June 2021 the purchase option was not exercised and the charter ended. She was renamed the CADENA 3. Between January and August 2022 chartered to *Wallenius SOL*.

CAPUCINE Built by the Kyokuyo Shipyard, Shimonoseki, Japan for *CLdN*. Initially operated on their Ipswich - Rotterdam service. This service was suspended in August 2012. In September, chartered to *Stena Line* and placed on the Harwich - Rotterdam service. Charter ended in January 2018. In February 2018 chartered to the *Italian Ministry of Defence*.

CATHERINE Built as the ROMIRA by Zhonghua Shipyard, Zhonghua, China for *Dag Engström Rederi* of Sweden. For six months engaged on a number of short-term charters, including *Cobelfret Ferries* who used her on both the Rotterdam - Immingham and Zeebrugge - Purfleet routes. In September 2002 purchased by *Cobelfret Ferries* and, in November 2002, renamed the CATHERINE and placed on the Rotterdam - Immingham service. In Spring 2003 chartered to the *US Defense Department* to convey materials to the Persian Gulf. Returned in late summer and operated thereafter on the Rotterdam - Immingham service. In January 2009 chartered to *CoTuNav* of Tunisia. In February 2010 returned to *Cobelfret* service and operated on the Rotterdam - Purfleet service. In March 2010 again chartered to *CoTuNav*. In March 2011 chartered to *RMR Shipping* to operate between Western Europe and Antwerpen, Eemshaven, Harwich and Dublin to Lagos (Nigeria). In May 2011 returned to *Cobelfret Ferries*. Between January and July 2022 chartered to *Wallenius SOL Line*.

CELANDINE, VICTORINE Built by Kawasaki Heavy Industries, Sakaide, Japan for *Cobelfret*. The CELANDINE was originally to be called the CATHERINE and the VICTORINE the CELANDINE. The names were changed before delivery. In May 2011 the CELANDINE was chartered to *RMR Shipping*. Returned in November 2013.

CELESTINE Built by Kawasaki Heavy Industries, Sakaide, Japan as the CELESTINE. In 1996 chartered to the *British MoD* and renamed the SEA CRUSADER. She was originally expected to return to *Cobelfret Ferries* in early 2003 and resume the name CELESTINE; however, the charter was extended because of the Iraq war. Returned in September 2003 and placed on the Zeebrugge - Immingham service. In November 2006 moved to the Zeebrugge - Purfleet route. In November 2008 moved to the Oostende - Dartford service. In April 2009 the route became Oostende - Purfleet. In April 2010 chartered to *RMR Shipping* and operated to West Africa In

May 2014 returned to *Cobelfret Ferries* and in May 2016 transferred to the Dagenham - Vlissingen service.

CELINE, DELPHINE Built by Hyundai Mipo Dockyard, Ulsan, South Korea. They are convertible to LPG propulsion and designed to be useable on deep sea ro-ro services as well as *CLdN's* current short sea routes. They mainly operate between Zeebrugge and Killingholme and Zeebrugge and Dublin.

CLEMENTINE Built by Kawasaki Heavy Industries, Sakaide, Japan for *Cobelfret Ferries*. Mainly used on the Zeebrugge - Immingham service. In 2007 moved to the Zeebrugge - Purfleet route. In March 2013 chartered to *RMR Shipping*. In July 2013 chartered to *DFDS* and placed on the Immingham - Cuxhaven service. In November 2014 returned to *Cobelfret Ferries.*

FAUSTINE, SERAPHINE Built by Hyundai Mipo Dockyard, Ulsan, South Korea. LNG powered.

GIUSEPPE LUCCHESI Built as the BERING STRAIT by Odense Staalskibsværft A/S, Odense, Denmark for *Pacific Basin Shipping Ltd Hong Kong* of the UK. In September 2012 sold to *Atlantica Di Navigation (Grimaldi)* of Italy and, in October, renamed the EUROCARGO BRINDISI. In March 2015 sold to *CLdN* and chartered to *Ekol Logistik AS* of Turkey and renamed the FADIQ. In July 2017 renamed the QUBRA. In January 2018 chartered to *Tirrenia* of Italy and renamed the GIUSEPPE LUCCHESI.

HERMINE, LAURELINE, SIXTINE, YSALINE Built by Hyundai Mipo Dockyard, Ulsan, South Korea. Used on a variety of routes. As part of the joint agreement with *DFDS* on Zeebrugge - Göteborg, one is always deployed on that route.

MARIA GRAZIA ONORATO Built by Flensburger Schiffbau-Gesellschaft for *Seven Yield Holding Pte. Ltd* of Singapore, an associated company of the yard's then owners, *Seim Industries* of Norway. Chartered to *Compagnia Italiana Di Navigazione SPA, (Tirrenia)*. In October 2021 sub-chartered to *CLdN*.

MAXINE Built as the SLINGEBORG by Flender Werft AG, Lübeck, Germany for *Wagenborg* of The Netherlands and time-chartered to *Cobelfret Ferries* to operate on the *Stora Enso* (a paper and card manufacturer)/*Cobelfret Ferries* service between Zeebrugge and Göteborg. In November 2014 the arrangement between *Stora Enso* and *Cobelfret Ferries* ended and she was chartered to *SOL Continent Line* who took over the operation of the service. In June 2019 the service was taken over by *DFDS Seaways* and she was purchased by them. She was renamed the GOTHIA SEAWAYS. In April 2021 purchased by *CLdN* and renamed the MAXINE. She was chartered back to *DFDS Seaways* and in June 2021 inaugurated a new service between Calais and Sheerness. In January 2022 returned to *CLdN*.

MAZARINE, PALATINE, PEREGRINE, VESPERTINE Built by Flensburger Schiffbau-Gesellschaft, Flensburg, Germany. Between Autumn 2019 and Spring 2020 an extra deck was added to the MAZARINE, PALATINE and VESPERTINE at Stocznia Remontowa, Gdansk, Poland, giving them a similar capacity to the AMANDINE and OPALINE. The extension of the PEREGRINE was deferred.

MELUSINE Built by Kawasaki Heavy Industries, Sakaide, Japan for *Cobelfret*. Similar to the CLEMENTINE. Normally operates between Zeebrugge and Cork.In August 2022 chartered to CoTuNav of Tunisia.

OPALINE Built by Flensburger Schiffbau-Gesellschaft, Flensburg, Germany. Operates mainly between Rotterdam and Killingholme and Rotterdam and Dublin.

PAULINE, YASMINE Built by Flensburger Schiffbau-Gesellschaft, Flensburg, Germany to operate on the Zeebrugge - Killingholme route. They now operate mainly on the Zeebrugge - Purfleet service.

SEVERINE Built by the Kyokuyo Shipyard, Shimonoseki, Japan. Initially operated on the Ipswich - Rotterdam service. This service was suspended in August 2012. In September, chartered to *Stena Line* and placed on the Harwich - Rotterdam service. Charter ended in January 2018. In June 2018 she was chartered to *GNV* of Italy. She returned in September 2018 and operated on *CLdN* services; in February 2020 she was chartered to *Grendi Trasporti Marittimi* of Italy to

Finnpulp (Miles Cowsill)

Finnwave (Philippe Holtoff)

operate between Marina di Carrara, Porto Torres and Cagliari. In March 2021 chartered to *GNV (Grandi Navi Veloci)* of Italy. In May 2021 chartered to *CoTuNv* of Tunisia.

WILHELMINE Built by the Kyokuyo Shipyard, Shimonoseki, Japan for *CLdN*. After completion, a additional deck and sponsons were retro-fitted at the Chengxi Shipyard, Jiangyin, China. Initially used on the Zeebrugge - Purfleet service. In January 2013 chartered to *P&O Ferries* to operate between Tilbury and Zeebrugge. After three weeks moved to the Middlesbrough - Rotterdam service. In November 2014 the charter ended and she was placed on the Zeebrugge - Purfleet service. She returned to *P&O Ferries* for five weeks during the refit period in January and February 2015 and again operated Middlesbrough - Rotterdam. In March 2019 chartered to *P&O Ferries* and placed on the Middlesbrough - Rotterdam route on a long-term basis although she has also operated between Zeebrugge and Tilbury. In February 2021 returned to *CLdN*.

CLdN also owns the SOMERSET, currently on charter to *Stena Line*.

Under Construction

| 32 | NEWBUILDING 1 | 74000t | 25 | 17.9k | 235.0m | 12P | - | 580T | A | MT | 9963578 |
| 33 | NEWBUILDING 2 | 74000t | 25 | 17.9k | 235.0m | 12P | - | 580T | A | MT | 9963566 |

NEWBUILDING 1, NEWBUILDING 2 Under construction by Hyundai Mipo Dockyard, Ulsan, South Korea. Similar to the CELINE and DELPHINE but Hybrid LNG/electric powered. Speed on electric power will be 16-17 knots.

FINNLINES

THE COMPANY *Finnlines PLC* is a Finnish private sector company owned by Grimaldi of Italy. Services to the UK are marketed by *Finnlines UK Ltd*, a British private sector company.

MANAGEMENT President & CEO Emanuele Grimaldi, **Head of Group Marketing, Sales and Customer Service, Line Manager Germany and North Sea ro-ro** Staffan Herlin.

ADDRESS *Finland* Komentosilta 1, 00980 Helsinki, Finland, **UK** Finnlines UK Ltd, Finhumber House, Queen Elizabeth Dock, Hedon Road, HULL HU9 5PB.

TELEPHONE Administration & Reservations *Finland* +358 (0)10 343 50, **UK** +44 (0)1482 377 655.

INTERNET *Email Finland* info.fi@finnlines.com **UK** info.uk@finnlines.com **Website** www.finnlines.com *(English, Finnish, German, Swedish, Russian)*

ROUTES OPERATED Helsinki - Hull (62 hrs; **FINNMASTER**; weekly), Helsinki - Kotka - Travemünde -Lübeck - Antwerpen - Zeebrugge - Bilbao - Zeebrugge - Antwerpen - Travemünde - Lübeck - Helsinki (3 week cycle, **FINNECO I, FINNECO II, FINNECO III**; weekly service), Zeebrugge - Rosslare (26 hrs; **FINNPULP**; 2 per week). Plus Baltic services - see website for details. Vessels may be switched between routes.

Ro-pax vessels on Baltic services are listed in Section 7.

1	FINNBREEZE	33816t	12	21.0k	217.8m	12P	600C	320T	A	FI	9468889
2	FINNECO I	64575t	22	-	238.0m	12P	-	410T	A	FI	9856830
3	FINNECO II	64575t	22	-	238.0m	12P	-	410T	A	FI	9856842
4	FINNECO III	64575t	22	-	238.0m	12P	-	410T	A	FI	9856854
5	FINNHAWK	11671t	01	20.0k	162.2m	12P	-	140T	A	FI	9207895
6	FINNKRAFT	11671t	00	20.0k	162.2m	12P	-	140T	A	FI	9207883
7	FINNMASTER	12433t	98	20.0k	154.5m	12P	-	124T	A2	FI	9132014
8	FINNMERCHANT	23235t	03	21.0k	193.0m	12P	-	180T	A	FI	9234082
9	FINNMILL	25732t	02	20.0k	187.6m	12P	-	190T	A	FI	9212656
10	FINNPULP	25732t	02	20.0k	187.6m	12P	-	190T	A	FI	9212644
11	FINNSEA	33816t	12	21.0k	217.8m	12P	600C	320T	A	FI	9468891
12	FINNSKY	33816t	12	21.0k	217.8m	12P	600C	320T	A	FI	9468906
13	FINNSUN	33816t	12	21.0k	217.8m	12P	600C	320T	A	FI	9468918
14	FINNTIDE	33816t	12	21.0k	217.8m	12P	600C	320T	A	FI	9468920
15	FINNWAVE	33816t	12	21.0k	217.8m	12P	600C	320T	A	FI	9468932

SECTION 3 - FREIGHT ONLY FERRIES

EUROCARGO SAVONA Built as the STRAIT OF MESSINA by Odense Staalskibsværft A/S, Odense, Denmark for *Pacific Basin Shipping Ltd* of the UK. Chartered to *CoTuNav* of Tunisia and operated between Marseille and Tunis. In September 2012 sold to *Grimaldi Line* of Italy and chartered back to *CoTuNav*. In April 2014 renamed the EUROCARGO SAVONA. In 2015 she began operating for *Grimaldi Line*. In April 2021 chartered to *Finnlines*.

FINNBREEZE, FINNSEA, FINNSKY, FINNSUN, FINNTIDE, FINNWAVE Built by Jinling Shipyard, Nanjing, China for *Finnlines*. The vessels were lengthened by approximately 30 metres at Remontowa Shipyard, Gdansk, Poland between November 2017 and December 2018.

FINNECO I, FINNECO II, FINNECO III Grimaldi Green 5th Generation (GG5G) Class hybrid built by China Merchants' Nanjing Jinling Shipyard. As well as the trailer deck capacity, there are 5,600 square metres of car decks and space for 300 TEU of containers on the weather deck.

FINNHAWK Built by Jinling Shipyard, Nanjing, China for the *Macoma Shipping Group* and chartered to *Finnlines*. In April 2008 purchased by *Finnlines*. Currently operates used on service between Finland and The Netherlands, Belgium, the UK and Spain.

FINNKRAFT Built by Jinling Shipyard, Nanjing, China for the *Macoma Shipping Group* and chartered to *Finncarriers*. In April 2008 purchased by *Finnlines*. Currently operates on services between Finland and Germany.

FINNMASTER Built as the UNITED TRADER by Fosen Mekaniske Verksteder A/S, Rissa, Norway for *United Shipping* (a subsidiary of *Birka Shipping*) of Finland and chartered to *Transfennica*. During 2000 used on their Kemi - Oulu - Antwerpen - Felixstowe service. In 2001 the route was transferred to *Finnlines* and the vessels used sub-chartered to them (charter later transferred to *Finnlines*). In 2002 *United Shipping* was renamed *Birka Cargo* and she was renamed the BIRKA TRADER. In 2006 the service ceased and she was transferred to other *Finnlines* routes. In 2008 the charter was extended a further four years. In January 2013 chartered to *Transfennica*. In July 2013 renamed the TRADER. In January 2015 sold to *Finnlines* but not delivered until the end of the year, when the charter ended. In January 2016 renamed the FINNMASTER. In November 2016 chartered to *DFDS*. Operated mainly between Immingham and Rotterdam. In July 2017 charter ended and she returned to *Finnlines*, operating on a new service between Oxelösund (Sweden) and Naantali (Finland). Now used on all *Finnlines* services.

FINNMERCHANT Built as the LONGSTONE by Flensburger Schiffbau-Gesellschaft, Flensburg, Germany for *AWSR Shipping* (later *Foreland Shipping*). Chartered to *Transfennica* and operated between Hanko (Finland) and Lübeck (Germany). In January 2009 chartered to *Finnlines* and placed on the Helsinki - Aarhus route. In January 2012 chartered to *North Sea RoRo*. In March 2013 the operation ceased and the charter was taken over by *DFDS* and she was placed on the Immingham - Cuxhaven route. In May took over the Zeebrugge - Rosyth route. In October 2013 sold to *C Bulk NV* of Belgium, an associated company of *CLdN/Cobelfret Ferries*. In April 2014 charter to *DFDS* ended and she was chartered to an Australian operator. In November 2014 renamed the DORSET. In December 2014 the charter ended and she returned to *CLdN*. In early January 2015 placed on the Zeebrugge - Purfleet service. Later in the month sold to *Finnlines* and renamed the FINNMERCHANT. In April 2022 chartered to the Dutch MoD for three years.

FINNMILL, FINNPULP Built by Jinling Shipyard, Nanjing, China for the *Macoma Shipping Group* and chartered to *Finnlines*. In 2008 purchased by *Finnlines*. During Winter 2008/09 extra ramps were added at STX Europe Helsinki shipyard to enable ro-ro traffic to be conveyed on the weather deck.

MANN LINES

THE COMPANY *Mann Lines* are owned by *Mann & Son (London) Ltd* of Great Britain.

MANAGEMENT CEO Bill Binks.

ADDRESS Mann & Son (London) Ltd, The Naval House, Kings Quay Street, Harwich CO12 3JJ.

TELEPHONE Administration & Reservations *UK* +44 (0)1255 245200, ***Germany*** +49 (0)421 1638 50, ***Finland*** +358 (0)2 275 0000, ***Estonia*** +372 (0)679 1450.

FAX Administration & Reservations *UK* +44 (0)1255 245219, *Germany* + 49 (0)421 1638 520, *Finland* +358 (0)2 253 5905, *Estonia* +372 (0)679 1455.

INTERNET Email enquiry@manngroup.co.uk **Website** www.mannlines.com *(English, Finnish, Estonian, German, Russian)*

ROUTES OPERATED Harwich (Navyard) - Rotterdam - Cuxhaven (Germany) – Paldiski (Estonia) - Turku (Finland) - Bremerhaven (Germany) – Harwich (**ML FREYJA**; weekly).

| 1 | ML FREYJA | 23000t | 17 | 19.0k | 190.8m | 12P | - | 180T | A | IT | 9799977 |

ML FREYJA Built by CN Visentini, Donada, Italy and chartered to *Mann Lines*. In June 2017 sub-chartered to *SOL Continent Line* for six months. In December 2017 entered service with *Mann Lines*.

NEPTUNE LINES

THE COMPANY *Neptune Lines Shipping & Managing Enterprises SA* is Greek company operating throughout Europe.

ADDRESS 5-9 Iassonos Street, 18537 Piraeus, Greece.

TELEPHONE +30 210 45 57 700.

FAX +30 210 42 83 858.

INTERNET Website www.neptunelines.com *(English)*

ROUTES OPERATED (Northern Europe only) *Circuit 1* Santander - Rosslare - Portbury - Zeebrugge - Le Havre - Southampton, *Circuit 2* Santander - Portbury - Zeebrugge - Le Havre - Southampton.

In addition, an extensive network of Mediterranean services is operated. Other vessels in the fleet outside of the scope of this book and which do not serve Northern Europe are the short sea feeder vessels NEPTUNE AVRA, NEPTUNE OKEANIS and NEPTUNE THELISIS and the PCTC type vessels NEPTUNE HELLAS, NEPTUNE BARCELONA, NEPTUNE KOPER, NEPTUNE THARROS, NEPTUNE PHOS and NEPTUNE KALLOS.

1	NEPTUNE AEGLI	21611t	02	20.0k	158.0m	12P	1500C	104T	AQ	MT	9240964
2	NEPTUNE DYNAMIS	21611t	02	20.0k	158.0m	12P	1500C	104T	AQ	MT	9240976
3	NEPTUNE GALENE	37692t	14	19.3k	169.6m	0P	3800C	56T	AQ	GR	9668491
4	NEPTUNE ILIAD	36825t	10	19.3k	169.6m	0P	3800C	56T	AQ	MT	9440100
5	NEPTUNE ITHAKI	36902t	10	19.3k	169.6m	0P	3800C	56T	AQ	MT	9440083
6	NEPTUNE KEFALONIA	36902t	09	19.3k	169.6m	0P	3800C	56T	AQ	MT	9438717
7	NEPTUNE ODYSSEY	36902t	10	19.3k	169.6m	0P	3800C	56T	AQ	MT	9440095
8	NEPTUNE THALASSA	37692t	14	19.3K	169.6m	0P	3800C	56T	AQ	MT	9668506

NEPTUNE AEGLI, NEPTUNE DYNAMIS Built by Barreras Shipyard, Vigo, Spain. Retractable mezzanine decks mean she can operate as a car carrier or a short sea ro-ro freight ferry. In winter 2017 NEPTUNE AEGLI operated for *P&O Ferries* during the refit period between Hull and Zeebrugge in order to maintain a daily freight service. In winters 2018, 2019 and 2020 NEPTUNE DYNAMIS operated for *P&O Ferries* during the refit period between Hull and Zeebrugge in order to maintain a daily freight service. One vessel is allocated to circuit 1, currently the NEPTUNE DYNAMIS.

NEPTUNE GALENE NEPTUNE ILIAD, NEPTUNE ITHAKI, NEPTUNE KEFALONIA, NEPTUNE ODYSSEY, NEPTUNE THALASSA Built by Built by Hyundai Mipo Dockyard, Ulsan, South Korea. One vessel is allocated to Circuit 2, currently the NEPTUNE GALENE.

SECTION 3 – FREIGHT ONLY FERRIES

SEA-CARGO

THE COMPANY *Sea-Cargo AS* of Norway is a subsidiary of *Seatrans AS* of Norway.

MANAGEMENT Managing Director Ole Saevild, **Director Business Development** Erik A Paulsen, **General Manager (Immingham)** Mark Brighton, **General Manager (Aberdeen)** Ian Shewan.

ADDRESS *Norway* Wernersholmvegen, 5232 Paradis, Norway, *Immingham* Sea-Cargo UK, West Riverside Road, Immingham Dock, Immingham DN40 2NT, *Aberdeen* Sea-Cargo Aberdeen Ltd, Matthews Quay, Aberdeen Harbour, Aberdeen, AB11 5PG.

TELEPHONE Administration & Bookings *Bergen* +47 55 10 84 84, *Immingham* +44 (0)1469 577119, *Aberdeen* +44 (0)1224 582360.

INTERNET Email mail@sea-cargo.no **Website** www.sea-cargo.no *(English)*

ROUTES OPERATED *Sea-Cargo* operate a network of services from West Norway to Amsterdam, Aberdeen, Immingham, Rotterdam, Esbjerg and Świnoujście. The schedule varies from week to week and is shown on the company website. The **SC CONNECTOR** and **BORE BAY** are generally used on the twice-weekly Immingham service and the **SEA-CARGO EXPRESS** on the weekly Aberdeen service.

1	BORE BAY	10572t	96	20.0k	138.8m	12P	-	105T	A2	FI	9122007
2	MISANA	14100t	07	20.0k	163.9m	12P	-	150T	A	FI	9348936
3	MISIDA	14100t	07	20.0k	163.9m	12P	-	150T	A	FI	9348948
4	SC AHTELA	8610t	91	14.8k	139.5m	12P	-	92T	AS	MT	8911736
5	SC CONNECTOR	12251t	97	15.0k	154.5m	12P	-	124T	AS	MT	9131993
6	SEA-CARGO EXPRESS	6693t	12	16.0k	117.4m	0P	-	35T	A	MT	9358060
7	TRANS CARRIER	9953t	94	14.5k	144.5m	0P	-	94T	AS	BS	9007879

BORE BAY Built as the HERALDEN by Umoe Sterkoder AS, Kristiansund, Norway for *Rederi AB Engship* of Finland and chartered to *Transfennica*. In 2006 *Rederi AB Engship* was taken over by *Rettig Group Bore*. In 2007 converted at COSCO Shipyard, Nantong, China to add a garage on top of the weather deck, renamed AUTO BAY and placed on long-term charter to *UECC*. Generally used on the Baltic or Iberian services. In 2017 converted back to conventional ro-ro format by Fayard, Odense, Denmark and renamed the BORE BAY. Chartered to *Grandi Navi Veloci (GNV)* of Italy. In February 2018 chartered to *Transfennica*. From April to August 2018 chartered to *Stena Line* to operate between, Gdynia and Nynäshamn. From August 2019 until December 2019 chartered to *Brittany Ferries* to replace the MN PELICAN which was undergoing a major refit. In January 2020 chartered to *Sea-Cargo*.

MISANA Built by J J Sietas, Hamburg, Germany for *Godby Shipping AB* of Finland and time-chartered to *UPM-Kymmene* of Finland to operate between Finland, Spain and Portugal. In July 2013 charter taken over by *Finnlines*. In January 2016 long-term chartered to *Stena RoRo*, who then sub-chartered them to *Transfennica*. In January 2018 sub-chartered to *Stena Line* and placed on the Harwich - Rotterdam service. In March 2020 charter ended. Laid up. In August 2020 chartered to *Sea-Cargo*.

MISIDA Until January 2020, details as the MISANA. In January 2020 charter ended. Chartered to *DFDS* for two weeks operating on the Vlaardingen - Immingham and Esbjerg - Immingham routes. In February chartered to *CoTuNav* of Tunisia to operate between Rades and Marseille. Charter terminated in April and laid up. In July 2020 chartered to *P&O Ferries* to operate between Liverpool and Dublin. In November 2020 chartered to *Sea-Cargo*.

SC AHTELA Built as the AHTELA by Brodogradiliste "Sava", Macvanska Mitrovica, Yugoslavia, completed by Fosen Mekaniske Verksteder, Rissa, Norway for *Rederi AB Gustav Erikson* of Finland. Chartered to *Transfennica*. In 1995 chartered to *DFDS Tor Line*. In 1996 chartered to *Finncarriers Oy* of Finland and in 1997 renamed the FINNOAK. In 1998, extended in Klaipėda, Lithuania by 17 metres. In 2007 sold to *Hollming Oy* of Finland and in 2008 the charter ended and she was renamed the AHTELA. Chartered to *Navirail* of Estonia to operate between Helsinki and Muuga (Estonia). Between February and May 2011 chartered to *Sea-Cargo* to operate

ML Freyja *(Rob de Visser)*

SC Connector *(Rob de Visser)*

between Esbjerg (Denmark) and Egersund (Norway). In October 2012 purchased by *Sea-Cargo* and renamed the SC AHTELA.

SC CONNECTOR Built as the UNITED EXPRESS by Fosen Mekaniske Verksteder A/S, Rissa, Norway for *United Shipping* (a subsidiary of *Birka Shipping*) of Finland and chartered to *Transfennica*. During 2000 used on their Kemi - Oulu - Antwerpen - Felixstowe service. In 2001 the route was transferred to *Finnlines* and the vessel used sub-chartered to them (charter later transferred to *Finnlines*). In 2002 *United Shipping* was renamed *Birka Cargo* and she was renamed the BIRKA EXPRESS. In 2008 the charter was extended a further four years. In June 2013 renamed the EXPRESS. In November 2013 chartered to *Transfennica*. In April 2014 sold to *Sea-Cargo* but initially continued to operate for *Transfennica*. During winter 2015 re-engined and modified to allow to side loading. In February 2015 renamed the SC CONNECTOR. Entered service in late April. In 2019 two 35m high rotors was installed in order that the diesel engines could be supplemented by wind power.

SEA-CARGO EXPRESS One of two vessels ordered in 2005 from Bharati Ratnagiri Ltd, Mumbai, India for *Sea-Cargo*. The order for the second ship was cancelled. Trailers are carried on the main deck only. Containers are carried on the weather deck and pallets on the lower decks. A crane is provided for the containers and a side door for pallets. She operates on the Aberdeen - Norway service.

TRANS CARRIER Built as the KORSNÄS LINK by Brodogradiliste Kraljevica, Kraljevica, Croatia for *SeaLink AB* of Sweden and due to be time-chartered to *Korsnäs AB*, a Swedish forest products company. However, due to the war in Croatia, delivery was seriously delayed and she was offered for sale. In 1994 sold to the *Swan Group* and renamed the SWAN HUNTER. She was placed on the charter market. In 1997 she was chartered to *Euroseabridge* and renamed the PARCHIM. In 1999 the charter ended and she resumed the name SWAN HUNTER. In 1999 she was sold to *SeaTrans* and renamed the TRANS CARRIER. She operated for *Sea-Cargo*. In 2005 chartered to *Finnlines* and used on the Finland to Spain/Portugal service. In 2006 returned to *Sea-Cargo*. In January and February 2009 lengthened by 18.9 metres in Poland.

SEATRUCK FERRIES

THE COMPANY *Seatruck Ferries Ltd* is a British private sector company. It is part of the *Clipper Group*.

MANAGEMENT Chairman Peter Lybecker, **CEO** Alistair Eagles.

ADDRESSES Heysham (HQ) North Quay, Heysham Port, Heysham, Morecambe, Lancs LA3 2UH, **Warrenpoint** Seatruck House, The Ferry Terminal, Warrenpoint, County Down BT34 3JR, **Liverpool:** Seatruck Ferry Terminal, Brocklebank Dock, Port of Liverpool, L20 1DB, **Dublin**: Seatruck Dublin, Terminal 5, Alexandra Road, Dublin 1 Irish Republic.

TELEPHONE Administration +44 (0)1524 855377, **Reservations Heysham** +44 (0)1524 853512. **Warrenpoint** +44 (0)28 754400, **Liverpool** + (0)151 9333660, **Dublin** + (0) 353 18230492.

FAX Administration +44 (0)28 4175 4545, **Reservations Warrenpoint** +44 (0)28 4177 3737, **Heysham** +44 (0)1524 853549.

INTERNET Email aje@seatruckgroup.co.uk **Website** www.seatruckferries.com *(English)*

ROUTES OPERATED Heysham - Warrenpoint (9 hrs; **SEATRUCK PERFORMANCE, SEATRUCK PRECISION**; 2 per day), Heysham - Dublin (9 hrs; **CLIPPER POINT**; 1 per day), Liverpool - Dublin (9 hrs;, **SEATRUCK PACE, SEATRUCK POWER, SEATRUCK PROGRESS**; up to 3 per day).

1	CLIPPER POINT	14759t	08	22.0k	142.0m	12P	-	120T	A	CY	9350666
2	SEATRUCK PACE	14759t	09	22.0k	142.0m	12P	-	120T	A	CY	9350678
3	SEATRUCK PERFORMANCE	19722t	12	21.0k	142.0m	12P	-	151T	A	IM	9506227
4	SEATRUCK POWER	19722t	11	21.0k	142.0m	12P	-	151T	A	IM	9506215
5	SEATRUCK PRECISION	19722t	12	21.0k	142.0m	12P	-	151T	A	IM	9506239
6	SEATRUCK PROGRESS	19722t	11	21.0k	142.0m	12P	-	151T	A	IM	9506203

Seatruck Progress *(Miles Cowsill)*

Seatruck Pace *(Miles Cowsill)*

CLIPPER POINT Built by Astilleros de Huelva SA, Huelva, Spain for *Seatruck Ferries*. In May 2012 chartered to *DFDS* and placed on the Immingham-Cuxhaven route. In April 2013 chartered to the organisers of the 'SATA Rally Azores 2013' car rally to take cars from Portugal to the Azores. In May began operating for *DFDS* in the Baltic. In October transferred to the Immingham - Cuxhaven route. In June 2015 the charter ended. In July she was chartered to *InterShipping*, of Morocco to operate between Algeciras and Tangiers. In September 2016 the charter ended and she returned to *Seatruck Ferries*.

SEATRUCK PACE Built as the CLIPPER PACE by Astilleros Sevilla SA, Sevilla, Spain for *Seatruck Ferries*. In March 2012 renamed the SEATRUCK PACE. In January 2013 chartered to *Blue Water Shipping* of Denmark to carry wind turbine parts between Mostyn (Wales) and Esbjerg. Now operates on the Liverpool - Dublin route.

SEATRUCK PERFORMANCE Built as the SEATRUCK PERFORMANCE by Flensburger Schiffbau-Gesellschaft, Flensburg, Germany for *Seatruck Ferries*. In September 2012 chartered to *Stena Line* and renamed the STENA PERFORMER. She operated on both the Heysham - Belfast and Birkenhead - Belfast services. In August 2018 returned to *Seatruck Ferries*, renamed the SEATRUCK PERFORMANCE and placed on the Heysham - Warrenpoint service.

SEATRUCK POWER, SEATRUCK PROGRESS Built by Flensburger Schiffbau-Gesellschaft, Flensburg, Germany for *Seatruck Ferries*.

SEATRUCK PRECISION Built as the SEATRUCK PRECISION by Flensburger Schiffbau-Gesellschaft, Flensburg, Germany for *Seatruck Ferries*. In September 2012 chartered to *Stena Line* and renamed the STENA PRECISION. She operated on the Heysham - Belfast service. In September 2015 moved to the Birkenhead - Belfast route. In August 2018 returned to *Seatruck Ferries*, renamed the SEATRUCK PRECISION and placed on the Heysham - Warrenpoint service.

Seatruck Ferries also own the CLIPPER PENNANT, currently on charter to *P&O Ferries* and the SEATRUCK PANORAMA, currently on charter to *Stena Line*. They manage the ARROW, currently on charter to *Isle of Man Steam Packet Company* on behalf of her owners.

TRANSFENNICA

THE COMPANY *Transfennica Ltd* is a Finnish private sector company wholly owned by *Spliethoff Bevrachtingskantoor* of The Netherlands.

MANAGEMENT Managing Director Dirk P Witteveen, **Sales Director (UK)** Andrew Clarke.

ADDRESSES *Finland* Eteläranta 12, 00130 Helsinki, Finland, *UK* Finland House, 47 Berth, Tilbury Port, Tilbury, Essex RM18 7EH.

TELEPHONE Administration & Reservations *Finland* +358 (0)9 13262, *UK* +44 (0)1375 363 900.

INTERNET Email *Finland* info@transfennica.com *UK* info.uk@transfennica.com **Website** www.transfennica.com *(English, Finnish, Russian)*

ROUTES OPERATED Tilbury (weekly) to various destinations in Finland and Russia. Please see the website. All *Transfennica* ships are listed below as ships are sometimes moved between routes.

1	BORE SEA	25586t	11	18.5k	195.0m	12P	-	210T	A2	NL	9443554
2	CORONA SEA	25609t	08	20.0k	184.8m	12P	-	250T	AS	UK	9357597
3	GENCA	28301t	07	22.0k	205.0m	12P	-	200T	A2	NL	9307372
4	HAFNIA SEA	25609t	08	20.0k	184.8m	12P	-	250T	AS	UK	9357602
5	KRAFTCA	28301t	06	22.0k	205.0m	12P	-	200T	A2	NL	9307360
6	PLYCA	28301t	09	22.0k	205.0m	12P	-	200T	A2	NL	9345398
7	PULPCA	28301t	08	22.0k	205.0m	12P	-	200T	A2	NL	9345386
8	SEAGARD	10488t	99	21.0k	153.5m	12P	-	134T	A2	FI	9198977
9	TIMCA	28301t	06	22.0k	205.0m	12P	-	200T	A2	NL	9307358
10	TRICA	28301t	07	22.0k	205.0m	12P	-	200T	A2	NL	9307384

BORE SEA Built by Flensburger Schiffbau-Gesellschaft, Flensburg, Germany for *Bore Shipowners (Rettig Group Bore)* of Finland. In May 2011 chartered to *Transfennica* and operated between Zeebrugge and Bilbao. In January 2013 chartered for three years to *Fret Cetam* of France and used for the conveyance of parts for Airbus aircraft. In September 2016 chartered to *CLdN/Cobelfret Ferries*. Initially used mainly on the Zeebrugge - Purfleet service but later also used on the Iberian routes. In January 2018 chartered to *Transfennica*.

CORONA SEA Built as the TOR CORONA by Jinling Shipyard, Nanjing, China for *Macoma Shipping Ltd* of the UK and time-chartered to *DFDS Tor Line* for ten years. Used on the Fredericia – København - Klaipėda service. In April 2012 renamed the CORONA SEAWAYS. In January 2018 chartered to *Transfennica* and, in February, renamed the CORONA SEA. In December 2018 sold to *Leomar RoRo* of Sweden.

GENCA, KRAFTCA, PLYCA, PULPCA, TIMCA, TRICA Built by New Szczecin Shipyard (SSN), Szczecin, Poland for *Spliethoff Bevrachtingskantoor*, owners of *Transfennica*.

HAFNIA SEA Built as the TOR HAFNIA by Jinling Shipyard, Nanjing, China for *Macoma Shipping Ltd* of the UK and time-chartered to *DFDS Tor Line* for ten years. Until 2013, mainly operated on the Immingham - Esbjerg route. In March 2011 renamed the HAFNIA SEAWAYS. In January 2015 chartered to *Cobelfret Ferries* for four weeks. In January 2018 chartered to *Transfennica* and in March 2018 renamed the HAFNIA SEA. In December 2018 sold to *Leomar RoRo* of Sweden.

SEAGARD Built by J J Sietas KG, Hamburg, Germany for *Bror Husell Chartering* of Finland (later acquired by *Bore Shipowning* of Finland) and chartered to *Transfennica*.

UECC

THE COMPANY *United European Car Carriers AS* is a Norwegian private sector company jointly owned in equal shares by *Nippon Yusen Kabushiki Kaisha (NYK)* of Japan and *Wallenius Lines* of Sweden. *UECC* consists of companies in Norway, Germany, Spain, France, Portugal and the UK. The fleet technical and ship management department is based in Grimsby (UK).

MANAGEMENT Chief Executive Officer Glenn Edvardsen.

ADDRESSES Norway Karenlyst Allè 57, 0277 Oslo, **UK** Units 5B & 5C Appian Way, Europa Park, Grimsby, DN31 2UT.

TELEPHONE Norway +47 21 00 98 00, **UK** +44 (0)1472 269429.

FAX Norway +47 21 00 98 01, **UK** +44 (0)207 628 2858.

INTERNET Email marketing@uecc.com, **Website** www.uecc.com *(English)*.

ROUTES OPERATED Atlantic Service Vigo – Le Havre – Zeebrugge – Sheerness – Portbury – Vigo, Vigo – Zeebrugge – Bremerhaven – Malmo – Drammen (*PCTC vessels; weekly*) **Baltic Service** Southampton – Zeebrugge – Bremerhaven – Gdansk – Hanko – Southampton (*AUTO ECO, AUTO ENERGY, AUTO STAR*; weekly), **Bristol Service** Portbury – Santander – Pasajes (*AUTOSUN*; weekly), **Biscay Services** Santander – Pasajes – Zeebrugge – Southampton – Santander (*AUTO ADVANCE*; weekly), Santander – Pasajes – Rotterdam – Zeebrugge – Santander (*AUTOSKY,* weekly), Santander – Bremerhaven –Zeebrugge – Southampton – Le Havre – Santander (*AUTOPRESTIGE*; weekly), **North Sea Service** Zeebrugge – Esbjerg – Gothenburg – Drammen (*MINCHAH*; weekly) **Norway Service** Bremerhaven – Oslo –Wallhamn – Bremerhaven (*AUTOPROGRESS*; twice weekly), **North – South Service** Bremerhaven – Zeebrugge – Portbury – Vigo – Sagunto – Tarragona – Savona – Livorno – Pireaus – Autoport – Bremerhaven (*PCTC vessels*; *every 9 days*).

Services listed carry large volumes of trade cars together with unaccompanied ro-ro cargo and often call at additional ports for an inducement. Vessels regularly transfer between routes and the following is a list of owned vessels currently in the *UECC* including those not presently serving the UK. The owned fleet is supplemented by chartered deep sea ocean-going PCTC vessels with side and quarter ramps many of which are owned by parent companies *NYK Line* and *Wallenius Lines* and Eukor (which is 40% owned by Wallenius*)*. Current chartered vessels

SECTION 3 – FREIGHT ONLY FERRIES

at the time of preparation and out of the scope of this book are the SPICA LEADER, CORAL LEADER, EMERALD LEADER, OPAL LEADER, VEGA LEADER and PROMETHEUS LEADER which belong to parent *NYK Line*, the VIKING AMBER chartered from *Gram Car Carriers*, the PASSERO chartered from German ship owning group *F. Laeisz* and the MONZA EXPRESS chartered from *Vroon*.

1	AUTO ACHIEVE	35667t	22	-	169.0m	0P	3600C	-	QRS	PT	9881304
2	AUTO ASPIRE	35667t	22	-	169.0m	0P	3600C	-	QRS	PT	9895812
3	AUTO ADVANCE	35667t	21	-	169.0m	0P	3600C	-	QRS	PT	9881299
4	AUTO ECO	43424t	16	18.6k	181.0m	0P	3800C	-	QRS	PT	9736365
5	AUTO ENERGY	43424t	16	18.6k	181.0m	0P	3800C	-	QRS	PT	9736377
6	AUTOPRESTIGE	11596t	99	20.0k	128.8m	0P	1220C	-	AS	PT	9190157
7	AUTOPROGRESS	11591t	98	20.0k	128.8m	0P	1220C	-	AS	PT	9131967
8	AUTOSKY	21010t	00	20.9k	140.0m	0P	2080C	-	AS	PT	9206774
9	AUTOSTAR	21010t	00	20.9k	140.0m	0P	2080C	-	AS	PT	9206786
10	AUTOSUN	21094t	00	20.9k	140.0m	0P	1220C	-	AS	PT	9227053

AUTO ACHIEVE, AUTO ADVANCE, AUTO ASPIRE Dual fuel LNG Battery Hybrid Ice Class 1A pure car and truck carrier with side and quarter ramps built by China Ship Building Trading Co Ltd and Jiangnan Shipyard Group Co. Ltd.

AUTO ECO, AUTO ENERGY Designated as E-Class both are Dual fuel LNG Ice Class 1A pure car and truck carriers with side and quarter ramps built by Kawasaki Heavy Industries at NACKS shipyard, Nantong, China for *UECC*. Used on Baltic services, the vessels are refuelled by a specialist barge in Zeebrugge. During the initial Covid-19 crisis the AUTOECO was temporarily deployed to the Biscay service in place of laid up P-class vessels but has now returned to the Baltic service.

AUTOPRESTIGE, AUTOPROGRESS, AUTOPRIDE Built by Frisian Shipyard, Harlingen, the Netherlands for *UECC*. Designated P-class, they are an enlarged version of the now scrapped R-class and built to a 'Grimsby-Max' specification with greater capacity for ro-ro cargo. Generally used on scheduled sailings between Iberia and the Benelux and UK or between Germany and Norway. In April 2020 *the* AUTOPRIDE and AUTOPROGRESS were laid up in the UK on the River Fal due to the Covid-19 crisis but have now returned to service. A fourth P-class the AUTOPREMIER was in the fleet until sold in 2021.

AUTOSKY, AUTOSTAR, AUTOSUN Built by Tsuneishi Zosen, Tadotsu, Japan for *UECC* Designated S-class, they are a further enlargement of the P-class and R-class designs and are normally used on Biscay services.

WAGENBORG

THE COMPANY *Wagenborg Shipping Sweden AB* is a subsidiary of *Royal* Wagenborg, a Dutch private sector company.

ADDRESS Wagenborg Shipping Sweden AB, Box 207, 201 22 Malmö, Sweden.

TELEPHONE +46 437 1 00.

INTERNET Email info.sweden@wagenborg.se **Website** www.wagenborg.com/shipping/roro-liner-service-baltic-europe *(English)*

ROUTES OPERATED Harraholmen (Sweden) - Bremen (Germany) - Sheerness (UK) - Terneuzen (Netherlands) - Cuxhaven (Germany) - Södertalje (Sweden) - Harraholmen (12 days; **BALTICBORG, BOTHNIABORG**; 1 per week),

1	BALTICBORG	12460t	04	16.5 k	153.1m	0P	-	104T	A	NL	9267716
2	BOTHNIABORG	12460t	04	16.5 k	153.1m	0P	-	104T	A	NL	9267728

BALTICBORG, BOTHNIABORG Built by Bodewes Volharding, Volharding, The Netherlands (hull built by Daewoo Mangalia Heavy Industries SA, Mangalia, Romania) for *Wagenborg Shipping* of The Netherlands. Time-chartered to *Kappa Packaging* (now *Smurfit Kappa Group*). Placed on service between Piteå and Northern Europe. Northbound journeys (Terneuzen - Piteå) marketed as *RORO2 Stockholm*, with a call at Södertälje (Sweden (near Stockholm)) and, from 2005, the section Bremen - Sheerness - Terneuzen marketed as *RORO2 London*. In 2007 these arrangements ceased and *Mann Lines* took over the marketing of northbound traffic, a northbound call at Harwich (Navyard) being introduced and the Södertälje call being replaced by a call at Paldiski in Estonia. This arrangement ceased in 2013 and they reverted to their previous schedules.

WALLENIUS SOL

THE COMPANY *Wallenius SOL* is a joint venture *Wallenius Lines* and *Swedish Orient Line*, both Swedish private sector companies.

MANAGEMENT Managing Director Ragnar Johansson, **Commercial Manager, Liner Service**

Kai Peränen, **Head Of Communications** Richard Jeppsson.

ADDRESSES Klippan 1A, 414 51 Gothenburg, Sweden.

TELEPHONE +46 (0)31 354 40 50.

INTERNET Email info@wallenius-sol.com **Website** wallenius-sol.com *(English)*

ROUTES OPERATED Kemi - Oulu - Pietarsaari - Lübeck - Zeebrugge - Tilbury - Zeebrugge - Kemi; *TAVASTLAND, THULELAND, TUNDRALAND*; 1 per week (2 of these are used, the other one is used on a purely Baltic ervice)), Kemi - Oulu - Husum - Zeebrugge - Antwerpen - Travemünde - Vaasa - Kemi; *BALTIC ENABLER, BOTNIA ENABLER* 1/2 per week).

1	BALTIC ENABLER	59761t	22	20.0k	242.0m	12P	-	420T	A	SE	9884681
2	BOTNIA ENABLER	59761t	22	20.0k	242.0m	12P	-	420T	A	SE	9884679
3	TAVASTLAND	23128t	06	16.0k	190.7m	12P	-	200T	A	SE	9334959
4	THULELAND	23128t	06	16.0k	190.7m	12P	-	200T	A	SE	9343261
5	TUNDRALAND	23128t	07	16.0k	190.7m	12P	-	200T	A	SE	9343273

BALTIC ENABLER, BOTNIA ENABLER Built by Yantai CIMC Raffles Shipyard, Yantai, China. Run on LNG.

TAVASTLAND Built as the TRANSPAPER by Aker Finnyards, Rauma, Finland for *Baltic Container Shipping* of the UK and chartered to *Rederi AB Transatlantic* of Sweden. Operated on services operated for Stora Enso Paper Group, mainly in the Baltic. In December 2016 chartered to *SOL Continent Line* and used on their Baltic service; she was renamed the TAVASTLAND. Usually operates on the Kemi - Oulu - Lübeck route but could be moved to a North Sea service.

THULELAND Built as the TRANSPULP by Aker Finnyards, Rauma, Finland for *Baltic Container Shipping* of the UK and chartered to *Rederi AB Transatlantic* of Sweden. Operated on service operated for Stora Enso Paper Group, mainly in the Baltic. In early 2011 transferred to the Göteborg - Tilbury (once weekly) and Göteborg - Zeebrugge (*CLdN* service) (once weekly) services. In January 2013 began operating twice weekly to Tilbury, replacing the SELANDIA SEAWAYS of *DFDS* . In January 2015 chartered to *SOL Continent Line*. In December 2016 renamed the THULELAND.

TUNDRALAND Built as the TRANSTIMBER by Aker Finnyards, Rauma, Finland for *Baltic Container Shipping* of the UK and chartered to *Rederi AB Transatlantic* of Sweden. Operated on service operated for Stora Enso Paper Group, mainly in the Baltic. In January 2015 chartered to *SOL Continent Line*. In August 2017 she was renamed the TUNDRALAND.

SECTION 4 - GB & IRELAND - RO-RO OPERATORS CONVEYING PRIVATE TRAFFIC

The following operators employ ro-ro freight ships for the conveyance of their own traffic or traffic for a limited number of customers and do not normally solicit general traffic from hauliers or shippers.

FORELAND SHIPPING

THE COMPANY *Foreland Shipping Limited* (formerly *AWSR Shipping Limited*) is a UK private sector company. The principal shareholder in *Foreland Shipping* is *Hadley Shipping Group*.

MANAGEMENT Chairman Peter Morton, **Managing Director** Paul Trudgeon, **Operations Director** Stuart Williams.

ADDRESS 4th Floor, 117-119 Houndsditch, London EC3A 7BT.

INTERNET Email enquiries@foreland-shipping.co.uk **Website** www.foreland-shipping.co.uk *(English)*

ROUTES OPERATED No public routes are operated. Ships are for charter to the *UK Ministry of Defence* for their 'Strategic Sealift Capability'.

1	ANVIL POINT	23235t	03	17.1k	193.0m	12P	-	180T	A	UK	9248540
2	EDDYSTONE	23235t	02	17.1k	193.0m	12P	-	180T	A	UK	9234070
3	HARTLAND POINT	23235t	03	17.1k	193.0m	12P	-	180T	A	UK	9248538
4	HURST POINT	23235t	02	17.1k	193.0m	12P	-	180T	A	UK	9234068

ANVIL POINT, HARTLAND POINT Built by Harland & Wolff, Belfast, UK for *AWSR Shipping*. To FSG design.

EDDYSTONE, HURST POINT Built by Flensburger Schiffbau-Gesellschaft, Flensburg, Germany for *AWSR Shipping*.

HOLMEN PAPER SHIPPING

THE COMPANY *Holmen Paper AB*, is an international company based in Sweden.

ADDRESS P.O. Box 5407, SE-114 84 Stockholm, Sweden.

TELEPHONE +46 8 666 21 00.

INTERNET Email info@holmen.com **Website** holmen.com *(English, Swedish)*

ROUTES OPERATED Hallstavik (Sweden) - Norrköping (Sweden) - Sheerness - Norrköping - Hallstavik (2 weeks); ***BALTIC BRIGHT***; 1 per fortnight).

| 1 | BALTIC BRIGHT | 9708t | 96 | 15.0k | 134.4m | 12P | - | 50T | A | FI | 9129263 |

BALTIC BRIGHT Built by Karlskronavarvet AB, of Sweden for *Ab Kungsvik & Rederi Ab Novator*, of Sweden and chartered to *Holmen Paper AB* to operate Hallstavik - Södertälje - Chatham (UK). Between 1997 and 2021 she undertook a variety of charters. In January 2021 she was sold to *Godby Shipping AB*, of Åland and in 2022 she was chartered to *Holmen Paper AB*.

SCA

THE COMPANY *SCA* is a Swedish company.

MANAGEMENT Managing Director (UK) Steve Harley.

ADDRESS Skepparplatsen, Sundsvall, Sweden.

TELEPHONE Administration & Reservations *Sweden* +46 (0)60 19 30 00, *UK* +44 (0)300 003 7160.

INTERNET Email info@sca.com **Website** www.sca.com/en/logistics *(English)*

ROUTE OPERATED Umeå - Sundsvall - Tilbury - Rotterdam (Eemhaven) - Helsingborg - Oxelösund - Umeå (8/9 day round trip; *SCA OBBOLA, SCA ORTVIKEN, SCA ÖSTRAND*; 1 per week).

1	SCA OBBOLA	20168t	96	16.0k	170.6m	OP	-	-	A	SE	9087350
2	SCA ORTVIKEN	20154t	97	16.0k	170.4m	OP	-	-	A	SE	9087374
3	SCA ÖSTRAND	20171t	96	16.0k	170.6m	OP	-	-	A	SE	9087362

SCA OBBOLA, SCA ORTVIKEN, SCA ÖSTRAND Built as the OBBOLA, ORTVIKEN and ÖSTRAND by Astilleros Españoles, Sevilla, Spain for *Gorthon Lines* and chartered to *SCA Transforest*. They are designed for the handling of forest products in non-wheeled 'cassettes' but can also accommodate trailers. The ORTVIKEN was lengthened during Autumn 2000 and the others during 2001. In June 2001 purchased by *SCA Transforest*. In spring 2016 renamed the SCA OBBOLA, SCA ORTVIKEN and SCA ÖSTRAND.

Hartland Point *(Frank Lose)*

SECTION 5 – GB & IRELAND - CHAIN, CABLE ETC FERRIES

CUMBRIA COUNTY COUNCIL (FROM 1 APRIL 2023 WESTMORLAND AND FURNESS COUNCIL)

Address Highways and Transport, Economy and Infrastructure Directorate, County Offices, Kendal, Cumbria LA9 4RQ **Tel** +44 (0)1539 713040, **Fax** +44 (0)1539 713035. Details will change e from 1 April 2023)

Internet **Email** george.sowerby@cumbria.gov.uk *(English* **Website** www.cumbria.gov.uk/roads-transport/highways-pavements/windmereferry.asp *(English)* Details will change e from 1 April 2023)

Route Bowness-on-Windermere - Far Sawrey.

1	MALLARD	-	90	-	25.9m	140P	18C	-	BA

MALLARD Cable ferry built by F L Steelcraft, Borth, Dyfed for *Cumbria County Council*.

DARTMOUTH – KINGSWEAR FLOATING BRIDGE CO LTD

Address DKFBC Ltd, Dart Marina, Sandquay Road, Dartmouth, Devon TQ6 9PH. **Tel** +44 (0)7866 531687.

Internet Website justbdartmouth.com/guestinfo/ferrytimes.html *(English)*

Route Dartmouth - Kingswear (Devon) across River Dart (higher route) (forms part of A379).

1	HIGHER FERRY	540t	09	-	52.7m	240P	32C	-	BA

HIGHER FERRY Built by Ravestein BV, Deest, The Netherlands under contract to Pendennis Shipyard, Falmouth, who fitted the vessel out between January and June 2009.

ISLE OF WIGHT COUNCIL (COWES FLOATING BRIDGE)

Address Cowes Floating Bridge, Medina Road, Cowes, Isle of Wight PO31 7BX. **Tel** +44 (0)1983 293041. **Internet Website** www.iwfloatingbridge.co.uk/timetable **Route** Cowes - East Cowes. **Note** the service is unable to operate at times of very low tide; a passenger service by launch is operated. Details are shown on the website.

1	FLOATING BRIDGE NO 6	-	17	-	38.0m	-	20C	-	BA
2•	NO 5	-	76	-	33.5m	-	15C	-	BA

FLOATING BRIDGE NO 6 Chain ferry built by Mainstay Marine Solutions Ltd, Pembroke Dock, UK.

NO 5 Chain ferry built by Fairey Marine, East Cowes, UK for *Isle of Wight County Council*, now *Isle of Wight Council*. In January 2017 withdrawn for sale. Laid up at Gosport.

KING HARRY FERRY AND CORNWALL FERRIES

Address 2 Ferry Cottages, Feock, Truro, Cornwall TR3 6QJ. **Tel** +44 (0)1326 741 194.

Internet Email info@falriver.co.uk **Website** www.falriver.co.uk *(English)*

Route Philliegh - Feock (Cornwall) (across River Fal).

1	KING HARRY FERRY	500t	06	-	55.2m	150P	34C	-	BA	UK	9364370

KING HARRY FERRY Chain ferry built by Pendennis Shipyard, Falmouth (hull constructed at Ravestein Shipyard, Deest, The Netherlands) to replace the previous King Harry ferry. Number is Lloyd's number, not IMO.

Bramble Bush Bay *(Andrew Cooke)*

Island Flyer and Barfleur *(Andrew Cooke)*

LUSTY BEG ISLAND FERRY

Address Lusty Beg, Boa Island, Kesh, County Fermanagh BT93 8AD.

Tel +44 (0)28 686 33300.

Internet Email info@lustybegisland.com **Website** www.lustybegisland.com *(English)*

Route Boa Island, County Fermanagh - Lusty Beg Island (Lower Lough Erne).

1	CORLOUGHAROO	-	-	-	10.0m	30P	2C	-	BA

CORLOUGHAROO Cable ferry, built for *Lusty Beg Island*.

REEDHAM FERRY

Address Reedham Ferry, Ferry Inn, Reedham, Norwich NR13 3HA. **Tel** +44 (0)1493 700429.

Internet Email info@reedhamferry.co.uk **Website** www.reedhamferry.co.uk *(English)*

Route Acle - Reedham - Norton (across River Yare, Norfolk).

1	REEDHAM FERRY	-	84	-	11.3m	20P	3C	-	BA

REEDHAM FERRY Chain ferry built by Newsons, Oulton Broad, Lowestoft, UK for *Reedham Ferry*. Maximum vehicle weight: 12 tons.

SANDBANKS FERRY

Address **Company** Bournemouth-Swanage Motor Road and Ferry Company, Shell Bay, Studland, Swanage, Dorset BH19 3BA. **Tel** +44 (0)1929 450203, **Ferry** Floating Bridge, Ferry Way, Sandbanks, Poole, Dorset BH13 7QN. **Tel** +44 (0)1929 450203.

Internet Email email@sandbanksferry.co.uk **Website** www.sandbanksferry.co.uk *(English)*

Route Sandbanks - Shell Bay (Dorset).

1	BRAMBLE BUSH BAY	625t	93	-	74.4m	400P	48C	-	BA	UK	9072070

BRAMBLE BUSH BAY Chain ferry, built by Richard Dunston (Hessle) Ltd, Hessle, UK for the *Bournemouth-Swanage Motor Road and Ferry Company*. Number is Lloyd's number, not IMO.

SOUTH HAMS DISTRICT COUNCIL

Address Lower Ferry Office, The Square, Kingswear, Dartmouth, Devon TQ6 0AA. **Tel** +44 (0)1803 861234.

Internet Website www.southhams.gov.uk/DartmouthLowerFerry *(English)*

Route Dartmouth - Kingswear (Devon) across River Dart (lower route).

1	THE TOM AVIS	-	94	-	33.5m	50P	8C	-	BA
2	THE TOM CASEY	-	89	-	33.5m	50P	8C	-	BA

THE TOM AVIS Float (propelled by tugs) built by C Toms & Sons, Fowey, UK for South Hams District Council.

THE TOM CASEY Float (propelled by tugs) built by Cosens, Portland, UK for South Hams District Council.

TORPOINT FERRY

Address 2 Ferry Street, Torpoint, Cornwall PL11 2AX. Tel +44 (0)1752 812233.

Internet Website www.tamarcrossings.org.uk *(English)*

Route Devonport (Plymouth) - Torpoint (Cornwall) across the Tamar. The three ferries operate in parallel, each on her own 'track'. Pre-booking is not possible and the above number cannot be used for that purpose.

1	LYNHER II	748t	06	-	73.0m	250P	73C	-	BA	UK	9310941
2	PLYM II	748t	04	-	73.0m	250P	73C	-	BA	UK	9310927
3	TAMAR II	748t	05	-	73.0m	250P	73C	-	BA	UK	9310939

LYNHER II, PLYM II, TAMAR II Chain ferries built by Ferguson Shipbuilders Ltd, Port Glasgow, UK to replace 1960s-built ships. Number is Lloyds number, not IMO.

WATERFORD CASTLE RESORT

Address The Island, Waterford, X91 Y722, Irish Republic. **Tel** +353 (0)51 878203.

Internet Email info@waterfordcastleresort.com **Website** www.waterfordcastleresort.com *(English)*

Route Grantstown - Little Island (in River Suir, County Waterford).

1	MARY FITZGERALD	122t	72	10.0k	35.0m	100P	14C	-	BA	IE	8985531

MARY FITZGERALD Built as the STEDINGEN by Abeking & Rasmussen, Lemwerder, Germany for *Schnellastfähre Berne-Farge GmbH* (from 1993 *Fähren Bremen-Stedingen GmbH*) to operate across the River Weser (Vegesack - Lemwerder and Berne - Farge). In 2004 sold to the *Lough Foyle Ferry Company Ltd* and renamed the FOYLE RAMBLER. Generally used on the Buncrana - Rathmullan (Lough Swilly) service, which did not resume in summer 2014. In 2014 sold to *Waterford Castle Hotel* and renamed the MARY FITZGERALD. Modified to be cable guided. Number is Lloyds number, not IMO.

SECTION 6 - GB & IRELAND - MAJOR PASSENGER-ONLY FERRIES

There are a surprisingly large number of passenger-only ferries operating in the British Isles, mainly operated by launches and small motor boats. There are, however, a few 'major' operators who operate only passenger vessels (of rather larger dimensions) and have not therefore been mentioned previously.

Alderney Ferry Services. CAUSEWAY EXPLORER 12.0m, 12 passengers. **Route operated** St Annes (Alderney) - St Peterport (Guernsey)**. Tel** +44 (0)7781 119796, **Email** info@alderneyferry.com **Web** alderneyferryservices.co.uk *(English)*

Appledore Instow Ferry LIZZIE M (2010, 6.7m, 12 passengers, SHEILA M (2019, 7.6m, 12 passengers). **Route operated** Appledore (Devon) - Instow (Devon) (across River Torridge). **Website** www.appledoreinstowferry.com *(English)*

Aran Island Ferries BANRÍON NA FARRAIGE (117t, 27.4m, 1984, 195 passengers, IMO 8407709) (ex ARAN EXPRESS 2007), CEOL NA FARRAIGE (234t, 2001, 37.4m, 294 passengers, IMO 9246750), DRAÍOCHT NA FARRAIGE (318t, 1999, 37.4m, 294 passengers, IMO 9200897), GLÓR NA FARRAIGE (170t, 1985, 33.5m, 244 passenger, IMO 8522391) (ex ARAN FLYER 2007), SAOIRSE NA FARRAIGE (424t, 2020, 39.9m, 392 passengers, IMO 9880881). **Routes operated** Galway – Inishmor, Rossaveal (Co Galway) – Inishmor, Rossaveal - Inis Meáin, Rossaveal - Inisheer. **Tel** +353 (0)91 568903, **Fax** +353 (0)91 568538, Email info@aranislandferries.com **Website** www.aranislandferries.com (English)

Blue Funnel Cruises HYTHE SCENE (66t, 1992, 21.3m, 162 passengers - catamaran) (ex GREAT EXPECTATIONS 2017), JENNY BLUE (ex OSSIAN OF STAFFA 2017) (1993, 13.7m, 65 passengers), JENNY R* (12t, 1984, 13.7m, 75 passengers), OCEAN SCENE (279t, 1994, 29.0m, 350 passengers - catamaran, IMO 8633865), OLIVER B* (21t, 1988, 12.2m, 62 passengers (ex SOLENT PRINCE 2001, JENNY ANN 1999, FINGAL OF STAFFA). Note: The HYTHE SCENE is the regular ferry. Other vessels in the fleet (which are used for charters and excursions) can cover as necessary. **Route Operated** Southampton - Hythe, **Tel** +44 (0)2380 239800 **Email** office@bluefunnel.co.uk **Website** www.bluefunnel.co.uk *(English)*. *The JENNY R is owned by Blue Funnel* but operated by *Solent and Wightline Cruises Ltd*, the OLIVER B is owned by *Solent and Wightline Cruises Ltd* but operated by *Blue Funnel Cruises*.

Cape Clear Ferries CARRAIG MHÓR (77t, 1989, 19.8m, 96 passengers) (ex HAPPY HOOKER 2022), DÚN AN OÍR II (61t. 1997 18 metres, 94 passengers), , **Routes operated** Baltimore (Co Cork) - Cape Clear, Schull (Co Cork) - Cape Clear, **Tel:** +353 (0)28 39159, **Email** info@capeclearferries.com **Website** www.capeclearferries.com *(English)*

Carmarthen Bay Ferries GLANSTEFFAN (2018, 8.0m, 10 passengers (amphibian)). **Route Operated** Ferryside - Llanstephan (Carmarthenshire, Wales). **Tel** +44 (0)7538 006 994. **Email** info@carmarthenbayferries.co.uk **Website** www.carmarthenbayferries.co.uk *(English, Welsh)*

Clydelink ISLAND TRADER (12 passengers), SILVER SWAN (12 passengers) **Route operated** Renfrew - Yoker (operated on behalf of *Strathclyde Partnership for Transport*). **Tel** +44 (0)871 705 0888, **Website** bustimes.org/services/clk-renfrew-ferry-yoker *(English)*.

Cremyll Ferry (Plymouth Boat Trips) EDGCUMBE BELLE (35t, 1957, 17.6m, 128 passengers) (ex HUMPHREY GILBERT 1978) **Route operated** Stonehouse, Plymouth, Devon - Cremyll, Cornwall. **Note:** River craft owned by this operator are also used for the ferry service on some occasions. **Tel** +44 (0)1752 253153 or, **Email** info@plymouthboattrips.co.uk **Website** www.plymouthboattrips.co.uk/ferries/cremyll-ferry *(English)*

Dartmouth Steam Railway & Riverboat Company DARTMOUTH PRINCESS (22t, 1990, 18.3m, 156 passengers), (ex DEVON BELLE II 2000) KINGSWEAR PRINCESS (27t, 1978, 19.1m, 150 passengers) (ex TWIN STAR II 2010). **Route operated** Dartmouth - Kingswear. **Note:** River craft owned by this operator are also used for the ferry service on some occasions. **Tel** +44 (0)1803 555872, **Email** sales@dsrrb.co.uk **Website** www.dartmouthrailriver.co.uk/tours/dartmouth-to-kingswear-passenger-ferry *(English)*

Doolin Ferry (O'Brien Line) ARAN ISLANDS EXPRESS (131t, 2013, 26.0m, 246 passengers, IMO 8346503) (ex DOUCE FRANCE 2020), DOOLIN DISCOVERY (2009, 15.2m, 72 passengers), DOOLIN EXPRESS, (161t, 2010, 24.5m, 194 passengers, IMO 8791966), (ex BLANCHE HERMINE 2016, ex SAINT VINCENT DE PAUL, 2014), JACK B (2005, 15.2m, 67 passengers), SPIRIT OF DOOLIN (115t, 2001, 24.0m, 200 passengers, IMO 8347935) (ex STAR RIVIERA 2020), STAR OF DOOLIN (121t, 2018, 24.0m, 200 passengers, IMO 8346565), TRANQUILITY (62t, 1988, 21.9m, 100 passengers). **Routes operated** Doolin - Inisheer, Doolin - Inishmaan, Doolin - Inishmore. Also cruises to Cliffs of Mohr. **Tel** +353 (0)65 707 5555, +353 (0)65 707 5618, **Email** info@doolinferry.com **Website** www.doolinferry.com *(English)*

Starcross – Exmouth Ferry ORCOMBE (23t, 1954, 14.3m, 90 passengers) **Route operated** Exmouth - Starcross. **Tel** +44 (0)7934 461672. **Website** www.facebook.com/StarcrossExmouthFerry *(English)*

Fleetwood – Knott End Ferry (operated by *Wyre Marine Services Ltd*) WYRE ROSE (2005, 10.0m length, 35 passengers). **Route operated** Fleetwood - Knott End. **Tel** +44 (0)1253 871113, **Ferry mobile** +44 (0) 7793 270934, **Email** info@wyremarine.co.uk **Website** www.wyre.gov.uk/info/200311/transport_and_parking/130/knott_end_to_fleetwood_ferry *(English)*

Gosport Ferry HARBOUR SPIRIT (293t, 2015, 32.8m, 297 passengers, IMO 9741669), SPIRIT OF GOSPORT (300t, 2001, 32.6m, 300 passengers, IMO 8972089), SPIRIT OF PORTSMOUTH (377t, 2005, 32.6m, 300 passengers, IMO 9319894). **Route operated** Gosport - Portsmouth. **Tel** +44 (0)23 9252 4551, **Email** admin@gosportferry.co.uk **Website** www.gosportferry.co.uk *(English)*

Gravesend – Tilbury Ferry (operated by the *JetStream Tours*) THAMES SWIFT (25.6t, 1995, 18.3m, 50 passengers (tri-maran)), (ex MARTIN CHUZZLEWIT 2001), JACOB MARLEY (29t, 1985, 15.5m, 98 passengers) (ex SOUTHERN BAY ROSE 2016, ex SEAWAYS EXPRESS 2006, ex CONDOR KESTREL), THAMES KESTREL (ex URIAH HEEP 2022) (25.6t, 1999, 18.3m, 60 passengers, (tri-maran)). **Note** the THAMES SWIFT is the regular ferry; the JACOB MARLEY and the THAMES KESTREL may substitute on occasions. **Route operated** Gravesend (Kent) - Tilbury (Essex), **Tel** +44 (0)1634 525202, **Email** bookings@jetstreamtours.com **Website** www.jetstreamtours.com *(English)*

Emily *(Nick Widdows)*

Hamble - Warsash Ferry CLAIRE (2.1t, 1985, 7.3m, 12 passengers), EMILY (3.7t, 1990, 8.5m, 12 passengers. **Route operated** Hamble - Warsash (across Hamble River). **Tel** +44 (0)23 8045 4512, **Mobile** +44 (0)7720 438402 Duty Ferryman +44 (0) 7827 157154. **Email** mike@hambleferry.co.uk, **Website** www.hambleferry.co.uk *(English)*

Harwich Harbour Foot & Bicycle Ferry HARBOUR FERRY (8t, 1969, 11.4m, 58 passengers) (ex lifeboat from the liner CANBERRA, ex TAURUS 2012, ex PUFFIN BILLI, 2016). **Routes operated** Harwich (Ha'penny Pier) - Shotley (Marina), Harwich - Felixstowe (Landguard Point) (Easter to end of September). **Tel** +44 (0)1728 666329, **Email** chris@harwichharbourferry.com **Website** www.harwichharbourferry.com *(English)*

Hayling Ferry (operated by **Baker Trayte Marine Ltd**). PRIDE OF HAYLING 1989, 11.9m, 63 passengers), **Route operated** Eastney – Hayling Island. **Tel/Fax:** +44 (0)23 9229 4800, **Ferry Mobile** +44 (0)7500 194854, **Website** www.haylingferry.net *(English)*

Hovertravel ISLAND FLYER (161t, 2016, 22.4m, 80 passengers, IMO 9737797, Griffon Hovercraft 12000TD/AP), SOLENT FLYER (161t, 2016, 40.0k, 22.4m, 80 passengers, IMO 9737785, Griffon Hovercraft 12000TD/AP). **Route operated** Southsea - Ryde. **Tel** +44 1983 617400, +44 (0)1983 811000, **Email** info@hovertravel.com **Website** www.hovertravel.co.uk

Isle of Sark Shipping Company CORSAIRE DE SERCQ (2007, 23.0m, 157 passengers) (ex CORSAIRE DES ILES 2021, ex ORAZUR II 2013). VENTURE (133t, 1986, 21.3m, 122 passengers, IMO 8891986), SARK VIKING (Cargo Vessel) (104t, 2007, 21.2m, 12 passengers, IMO 8648858). **Route operated** St Peter Port (Guernsey) - Sark. **Tel** +44 (0) 1481 724059, **Email** info@sarkshipping.gg **Website** www.sarkshippingcompany.com *(English)*

John O'Groats Ferries PENTLAND VENTURE (186t, 1987, 29.6m, 250 passengers, IMO 8834122). **Route operated** John O'Groats – Burwick (Orkney). **Tel** +44 (0)1955 611353, **Email** Office@jogferry.co.uk **Website** www.jogferry.co.uk *(English)*

Kintyre Express KINTYRE EXPRESS 5 (2012, 13.3m, 12 passengers), **Routes operated** Campbeltown - Ballycastle, Port Ellen (Islay) - Ballycastle. **Tel** +44 (0)1586 555895, **Email** info@kintyreexpress.com **Website** www.kintyreexpress.com *(English)*

Lundy Company OLDENBURG (294t, 1958, 43.6m, 267 passengers, IMO 5262146**). Routes operated** Bideford - Lundy Island, Ilfracombe - Lundy Island. Also North Devon coastal cruises and River Torridge cruises. **Tel** +44 (0)1237 470074, **Email** info@lundyisland.co.uk **Website** www.lundyisland.co.uk *(English)*

Manche Iles Express (trading name of Société Morbihannaise de Navigation) GRANVILLE (325t, 2006, 41.0m, 245 passengers, IMO 9356476 - catamaran) (ex BORNHOLM EXPRESS 2014), VICTOR HUGO (387t, 1997, 35.0m, 236 passengers, IMO 9157806 - catamaran) (ex SALTEN 2003). **Routes operated** Jersey - Guernsey, Granville – Jersey - Sark - Guernsey, Portbail or Carteret – Jersey, Guernsey and Sark, Diélette - Alderney - Guernsey. **Tel** *France* +33 0825 131 050, **Guernsey** +44 (0)1481 701316, *Jersey* +44 (0)1534 880756, **Website** www.manche-iles-express.com *(French, English)*

Mersey Ferries ROYAL IRIS OF THE MERSEY (464t, 1960, 46.3m, 650 passengers, IMO 8633712) (ex MOUNTWOOD 2002), SNOWDROP (670t, 1960, 46.6m, 650 passengers, IMO 8633724) (ex WOODCHURCH 2004). **Routes operated** Liverpool (Pier Head) - Birkenhead (Woodside), Liverpool - Wallasey (Seacombe) with regular cruises from Liverpool and Seacombe to Salford along the Manchester Ship Canal. **Tel** +44 (0)151 330 1003, **Website** www.merseyferries.co.uk *(English)*

Mudeford Ferry (Derham Marine) FERRY DAME (4t, 1989, 9.1m, 48 passengers), JOSEPHINE (10.5t, 1997, 10.7m, 70 passengers - catamaran), JOSEPHINE II (10.5t, 2013, 11.0m, 86 passengers - catamaran), SENSATION (9.0m, 12 passengers - RIB for private or commercial hire). **Route operated** Mudeford Quay - Mudeford Sandbank. **Tel** +44 (0)7968 334441 **Email** information@mudefordferry.co.uk **Website** www.mudefordferry.co.uk *(English)*

Nexus (trading name of Tyne & Wear Integrated Transport Authority) PRIDE OF THE TYNE (222t, 1993, 24.0m, 240 passengers, IMO 9062166), SPIRIT OF THE TYNE (174t, 2006, 25.0m, 200 passengers). Route operated North Shields - South Shields. Also cruises South Shields - Newcastle. Tel +44 (0)191 2020747, **Website** www.nexus.org.uk/ferry *(English)*

O'Malley Ferries, Clare Island NAOMH CIARAN II (35t, 1982, 17.7m, 97 passengers, TORMORE (67t, 1992, 17.7m, 75 passengers), TRUE LIGHT (19t, 2002, 12.8m, 38 passengers). Routes Operated Roonagh (Co Mayo) - Inishturk, (50 mins), Roonagh - Clare, Island. Tel +353(0)98 25045, Mobiles +353(0)87 660 0409, +353(0)86 887 0814, Email enquiry@omalleyferries.com Website www.omalleyferries.com *(English)*

Travel Trident HERM TRIDENT V (79t, 1989, 25.9m, 250 passengers), TRIDENT VI (79t, 1992, 22.3m, 250 passengers). **Route operated** St Peter Port (Guernsey) - Herm. **Tel** +44 (0)1481 721379, **Email** peterwilcox@cwgsy.net **Website** www.traveltrident.com *(English)*

Uber Boat by Thames Clippers (trading name of Collins River Enterprises Ltd) AURORA CLIPPER (181t, 2007, 37.8m, 27.5k, 220 passengers, IMO 9451824), CYCLONE CLIPPER (181t, 2007, 37.8m, 27.5k, 220 passengers, IMO 9451880), GALAXY CLIPPER (155t, 2015, 34.0m, 155 passengers, IMO 9783784), HURRICANE CLIPPER (181t, 2002, 37.8m, 27.5k, 220 passengers, IMO 9249702), JUPITER CLIPPER (155t, 2017, 35.0 m, 28.0k, 170 passengers, IMO 9223796), MERCURY CLIPPER (155t, 2017, 35.0 m, 28.0k, 170 passengers, IMO 9223801), METEOR CLIPPER (181t, 2007, 37.8m, 27.5k, 220 passengers, IMO 9451812), MONSOON CLIPPER (181t, 2007, 37.8m, 27.5k, 220 passengers, IMO 9451795), MOON CLIPPER (98t, 2001, 32.0m, 25.0k, 138 passengers, IMO 9245586) (ex DOWN RUNNER 2005), NEPTUNE CLIPPER (155t, 2015, 34.0m, 155 passengers, IMO 9783796), SKY CLIPPER (60t, 1992, 25.0m, 62 passengers) (ex VERITATUM 1995, SD10 2000), STAR CLIPPER (60t, 1992, 25.0m, 62 passengers) (ex CONRAD CHELSEA HARBOUR 1995, SD9 2000), STORM CLIPPER (60t, 1992, 25.0m, 62 passengers) (ex DHL WORLDWIDE EXPRESS 1995, SD11 2000), SUN CLIPPER (98t, 2001, 32.0m, 25.0k, 138 passengers, IMO 9232292) (ex ANTRIM RUNNER 2005), TORNADO CLIPPER (181t, 2007, 37.8m, 27.5k, 220 passengers, IMO 9451783), TWIN STAR (45t, 1974, 19.2m, 120 passengers), TYPHOON CLIPPER (181t, 2007, 37.8m, 27.5k, 220 passengers, IMO

9451771, (2015, 34.0m, 154 seats), VENUS CLIPPER (172t, 2019, 38.0m, 25.0k, 220 passengers, IMO 9867736) The 'Typhoon', 'Tornado', 'Cyclone' and 'Monsoon', 'Aurora' and 'Meteor' Clippers were designed by AIMTEK and built by Brisbane Ship Constructions in Australia in 2007. 'Galaxy' and 'Neptune' were designed by One2three Naval Architects and built by Incat Tasmania, Hobart, Australia, 'Jupiter', 'Mercury' and 'Venus' were also designed by One2three Naval Architects but were built by Wight Shipyard, East Cowes, Isle of Wight. **Under Construction** NEWBUILDING 1 (200t, 2022, 38.0m, 25.0k, 220 passengers, IMO 9963499, NEWBUILDING 2 (200t, 2023, 38.0m, 25.0k, 220 passengers, IMO 9963504.Under construction by Wight Shipyard, East Cowes, Isle of Wight. Hybrid diesel/electric. **Routes operated** Embankment - Waterloo - Blackfriars – Bankside - London Bridge - Tower - Canary Wharf – Greenland - Masthouse Terrace - Greenwich - North Greenwich – Royal Wharf - Woolwich, Bankside – Millbank - St George (Tate to Tate Service), Putney - Wandsworth – Plantation Wharf - Chelsea Harbour - Cardogan - Embankment - Blackfriars, Canary Wharf - Rotherhithe DoubleTree by Hilton Docklands Hotel (TWIN STAR). **Tel** +44 (0)870 781 5049, **Fax** +44 (0)20 7001 2222, **Email** web@thamesclippers.com **Website** www.thamesclippers.com *(English)*

Waverley Excursions WAVERLEY (693t, 1946, 73.13m, 860 passengers, IMO 5386954). **Routes operated** Excursions all round British Isles operate between May and October annually. However, regular cruises in the Clyde, Bristol Channel, South Coast and Thames provide a service which can be used for transport purposes and therefore she is in a sense a ferry. She is the last seagoing paddle steamer in the world. **Tel** +44 (0)141 243 2224, **Email** info@waverleyexcursions.co.uk **Website** www.waverleyexcursions.co.uk *(English)*.

Western Isles Cruises Ltd ARWEN (12.6t, 1992, 12m, 12 passengers) (ex MOIRA BARRIE 2020 - former RNLI lifeboat)), LARVEN (21t, 2017, 14.2m, 40 passengers (catamaran)), WESTERN ISLES (54t, 1960, 18.0m, 82 passengers). **Route Operated** Mallaig - Inverie (Knoydart) - Tarbet Loch Nevis - Inverie and Tarbet, Mallaig - Small Isles ferry service for school children Fridays and Sundays. **Tel** +44 (0)1687 462233, **Email** info@westernislescruises.co.uk, **Website** www.westernislescruises.co.uk *(English)*

Western Lady Ferry Service DART VENTURER (94t, 1982, 25.0m, 300 passengers), DITTISHAM PRINCESS (1995, 21.3m, 181 passengers) (ex PLYMOUTH VENTURER), **Route Operated** Torquay - Brixham. **Tel** +44 (0)1803 293797, **Website** www.westernladyferry.com *(English)* Note: The service is now part of *Dartmouth Steam Railway & Riverboat Company* but is marketed separately.

White Funnel BALMORAL (735t, 1949, 62.2m, 800 passengers, IMO 5034927) Excursions in Bristol Channel, North West, South Coast, Thames and Clyde. However, no services operated in 2018, 2019, 2020, 2021 and 2022. Services may resume in 2023. **Email** via website **Website** www.thebalmoral.org.uk *(English)*.

Windermere Lake Cruises (major units only) SWAN (251t, 1938, 42.0m, 533 passengers, SWIFT (2020, 34.4m, 300 passengers, TEAL (251t, 1936, 42.0m, 533 passengers, TERN (120t, 1938, 42.8m, 350 passengers. **Route Operated** Ambleside - Bowness - Lakeside (Windermere) **Tel** +44 (0)15394 43360, **Website** www.windermere-lakecruises.co.uk *(English)*

SECTION 6 – MAJOR PASSENGER ONLY FERRIES

SCR - Improve Air Quality

Battery Power

Conn

for a

SCANDINAVIAN AND NORTHERN EUROPE REVIEW 2021/22

The following geographical review again takes the form of a voyage along the coast of the Netherlands and Germany, round the Southern tip of Norway, down the Kattegat, through the Great Belt and into the Baltic, then up to the Gulf of Finland and Gulf of Bothnia.

At long last it appears as though the COVID-19 pandemic is waning and most services have been returning to something approaching normal operations since the start of the year. However, the Baltic cruise ferry services of Viking Line and in particular Tallink Silja are operating significantly reduced services with the latter operator sending vessels on charter for the summer season.

The region has also benefitted from the arrival of several ro-pax and cruise ferries that were ordered before the pandemic started and are now coming into service. However, no new vessels have been ordered since the pandemic hit and it is likely that traffic (and therefore the orderbook) will remain suppressed for the foreseeable future.

NETHERLANDS, FRISIAN ISLANDS & ELBE

Holland Norway Lines, a new company linking the Dutch port of Eemshaven with the Norwegian port of Kristiansand commenced operations on 7 April. Tallink's *Romantika* has been chartered to the new operator and makes three return crossings per week.

The attempt by Elbferry to re-open the Cuxhaven and Brunsbüttel operation in early 2021 ended in failure as the company was declared insolvent in November 2021 and the *Greenferry 1* was returned to her owners. This was the second attempt to restart the service in recent years following the failure of Elblink in 2017.

NORWEGIAN DOMESTIC

Havila commenced its new Norwegian Coastal Express service in December with the much delayed delivery of *Havila Capella*. However, the Russian invasion of Ukraine had a major impact on the operations of Havila Voyages who had to cease operations due to the Russian financing of the ship. The vessel was forced to stop sailing in early April when the Russian financing company GTLK which owns the vessel was included in the EU list of sanctioned institutions. GTLK own *Havila Capella* – and was intended to own its three sisters – and as a result, '*Capella*' was effectively impounded by the sanctions. Havila applied to the Norwegian government for an exemption to the sanctions in early April which was granted whilst the company sought additional financing. However, the company then discovered it was unable to insure the ship and an application to the government for an exemption for this was rejected. It is understood that the company is also unable to purchase the vessel outright as that effectively involves transferring money to the banned GTLK. This action has been taken due to the unwillingness of GTLK to find an amicable solution, according to a Havila press release in June.

In mid-June, the company then started legal action at the High Court in London to ensure it could take ownership of '*Capella*'. It had a purchase option from the leasing company two years after delivery and a purchase obligation at the end of the contract with the Norwegian Ministry of Transport. The plan was for the company to pay the value of the vessel to a blocked account which will then be paid to GTLK once the sanctions are lifted. On 20 June, it was announced that the company had been granted full ownership rights as administrators of the vessel and *Havila Capella* re-entered service on 28 June.

Fortunately, GTLK had not yet taken delivery of the second vessel *Havila Castor* which has been purchased directly from the shipyard by Havila. The ship arrived in Norway in early May and was rapidly prepared to enable a maiden departure from Bergen on Tuesday 7 May. It is believed that the final pair of vessels – *Havila Polaris* and *Havila Pollux* – will be able to be acquired by Havila or an alternative leasing company thus allowing the company to operate more departures when they are delivered in September and December respectively. Havila has suffered a run of misfortune with its new operation with the 'P' pair order originally going to

Stena Flavia *(Philippe Holthof)*

Fynshav *(Frank Lose)*

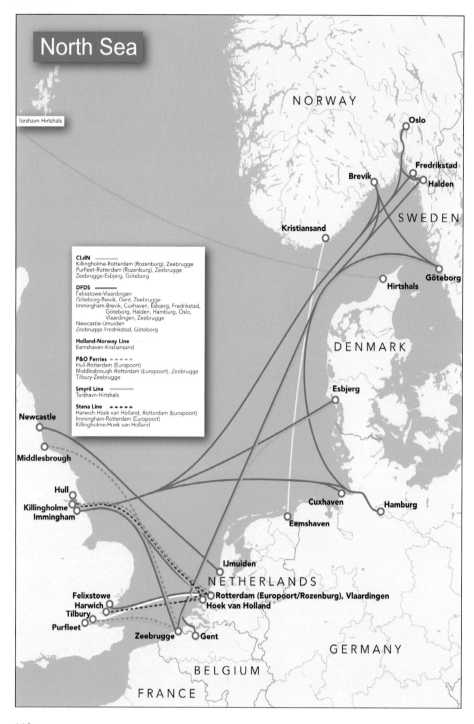

North Sea

Torshavn-Hirtshals

CLdN
Killingholme-Rotterdam (Rozenburg), Zeebrugge
Purfleet-Rotterdam (Rozenburg), Zeebrugge
Zeebrugge-Esbjerg, Göteborg

DFDS
Felixstowe-Vlaardingen
Göteborg-Brevik, Gent, Zeebrugge
Immingham-Brevik, Cuxhaven, Esbjerg, Fredrikstad,
          Göteborg, Halden, Hamburg, Oslo,
          Vlaardingen, Zeebrugge
Newcastle-IJmuiden
Zeebrugge-Fredrikstad, Göteborg

Holland-Norway Line
Eemshaven-Kristiansand

P&O Ferries - - - - -
Hull-Rotterdam (Europoort)
Middlesbrough Rotterdam (Europoort), Zeebrugge
Tilbury-Zeebrugge

Smyril Line
Torshavn-Hirtshals

Stena Line - - - - -
Harwich-Hoek van Holland, Rotterdam (Europoort)
Immingham-Rotterdam (Europoort)
Killingholme-Hoek van Holland

NORWAY
Oslo
Fredrikstad
Brevik
Halden
Kristiansand
SWEDEN
Göteborg
Hirtshals
DENMARK
Esbjerg
Newcastle
Middlesbrough
Cuxhaven
Hamburg
Hull
Killingholme
Immingham
Eemshaven
IJmuiden
NETHERLANDS
Felixstowe
Harwich
Rotterdam (Europoort/Rozenburg), Vlaardingen
Tilbury
Hoek van Holland
Purfleet
Zeebrugge
Gent
GERMANY
BELGIUM
FRANCE

the Barreras shipyard which eventually resigned the order and then COVID caused significant delays to the completion of all four vessels.

SKAGERRAK & KATTEGAT

Stena Saga was chartered to Adria Ferries for a short season of operation between Ancona and Durrës. She started operations in late July 2021 and finished for the summer in early September when she moved to Piraeus for drydocking and then charter to the Far East as an accommodation vessel.

DANISH DOMESTIC

Molslinjen has introduced a new electric ferry between Esbjerg and Fanø. The *Grotte* was constructed at Hvide Sande Shipyard. Other than its power source, the new vessel is the same design as the 1998-built *Fenja* and *Menja*. Both these vessels have recently been converted to run on HVO biodiesel to enable the operation to become almost completely fossil-free, reducing emissions by 96%.

SOUTHERN BALTIC

Scandlines has ordered a new zero-emission freight ferry for operation between Puttgarden and Rødbyhavn. The new vessel will be 147 metres in length and offer capacity for 66 lorries and 140 passengers. Freight loading will for the first time on the route be over both upper and lower decks which will require the rebuilding of berth three in Rødbyhavn and berth one in Puttgarden. The ferry will enter service in 2024, primarily operating in freight-only mode but with the ability to provide back-up to the other members of the fleet should circumstances require this. The vessel will have hybrid power with both diesel and electric propulsion with the ability to operate fully on battery power at 10 knots, completing the crossing in 60 minutes. Alternatively, it will be able to operate in hybrid mode at 16 knots and complete the crossing in 45 minutes. On its arrival in 2024 it will replace *Kronprins Frederik*.

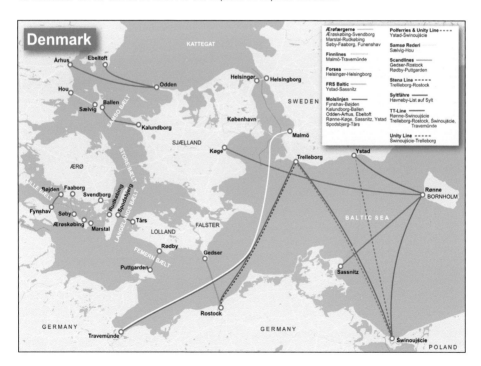

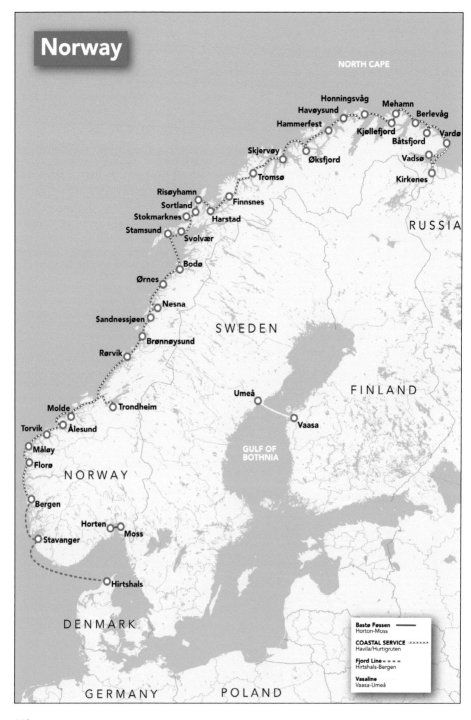

Norway

NORTH CAPE

Honningsvåg
Havøysund
Hammerfest
Mehamn
Berlevåg
Kjøllefjord
Båtsfjord
Vardø
Skjervøy
Øksfjord
Vadsø
Tromsø
Kirkenes

RUSSIA

Risøyhamn
Sortland
Finnsnes
Stokmarknes
Harstad
Stamsund
Svolvær
Bodø
Ørnes
Nesna
SWEDEN
Sandnessjøen
Brønnøysund
Rørvik

FINLAND

Umeå
Molde
Trondheim
Torvik
Ålesund
Måløy
Vaasa
Florø
GULF OF
BOTHNIA
NORWAY
Bergen
Horten
Stavanger
Moss

Hirtshals

DENMARK

Bastø Føssen	
Horton-Moss	
COASTAL SERVICE	
Havila/Hurtigruten	
Fjord Line	
Hirtshals-Bergen	
Vasaline	
Vaasa-Umeå	

GERMANY   POLAND

Greenferry 1 *(Frank Lose)*

TT-Line took delivery of its new flagship and latest *Nils Holgersson* on 7 March and the vessel started her delivery voyage on 10 March with the vessel entering service in early May. Along with sister *Peter Pan*, the vessels will be 230 metres in length and will carry 800 passengers and 4,600 lane metres of freight. The previous *Nils Holgersson* was renamed *Akka* in early 2022 in anticipation of the new arrival.

In late 2021 Polskie Promy announced an order for three new ro-pax vessels with the Remontowa shipyard at Gdańsk. The company is an investment vehicle co-owned by the Polish Finance Ministry and Polska Żegluga Morska, the parent company of Unity Line. Two of the three vessels will be operated by Unity Line whilst the third, along with an optional fourth, are believed to be earmarked for Polferries although this has not been confirmed. The vessels will be 195.6 metres in length and will offer capacity for 4,100 lane metres and 400 passengers. The ships will be powered by four LNG engines with battery support; they will be equipped with four azimuth thrusters and will have a service speed of 19 knots.

The new ferry terminal at the Polish Port of Gdynia was inaugurated on 23 September with the switch of Stena Line's operation to the outer harbour berths. Stena also announced a change of plan to the previous decision to introduce the longer E-Flexers onto the Ventspils route and instead they have been earmarked for the Karlksrona – Gdynia service. The first vessel has been given the name *Stena Estelle* and began operation in mid-August. The second will be called *Stena Ebba* and will enter service in early 2023.

NORTHERN BALTIC

Rederi AB Gotland launched a new service linking Nynäshamn and Rostock on Monday 30 August with a departure from the Swedish port to Germany, following a ceremony attended by the Swedish Deputy Prime Minister Per Bolund. The company chose to use *Drotten* for the new route and she has received a modified livery featuring the brand 'Hansa Destinations'. The

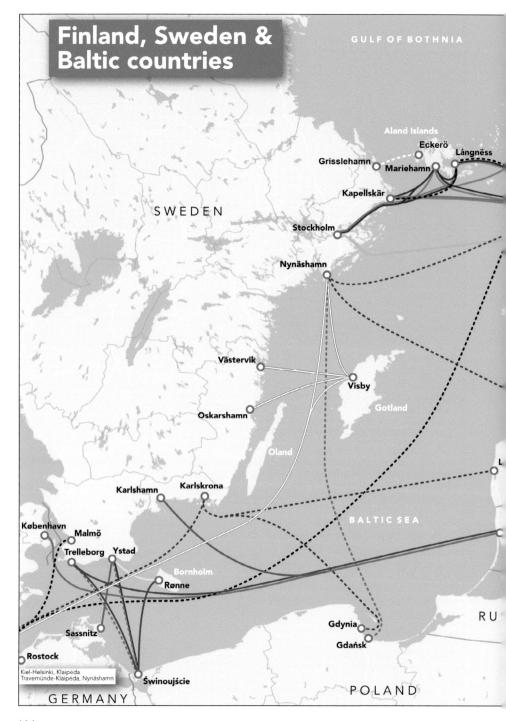

Finland, Sweden & Baltic countries

GULF OF BOTHNIA

Aland Islands

Eckerö

Långnëss

Grisslehamn

Mariehamn

Kapellskär

S W E D E N

Stockholm

Nynäshamn

Västervik

Visby

Gotland

Oskarshamn

Oland

Karlshamn

Karlskrona

København

Malmö

Trelleborg

Ystad

Bornholm

Rønne

BALTIC SEA

RU

Sassnitz

Gdynia

Rostock

Gdańsk

Kiel-Helsinki, Klaipėda
Travemünde-Klaipėda, Nynäshamn

Świnoujście

POLAND

R U

GERMANY

FINLAND

ntali

Turku

Helsinki

Hanko

GULF OF FINLAND

St Petersburg

Paldiski

Tallinn

RUSSIA

Heltermaa

Hiiumaa

Rohukula

ESTONIA

Kulvastu

Virtsu

GULF OF RIGA

Ventspils

LATVIA

Destination Gotland/Hansa Destinations
Nynäshamn-Rostock, Visby
Visby-Oskarshamn, Västervik

DFDS
Karlshamn-Klaipėda
København-Klaipėda
Paldiski-Kapellskär

Eckerö Line · · · · ·
Helsinki-Tallinn
Eckerö-Grisslehamn

Finnlines ▪ ▪ ▪ ▪ ▪
Helsinki-Travemünde
Naantali-Långnäss-Kapellskär
Malmö-Travemünde

FRS Baltic
Ystad-Sassnitz

Moby
Tallinn-Stockholm-Helsinki

Molslinjen
Rønne-Ystad

Polferries ▪ ▪ ▪ ▪
Ystad-Świnoujście
Nynäshamn Gdańsk

Praamid
Kuivastu-Virtsu
Rohokula-Heltermaa

Stena Line ▪ ▪ ▪ ▪ ▪
Travemünde-Karlskrona-Liepaja
Nynäshamn-Hanko, Ventspils
Karlskrona-Gdynia

Tallink/Silja Line
Helsinki-Mariehamn, Tallinn
Turku-Mariehamn, Långnäss
Stockholm-Långnäss, Mariehamn
Kapellskär-Paldiski

TT-Line
Rønne-Świnoujście
Trelleborg-Klaipėda, Świnoujście

Unity Line ▪ ▪ ▪ ▪ ▪
Świnoujście-Trelleborg, Ystad

Viking Line
Helsinki-Mariehamn, Tallinn
Kapellsakr-Mariehamn
Stockholm-Långnäss, Mariehamn
Turku-Långnäss, Mariehamn

LITHUANIA

BELARUS

165

Cracavia *(Frank Lose)*

Selandia Seaways *(Frank Lose)*

vessel has had additional cabins installed and an additional further restaurant created in place of a reclining lounge. The service departs Nynäshamn at 1900 on Mondays, Wednesdays and Fridays arriving at Rostock at 1300 the following day. The return journeys take place on Tuesdays, Thursdays and Saturdays, departing 1900 and arriving at 1330. The Friday departure ex- Nynäshamn calls in at Visby at 2115 (departing 25 minutes later) with the return call occurring on the Saturday crossing from 0930 to 1000 on Sunday morning. The company later introduced a second ro-ro vessel to allow six freight departures a week. The ship in question is the *Eliana Marino*.

DFDS introduced both new Chinese-built ro-paxes since the start of 2022 with *Aura Seaways* entering service on the Karlshamn – Klaipėda route on January 23. Sister *Luna Seaways* departed China a couple of weeks later and entered service in April. The vessels offer passenger capacity for 600 people and freight space of 4,500 lane metres.

Stena Line has invested heavily in their Baltic States services in the last few years and 2022 sees this trend continue. The arrival of the rebuilt *Stena Scandica* in 2021 on the Nynäshamn – Ventspils service significantly enhanced capacity on that operation and sister vessel *Stena Baltica* took up the service at the start of 2022. Both ultimately released *Stena Flavia* and *Stena Livia* for the Travemünde – Liepāja service, in turn releasing *Urd* and *Stena Gothica*.

Stena Line therefore opened a new route between Nynäshamn and Hanko in Finland utilising both these vessels. The new ro-pax service commenced operation on 1 February 2022 with *Urd* and she was joined by *Stena Gothica* from 1 May and frequency increased to daily departures on the 13 hour service.

Viking Line's new *Viking Glory* entered service on March 1 following her christening at Turku on 28February. The displaced *Amorella* was then moved to the Stockholm – Helsinki service to fill the gap left by the sale of *Mariella* to Corsica Ferries last year. However, it was announced in early August that *Amorella* had also been sold to Corsica Ferries for delivery in October 2022.

Although Tallink has restored the Stockholm – Helsinki and Stockholm – Turku routes to full operation by Summer 2022, the services to Tallinn was reduced to a single ship operation utilising *Baltic Queen* and that to Riga remained suspended. The redundant ships *Victoria 1* and *Romantika* have thus spent the last two seasons on the charter market. The Moroccan Government-owned Inter Shipping took both vessels to participate in Operación Paso del Estrecho during summer 2021. Due to the higher incidence of the COVID virus in Spain, the Moroccan Government has routed all ferry services to France or Italy, thus requiring additional tonnage with overnight capabilities. Both ships left layup in early July 2021 for the Mediterranean where they were placed into service between Sète and Tangier Med with the charter expected to last into the early Autumn. For summer 2022, *Romantika* was chartered to a new operation called Holland Norway Lines which placed her on a route between Eemshaven and Kristiansand, *Victoria 1* became an accommodation vessel at Leith in Scotland for Ukranian refugees and *Isabelle* was performing the same function at Tallinn. Both *Silja Europa* and *Romantika* visited Glasgow as accommodation vessels for the UN Climate Change Conference in autumn 2021 and *Silja Europa* and *Galaxy* are due to be chartered to the Dutch government in autumn 2022 as accommodation vessels. This will reduce the Stockholm – Turku operation to single-ship for the winter season. Tallink has sold *Sea Wind* for further service in the Mediterranean with her place on the Muuga – Vuosaari being taken by *Regal Star*.

Finnlines introduced *Europalink* onto its Kapellskär – Naantali service in January, replacing *Finnfellow* and joining sistership *Finnswan*. The new 'Superstar' class ships will arrive in 2023. *Finnfellow* switched to the Travemünde – Malmö, replacing *Finnclipper* which was deployed to the Mediterranean.

Matthew Punter

SECTION 7 – NORTHERN EUROPE

ÆRØFÆRGERNE

THE COMPANY *Ærøfærgerne* is a Danish company, owned by the municipality of Ærø.

MANAGEMENT Managing Director Kelda Møller, **Marketing Coordinator** Jeanette Erikson.

ADDRESS Vestergade 1A, 5970 Ærøskøbing, Denmark.

TELEPHONE Administration & Reservations +45 62 52 40 00.

INTERNET Email info@aeroe-ferry.dk **Website** www.aeroe-ferry.dk *(Danish, English, German)*

ROUTE OPERATED Ærøskøbing (Ærø) - Svendborg (Funen) (1hr 15mins; **ÆRØSKØBING, MARSTAL**; every 1/2 hours), Søby (Ærø) - Faaborg (Funen) (1hr; **SKJOLDNÆS**; 3 per day), Søby (Ærø) - Funenshav (Als) (1hr 10mins; **ELLEN**; 3 per day).

1	ÆRØSKØBING	1617t	99	12.0k	49.0m	395P	42C	-	BA	DK	9199086
2	ELLEN	996t	18	13.0k	59.4m	198P	31C		BA	DK	9805374
3	MARSTAL	1617t	99	12.0k	49.0m	395P	42C	-	BA	DK	9199074
4	SKJOLDNÆS	986t	79	11.0k	47.1m	245P	31C	-	BA	DK	7925649

ÆRØSKØBING, MARSTAL Built by EOS, Esbjerg, Denmark for *Ærøfærgerne*.

ELLEN Built by Søby Vaerft, Søby, Ærø, Denmark for *Ærøfærgerne*. Hybrid electric powered. Entered service in August 2019.

SKJOLDNÆS Built as the SAM-SINE by Søren Larsen & Sønner Skibsværft A/S, Nykøbing Mors, Denmark for *Hou-Sælvig Ruten Aps* of Denmark. Operated between Hou (Jylland) and Sælvig (Samsø). In 1995 she was taken over by *Samsø Linien*. In 2001 she was lengthened by Ørskov Christensen's Staalskibsværft, Frederikshavn, Denmark. In 2009 sold to *Ærøfærgerne* and renamed the SKJOLDNÆS.

ÆRØXPRESSAN

THE COMPANY ÆrøXpressan A/S is a Danish private sector company.

ADDRESS Havnepladsen 8, 5960 Marstal, Ærø, Denmark.

TELEPHONE +45 73 70 78 00.

INTERNET Email info@aeroexpressen.dk **Website** www.aeroexpressen.dk *(Danish)*

ROUTE OPERATED Marstal (Ærø, Denmark) - Rudkøbing (Langeland, Denmark) (50 mins; **ÆRØXPRESSAN**; up to 7 per day).

| 1 | ÆRØXPRESSAN | 600t | 19 | 11.4k | 50.0m | 300P | 30C | 0L | BA | DK | 9861500 |

ÆRØXPRESSAN Built by the Hvide Sande Shipyard, Denmark.

BASTØ FOSEN

THE COMPANY *Bastø Fosen* is a Norwegian private sector company, a subsidiary of *Torghatten ASA - Brønnøysund*.

MANAGEMENT Managing Director Øyvind Lund.

ADDRESS PO Box 94, 3191 Horten, Norway.

TELEPHONE Administration +47 33 03 17 40.

INTERNET Email post@fosen.no **Website** basto-fosen.no *(Norwegian, English)*

ROUTE OPERATED Moss - Horten (across Oslofjord, Norway) (30 mins; **BASTØ I, BASTØ II, BASTØ IV, BASTØ V, BASTØ VI, BASTØ ELECTRIC**; up to every 15 mins), Svelvik - Verket (5 mins; **SVELVIK**; up to every 20 minutes).

1	BASTØ I	5505t	97	17.0k	109.0m	600P	200C	18L	BA	NO	9144081
2	BASTØ II	5505t	97	17.0k	109.0m	600P	200C	18L	BA	NO	9144093
3	BASTØ IV	7700t	16	18.0k	142.9m	600P	200C	30L	BA	NO	9771420
4	BASTØ V	7700t	17	18.0k	142.9m	600P	200C	30L	BA	NO	9771432
5	BASTØ VI	7870t	16	18.0k	142.9m	600P	200C	30L	BA	NO	9769219
6	BASTØ ELECTRIC	7911t	21	18.0k	142.9m	600P	200C	24L	BA	NO	9878993
7	SVELVIK	983t	21	-	54.0m	99P	30C	-	BA	NO	9907990

BASTØ I, BASTØ II Built by Fosen Mekaniske Verksteder, Frengen, Norway.

BASTØ IV, BASTØ V Built by Sefine Shipyard, Yalova, Turkey. BASTØ IV is to be converted to full electric power.

BASTØ VI Built by Cemre Shipyard, Yalova, Turkey. To be converted to full electric power.

BASTØ ELECTRIC Built by Sefine Shipyard, Yalova, Turkey. Hybrid diesel/electric but can operate in 100% electric mode when shore infrastructure is completed.

SVELVIK Built by Sefine Shipyard, Yalova, Turkey. Operated across Drammensfjorden (south of Oslofjord) between Svelvik and Verket from January 2022.

COLOR LINE

THE COMPANY *Color Line ASA* is a Norwegian private sector stock-listed limited company. The company merged with *Larvik Scandi Line* of Norway (which owned *Larvik Line* and *Scandi Line*) in 1996. In 1997 the operations of *Larvik Line* were incorporated into *Color Line*; *Scandi Line* continued as a separate subsidiary until 1998, when it was also incorporated into *Color Line*. The marketing name *Color Scandi Line* was dropped at the end of 2000.

MANAGEMENT President & CEO Trond Kleivdal.

ADDRESS *Commercial* Postboks 1422 Vika, 0115 Oslo, Norway, *Technical Management* Color Line Marine AS, PO Box 2090, 3210 Sandefjord, Norway.

TELEPHONE Administration & Reservations +45 99 56 19 00.

INTERNET Website www.colorline.com *(English, Danish, German, Norwegian, Swedish)*

ROUTES OPERATED Conventional Ferries Oslo (Norway) - Kiel (Germany) (19 hrs 30 mins; **COLOR FANTASY, COLOR MAGIC**; 1 per day), Kristiansand (Norway) - Hirtshals (3 hrs 15 mins; **SUPERSPEED 1**; 2 per day), Larvik (Norway) - Hirtshals (Denmark) (3 hrs 45 mins; **SUPERSPEED 2**; up to 2 per day), Sandefjord (Norway) - Strömstad (Sweden) (2 hrs 30 mins; **COLOR HYBRID, COLOR VIKING**; up to 4 per day). **Freight ferry** Oslo - Kiel (21 hrs; **COLOR CARRIER**; 3 per week).

1F	COLOR CARRIER	12433t	98	20.0k	154.5m	12P	-	124T	A2	NO	9132002
2	COLOR FANTASY	74500t	04	22.3k	224.0m	2605P	750C	90T	BA	NO	9278234
3	COLOR HYBRID	27000t	19	25.3k	160.0m	2000P	500C	-	BA	NO	9824289
4	COLOR MAGIC	75100t	07	22.3k	224.0m	2812P	550C	90T	BA	NO	9349863
5	COLOR VIKING	19763t	85	16.4k	137.0m	1773P	370C	40T	BA	NO	8317942
6	SUPERSPEED 1	36821t	08	27.0k	211.3m	2400P	750C	121T	BA2	NO	9374519
7	SUPERSPEED 2	33500t	08	27.0k	211.3m	2000P	764C	121T	BA2	NO	9378682

COLOR CARRIER Built as the UNITED CARRIER by Fosen Mekaniske Verksteder A/S, Rissa, Norway for *United Shipping* (a subsidiary of *Birka Shipping*) of Finland and chartered to *Transfennica*. During 2000 she was used on their Kemi - Oulu - Antwerpen - Felixstowe service. In 2001 the route was transferred to *Finnlines* and the vessel used sub-chartered to them (charter later transferred to *Finnlines*). In 2002 *United Shipping* was renamed *Birka Cargo* and the ship was renamed the BIRKA CARRIER. In 2006 the service ceased. In 2008 the charter was extended a further four years. In January 2013 chartered to *Transfennica*. In June 2013 she was renamed the CARRIER. In January 2015 sold to *Finnlines* but not delivered until the end of the year, when the charter ended. In January 2016 renamed the FINNCARRIER. In July 2018 sold to *Color Line* and chartered back to *Finnlines*. In January 2019 renamed the COLOR CARRIER and entered service between Oslo and Kiel.

COLOR FANTASY Built by Kværner Masa-Yards, Turku, Finland for *Color Line* to replace the PRINSESSE RAGNHILD on the Oslo – Kiel service.

COLOR HYBRID Built by Ulstein Verft A/S, Ulsteinvik, Norway, to replace the BOHUS on the Sandefjord - Strömstad route in August 2019. She is a hybrid vessel, operating in both battery and diesel-electric mode.

COLOR MAGIC Built by Aker Yards, Turku, Finland (hull construction) and Rauma, Finland (fitting out), for the Oslo - Kiel route.

COLOR VIKING Built as the PEDER PAARS by Nakskov Skibsværft A/S, Nakskov, Denmark for *DSB (Danish State Railways)* for their service between Kalundborg (Sjælland) and Århus (Jylland). In 1990 purchased by *Stena Line* of Sweden for delivery in 1991. In that year renamed the STENA INVICTA and entered service on the *Sealink Stena Line* Dover - Calais service. She was withdrawn from the route in February 1998, before the formation of *P&O Stena Line,* but ownership was transferred to that company. In Summer 1998, she was chartered to *Silja Line* to operate between Vaasa and Umeå under the marketing name 'WASA JUBILEE'. In Autumn 1998 she was laid up at Zeebrugge. She remained there until Autumn 1999 when she was chartered to *Stena Line* to operate between Holyhead and Dublin. In 2000 she was chartered to *Color Line*, renamed the COLOR VIKING and in April entered service on the Sandefjord - Strömstad service. In 2002 purchased by *Color Line*.

SUPERSPEED 1, SUPERSPEED 2 Built by Aker Yards, Rauma, Finland for the Kristiansand - Hirtshals and Larvik - Hirtshals routes. In January 2011, the SUPERSPEED 1 was modified to provide additional facilities and increase passenger capacity.

DESTINATION GOTLAND (REDERI AB GOTLAND)

THE COMPANY *Rederi AB Gotland. (Gotlandsbolaget)* is a Swedish private sector company whose ferry operations are branded as *Destination Gotland* and *Hansa Destinations*.

MANAGEMENT Managing Director Marcus Risberg, **Marketing Manager** Adam Jacobsson.

ADDRESS Korsgatan 2, PO Box 1234, 621 23 Visby, Gotland, Sweden.

TELEPHONE Rederi AB Gotland +46 (0)498-20 00 00 **Destination Gotland** +46 (0)498-20 18 00, **Hansa Destinations** +46 (0)771 702 550.

INTERNET Email info@destinationgotland.se **Websites** gotlandsbolaget.se/en www.destinationgotland.se www.hansadestinations.com *(Swedish, English, German)*

ROUTES OPERATED Destination Gotland services *Fast Conventional Ferries* Visby (Gotland) - Nynäshamn (Swedish mainland) (3 hrs 15 mins; *DROTTEN, GOTLAND, VISBORG*; up to 7 per day), Visby - Oskarshamn (Swedish mainland) (2 hrs 55 mins; *DROTTEN, GOTLAND, VISBORG*; up to 3 per day), *Fast Ferries (Summer only)* Visby (Gotland) - Nynäshamn (3 hrs 15 mins; *GOTLANDIA II*; 1 per week), Visby - Vastervik (2 hrs 30 mins; *GOTLANDIA II*; 1 per day).

Hansa Destinations service *Fast Conventional Ferries* Nynäshamn-Rostock (18 hrs; *DROTTEN*; 2/3 per week). *Freight service* Nynäshamn-Rostock (18 hrs; *ELIANA MARINO*; 3 per week)

1	DROTTEN	29746t	03	28.5k	195.8m	1500P	500C	118T	BAS2	SE	9223796
2F	ELIANA MARINO	18265t	00	23.5k	174.0m	12P	-	171T	A	IT	9226360
3	GOTLAND	32447t	19	28.5k	200.0m	1650P	500C	110L	BAS2	SE	9783071
4»•	GOTLANDIA	5632t	99	35.0k	112.5m	700P	140C	-	A	SE	9171163
5»	GOTLANDIA II	6554t	06	36.0k	122.0m	780P	160C	-	A	SE	9328015
6	VISBY	32000t	18	28.5k	200.0m	1650P	500C	110L	BAS2	SE	9763655

ELIANA MARINO Launched by J J Sietas Schiffswerft, Hamburg, Germany as the LOUISE RUSS for *Ernst Russ* of Germany. On completion, renamed the PORTO EXPRESS and chartered to *ROROExpress* to operate between Southampton, Oporto and Tangier. The service ceased in Autumn 2001 when she was returned to her owners and resumed the name LOUISE RUSS. In March 2002 chartered to *Cobelfret Ferries*. The charter ended in February 2011 and in March

Color Carrier *(Richard Seville)*

Drotten *(Frank Lose)*

she was chartered to *Transfennica*. In September 2019 she was chartered to *Moby Line* of Italy and in January 2016 she was renamed the ELIANA MARINO. In October2021 sub-chartered to *DFDS* to operate between Trieste and Mersin. In March 2022 chartered to *Rederi AB Gotland* and placed on the Nynäshamn-Rostock service.

DROTTEN Built as the GOTLAND by Guangzhou Shipyard International, Guangzhou, China for *Rederi AB Gotland* for use on *Destination Gotland* services. In February 2020 renamed the DROTTEN. Between January and March 2021 chartered to *DFDS* to operate between Dunkerque and Rosslare. From August 2021 operated Nynäshamn-Rostock.

GOTLAND Built as the THJELVAR in 2019 by Guangzhou Shipyard International, Guangzhou, China for *Rederi AB Gotland* for use on *Destination Gotland* services. LNG powered. In June 2020 renamed the GOTLAND.

GOTLANDIA Alstom Leroux Corsair 11500 monohull vessel built as the GOTLAND at Lorient, France for *Rederi AB Gotland* and chartered to *Destination Gotland*. In 2003 renamed the GOTLANDIA. Now laid up.

GOTLANDIA II Fincantieri SF700 monohull fast ferry built at Riva Trigoso, Italy for *Rederi AB Gotland* for use by *Destination Gotland*.

VISBY Built by as the VISBORG Guangzhou Shipyard International, Guangzhou, China for *Rederi AB Go.tland* for use on *Destination Gotland* services. LNG Powered. In December 2021 renamed the VISBY.

Rederi ABGotland also owns the VISBORG on charter to *DFDS* to operate accompanied freight services between Dunkerque and Rosslare.

DFDS FERRY

THE COMPANY *DFDS Ferry* is a division of *DFDS A/S*, a Danish private sector company.

MANAGEMENT CEO DFDS A/S Torben Carlsen, **Executive Vice-President Shipping Division** Peder Gellert Pedersen, **Head of Business Unit Passenger** Kasper Moos, **Head of the Business Unit Baltic** Anders Refsgaard.

ADDRESS *København* Sundkrogsgade 11, 2100 København Ø, Denmark.

TELEPHONE Administration +45 33 42 33 42, **Reservations *Denmark*** +45 78 79 55 36, **Germany** +49 (0)40-389030, **Lithuania** +370 46 393616, **Sweden** +46 454 33680.

FAX Administration +45 33 42 33 41.

INTERNET Administration incoming@dfdsseaways.dk, **Reservations *Denmark*** incoming@dfdsseaways.dk **Germany** service.de@dfds.com **Lithuania** booking.lt@dfds.com, **Sweden** pax@dfds.com **Website** www.dfds.com (*English, Danish, Dutch, German, Italian, Japanese, Norwegian, Polish, Swedish*)

ROUTES OPERATED *Passenger services* København - Fredrikshavn - Oslo (Norway) (19 hrs 30; ***CROWN SEAWAYS, PEARL SEAWAYS***; 1 per day), Klaipėda (Lithuania) - Kiel (Germany) (21 hrs; ***VICTORIA SEAWAYS***; 7 per week), Klaipėda - Karlshamn (Sweden) (14 hrs; ***AURA SEAWAYS, LUNA SEAWAYS***; 10 per week), Paldiski (Estonia) - Kapellskär (Sweden) (10 hrs; ***PATRIA SEAWAYS, SIRENA SEAWAYS***; 11 per week). ***Freight-only service*** Fredericia - København - Klaipėda (***BELGIA SEAWAYS***; 2 per week).

See Section 1 for services operating to Great Britain & Ireland.

1F	ARK FUTURA	18725t	96	19.7k	183.3m	12P	-	164T	AS	DK	9129598
2	ATHENA SEAWAYS	24950t	07	23.0k	199.1m	500P	-	190T	A	LT	9350680
3	AURA SEAWAYS	56043t	21	23.0k	230.0m	600P	-	270L	A2	DK	9851036
4F	BELGIA SEAWAYS	21005t	00	18.0k	183.4m	12P	-	180T	A	LT	9188233
5	CROWN SEAWAYS	35498t	94	22.0k	169.4m	1940P	450C	50T	BA	DK	8917613
6F	FINLANDIA SEAWAYS	11530t	00	20.0k	162.2m	12P	-	140T	A	DK	9198721
7	LUNA SEAWAYS	56043t	22	23.0k	230.0m	600P	-	270L	A2	DK	9851048
8	OPTIMA SEAWAYS	25206t	99	21.5k	186.3m	327P	164C	150T	A	LT	9188427

9	PATRIA SEAWAYS	18332t	92	17.0k	154.0m	242P	-	114T	BA2	LT	8917390
10	PEARL SEAWAYS	40039t	89	21.0k	178.4m	2090P	350C	70T	BA	DK	8701674
11	SIRENA SEAWAYS	22382t	03	22.0k	199.4m	596P	316C	154T	A	LT	9212163
12	VICTORIA SEAWAYS	24950t	09	23.0k	199.1m	600P	-	190T	A	LT	9350721

ARK FUTURA Built as the DANA FUTURA by C N Visentini di Visentini Francesco & C, Donada, Italy for *DFDS*. In 2001 she was renamed the TOR FUTURA. Initially operated mainly between Esbjerg and Harwich, but latterly operated mainly between Esbjerg and Immingham. In 2004 chartered to *Toll Shipping* of Australia. Later time-chartered to the *Danish MoD* for 5.5 years. However, when not required for military service she has been chartered to other operators such as *P&O Ferries*, *Cobelfret Ferries* and *Van Uden Ro-Ro* and used on *DFDS Tor Line* services. In 2006 sold to *DFDS Lys Line Rederi A/S* of Norway, a *DFDS* subsidiary and chartered back. In April 2011 renamed the ARK FUTURA. In November 2020 ceased to be part of the ARK Project.

ATHENA SEAWAYS Built as the CORAGGIO by Nuovi Cantieri Apuani, Marina di Carrara, Italy. First of an order of eight vessels for *Grimaldi Holdings* of Italy. Used on *Grimaldi Lines* Mediterranean services. In September 2010, bare-boat chartered to *Stena Line* to operate between

Hoek van Holland and Killingholme. In November 2011 replaced by the new STENA TRANSIT and returned to Mediterranean service. In December 2013 renamed the ATHENA SEAWAYS, chartered to *DFDS* and replaced the LIVERPOOL SEAWAYS on the Klaipėda - Kiel service. In May 2016 purchased by *DFDS*.

AURA SEAWAYS, LUNA SEAWAYS Built by Guangzhou Shipyard International, Guangzhou, China. They operate on the Klaipėda to Karlshamn route.

BELGIA SEAWAYS Built as the SCHIEBORG by Flender Werft AG, Lübeck, Germany for *Wagenborg* of The Netherlands and time-chartered to *Cobelfret Ferries* to operate on the *Stora Enso* (a paper and card manufacturer)/*Cobelfret Ferries* service between Zeebrugge and Göteborg. In November 2014 the arrangement between *Stora Enso* and *Cobelfret Ferries* ended and she was chartered to *SOL Continent Line* who took over the operation of the service. In June 2019 the service was taken over by *DFDS Seaways* and she was purchased by that company and renamed the BELGIA SEAWAYS.

CROWN SEAWAYS Launched as the THOMAS MANN by Brodogradevna Industrija, Split, Croatia for *Euroway AB* for their Lübeck - Travemünde - Malmö service. However, political problems led to serious delays and, before delivery, the service had ceased. She was purchased by *DFDS*, renamed the CROWN OF SCANDINAVIA and introduced onto the København - Oslo service. In January 2013 renamed the CROWN SEAWAYS.

FINLANDIA SEAWAYS Launched as the FINNMAID but renamed the FINNREEL before delivery. Built by Jinling Shipyard, Nanjing, China for the *Macoma Shipping Group* and chartered to *Finnlines*. In 2008 sold to *DFDS Lisco* and in January 2009 delivered, chartered to *DFDS Tor Line* and renamed the TOR FINLANDIA. Operated on the Immingham - Rotterdam route until January 2011 when she was transferred to the Rosyth - Zeebrugge route. In May 2012 moved to the Cuxhaven - Immingham service but returned in July. In December 2012 renamed the FINLANDIA SEAWAYS. In October 2013 moved to the Kiel - St Petersburg service. In April 2014 returned to the Rosyth - Zeebrugge route. In April 2018 she had a serious engine room fire and the route closed. She returned to service in November 2018 on the Immingham - Cuxhaven service.

OPTIMA SEAWAYS Ro-pax vessel built as the ALYSSA by C N Visentini di Visentini Francesco & C Donada, Italy for *Levantina Trasporti* of Italy for charter. Initially chartered to *CoTuNav* of Tunisia for service between Marseilles, Génova and Tunis and in 2000 to *Trasmediterranea* of Spain for service between Barcelona and Palma de Mallorca. In 2001 chartered to *Stena Line Scandinavia AB*, renamed the SVEALAND and placed as second vessel on the *Scandlines AB* freight-only Trelleborg - Travemünde service. In 2003 sub-chartered to *Scandlines AG* and placed on the Kiel - Klaipėda route, replacing the ASK and PETERSBURG. In 2004 sold to *Rederia AB Hornet*, a *Stena* company. In late 2005 the *Scandlines* Kiel - Klaipėda service ended.

In early 2006 she was chartered to *TT-Line* to cover for the rebuilding of the engines of their four newest vessels. Later sold to *DFDS*, renamed the LISCO OPTIMA. In April 2012 renamed the OPTIMA SEAWAYS.

PATRIA SEAWAYS Ro-pax vessel built as the STENA TRAVELLER by Fosen Mekaniske Verksteder, Trondheim, Norway for *Stena RoRo*. After a short period with *Stena Line* on the Hoek van Holland - Harwich service, she was chartered to *Sealink Stena Line* for their Southampton - Cherbourg route, initially for 28 weeks. At the end of the 1992 summer season she was chartered to *TT-Line* to operate between Travemünde and Trelleborg and was renamed the TT-TRAVELLER. In late 1995, she returned to *Stena Line*, resumed the name STENA TRAVELLER and inaugurated a new service between Holyhead and Dublin. In Autumn 1996 she was replaced by the STENA CHALLENGER (18523t, 1991). In early 1997 she was again chartered to *TT-Line* and renamed the TT-TRAVELLER. She operated on the Rostock - Trelleborg route. During Winter 1999/2000 her passenger capacity was increased to 250 and passenger facilities renovated. In early 2002 the charter ended and she was renamed the STENA TRAVELLER, chartered to *Stena Line* and placed on their Karlskrona - Gdynia service. This charter ended in May 2003 and she was sold to *Lisco Baltic Service* and renamed the LISCO PATRIA. Placed on the Klaipėda - Karlshamn service. In January 2006 transferred to the Klaipėda - Kiel service to replace the *Scandlines* vessel SVEALAND following that company's withdrawal from the joint route. In Spring 2006 returned to the Klaipėda – Karlshamn route. In May 2011 chartered to *Baltic Scandinavia Lines* and placed on their Paldiski - Kapellskär service. In September 2011 a controlling interest in this service was acquired by *DFDS*. In January 2012 renamed the PATRIA SEAWAYS. In September 2014 replaced by the SIRENA SEAWAYS and became a relief vessel. In April 2015 chartered as a windfarm accommodation vessel off Esbjerg. In January 2016 chartered to *P&O Ferries* to cover for refits on the Hull routes. In April 2016 became third vessel on the Klaipėda – Karlshamn route.

PEARL SEAWAYS Built as the ATHENA by Wärtsilä Marine, Turku, Finland for *Rederi AB Slite* of Sweden (part of *Viking Line*) and used on 24-hour cruises from Stockholm to Mariehamn (Åland). In 1993 the company went into liquidation and she was sold to *Star Cruises* of Malaysia for cruises in the Far East. She was renamed the STAR AQUARIUS. Later that year she was renamed the LANGKAPURI STAR AQUARIUS. In February 2001 sold to *DFDS* and renamed the AQUARIUS. After rebuilding, she was renamed the PEARL OF SCANDINAVIA and introduced onto the København - Oslo service. In January 2011 renamed the PEARL SEAWAYS.

SIRENA SEAWAYS Built as the GOLFO DEI DELFINI by Stocznia Szczecinska, Szczecin, Poland for *Lloyd Sardegna* of Italy for service between Italy and Sardinia. However, due to late delivery the order was cancelled. In 2002 purchased by *DFDS* and, during Winter 2002/03, passenger accommodation was enlarged and refitted, increasing passenger capacity from 308 to 596. In June 2003, renamed the DANA SIRENA, she replaced unmodified sister vessel, the DANA GLORIA on the Esbjerg – Harwich service. In February 2013 she was renamed the SIRENA SEAWAYS. At the end of September 2014 the route ceased and she moved to the Paldiski (Estonia) - Kapellskär route, replacing the PATRIA SEAWAYS. In December she was replaced by the LIVERPOOL SEAWAYS and laid up. During the early part of 2015 she performed relief work in the Baltic. In April 2015 she was chartered to *Brittany Ferries* for five years and renamed the BAIE DE SEINE. She entered service in May 2015. In March 2020 returned to *DFDS* and in April renamed the SIRENA SEAWAYS and placed on the Klaipėda - Karlshamn route.

VICTORIA SEAWAYS Built by Nuovi Cantieri Apuani, Marina di Carrara, Italy. Launched as the FORZA. Fifth of an order of eight vessels for *Grimaldi Holdings* of Italy. Whilst under construction, sold to *DFDS Tor Line*. On delivery renamed the LISCO MAXIMA. In March/April 2012 renamed the VICTORIA SEAWAYS. Operates between Kiel and Klaipėda.

Aura Seaways *(Frank Lose)*

Crown Seaways *(Richard Seville)*

REDERIJ DOEKSEN

THE COMPANY *BV Rederij G. Doeksen en Zn BV* is a Dutch private sector company. Ferries are operated by subsidiary *Terschellinger Stoomboot Maatschappij*, trading as *Rederij Doeksen*.

MANAGEMENT Managing Director D. Spoor, **Manager Nautical Services** J. de Vries, **Manager Technical Services** M. Schouwenaar **Manager Finance and ICT** R. Herrema, **Manager HR** A. Speerstra, **Manager Commercial Affairs** A. van Brummelen-van Dam.

ADDRESS Waddenpromenade 5, 8861 NT Harlingen, The Netherlands.

TELEPHONE +31 088 9000 888

INTERNET Email info@rederij-doeksen.nl **Website** www.rederij-doeksen.nl *(Dutch, English, German)*

ROUTES OPERATED Conventional Ferries Harlingen (The Netherlands) - Terschelling (Frisian Islands) (2 hrs; *FRIESLAND, WILLEM BARENTSZ*, *WILLEM DE VLAMINGH*; up to 6 per day), Harlingen - Vlieland (Frisian Islands) (1 hr 45 mins; *VLIELAND*; 3 per day). **Fast Passenger Ferries** Harlingen - Terschelling (45 mins; *KOEGELWIECK, TIGER*; 3 to 6 per day), Harlingen - Vlieland (45 mins; *KOEGELWIECK, TIGER*; 2 per day), Vlieland - Terschelling (30 mins; *KOEGELWIECK, TIGER*; 2 per day). **Freight Ferry** Harlingen - Terschelling (2 hrs; *NOORD-NEDERLAND*), Harlingen - Vlieland (1hr 45 mins; *NOORD-NEDERLAND*).

1	FRIESLAND	3583t	89	14.0k	69.0m	1100P	122C	12L	BA	NL	8801058
2»p	KOEGELWIECK	439t	92	33.0k	35.5m	315P	0C	0L	-	NL	9035527
3F	NOORD-NEDERLAND	361t	02	14.0k	68.0m	12P	-	-	BA	NL	9269611
4»p	TIGER	660t	02	37.0k	52.0m	414P	0C	0L	BA	NL	9179191
5	VLIELAND	2726t	05	15.0k	64.1m	1300P	58C	4L	BA	NL	9303716
6	WILLEM BARENTSZ	3744t	19	14.0k	70.0m	700P	64C	-	BA	NL	9807578
7	WILLEM DE VLAMINGH	3744t	19	14.0k	70.0m	700P	64C	-	BA	NL	9807580

FRIESLAND Built by Van der Giessen de Noord, Krimpen aan den IJssel, Rotterdam, The Netherlands for *Rederij Doeksen*. Used on the Harlingen - Terschelling route.

KOEGELWIECK Harding 35m catamaran built at Rosendal, Norway for *Rederij Doeksen* to operate between Harlingen and Terschelling, Harlingen and Vlieland and Terschelling and Vlieland.

NOORD-NEDERLAND Catamaran built by ASB, Harwood, New South Wales, Australia for *Rederij Doeksen*. Used on freight services from Harlingen to Terschelling and Vlieland. In spring 2017 lengthened by 20 metres.

TIGER Catamaran built as the SUPERCAT 2002 by FBMA Babcock Marine, Cebu, Philippines for *SuperCat* of the Philippines. In 2007 purchased by *Rederij Doeksen* and renamed the TIGER. Operates from Harlingen to Terschelling and Vlieland.

VLIELAND Catamaran built by FBMA Babcock Marine, Cebu, Philippines for *Rederij Doeksen* to operate between Harlingen and Vlieland.

WILLEM BARENTSZ, WILLEM DE VLAMINGH Built by Strategic Marine, Vung Tau, Vietnam and fitted out at Nesta Shipping, Harlingen, Netherlands. They are aluminium catamarans and LNG powered. They arrived in the Netherlands in May 2019 but entered service in July and October 2020 respectively. These vessels are the first single fuel LNG ferries in the Netherlands and the very first ships in the world where single fuel LNG engines directly drive a fixed propeller.

REDERI AB ECKERÖ

THE COMPANY *Rederi AB Eckerö* is an Åland Islands company. It operates two ferry companies, a ro-ro time chartering company *(Eckerö Shipping)* and a bus company on Åland *(Williams)*.

ADDRESS PO Box 158, AX-22101 Mariehamn, Åland, Finland.

TELEPHONE Administration +358 (0)18 28 030.

INTERNET Email info@rederiabeckero.ax **Website** www.rederiabeckero.ax *(English, Swedish)*

ECKERÖ LINE

THE COMPANY *Eckerö Line Ab Oy* is a Finnish company, 100% owned by *Rederi Ab Eckerö* of Åland, Finland. Until January 1998, the company was called *Eestin-Linjat*.

MANAGEMENT Managing Director Taru Keronen, **Marketing Director** Ida Toikka-Everi.

ADDRESS PO Box 307, 00181 Helsinki, Finland.

TELEPHONE Administration & Reservations *Finland* 06000 4300, *International* +358 9 2288 544.

INTERNET Email info@eckeroline.fi **Website** www.eckeroline.fi *(Swedish, Finnish, English)*

ROUTE OPERATED Passenger & Freight Service Helsinki (JetStar) - Tallinn (Estonia) (2 hrs 30 mins; *FINLANDIA*; up to 3 per day), **Freight and Car Passengers only** Helsinki (Vuosaari Port) - Tallinn (Muuga); *FINBO CARGO*; 3 per day.

1	FINBO CARGO	22152t	00	22.5k	180.0m	366P	-	120L	BA2	FI	9181106
2	FINLANDIA	36093t	01	27.0k	175.0m	1880P	665C	116T	BA	FI	9214379

FINBO CARGO Built as the MIDNIGHT MERCHANT by Astilleros Españoles SA, Sevilla, Spain for *Cenargo* (then owners of *NorseMerchant Ferries*). On delivery, chartered to *Norfolkline* to operate as second vessel on the Dover - Dunkerque (Ouest) service. In 2002 modified to allow two-deck loading. In 2006 chartered to *Acciona Trasmediterranea* of Spain and renamed the EL GRECO. Used on Mediterranean and Canary Island services. In 2007 sold to *P&O Ferries* and renamed the EUROPEAN ENDEAVOUR. Operated on The Dover - Calais route and as a re-fit relief vessel on Irish Sea routes. In May 2010 laid up. In February 2011 moved to the Liverpool - Dublin route. In May 2019 sold to *Rederi AB Eckerö*, renamed the FINBO CARGO and, in June 2019, placed on a new Helsinki - Muuga freight route. Between January and March 2020 converted to full 1A Ice Class at Öresund Drydocks in Landskrona.

FINLANDIA Built as the MOBY FREEDOM by Daewoo Shipbuilding & Heavy Machinery Ltd, Okpo, South Korea for *Moby SpA (Moby Line)* of Italy. Operated on their Génova/Civitavecchia/Livorno - Olbia routes. In March 2012 sold to *Eckerö Line*, and renamed the FREEDOM. Refitted at Landskrona and, in June, renamed the FINLANDIA. She entered service on 31st December 2012.

ECKERÖ LINJEN

THE COMPANY *Eckerö Linjen* is an Åland Islands company 100% owned by *Rederi AB Eckerö*.

MANAGEMENT Managing Director Tomas Karlsson, **Marketing Director** Maria Hellman-Aarnio.

ADDRESS Torggatan 2, Box 158, AX-22100 Mariehamn, Åland.

TELEPHONE Administration +358 (0)18 28 000, **Reservations** +358 (0)18 28 300.

INTERNET Email info@eckerolinjen.ax **Website** www.eckerolinjen.se *(Swedish, Finnish, English)*

ROUTE OPERATED Eckerö (Åland) - Grisslehamn (Sweden) (2 hrs; *ECKERÖ*; 3 per day).

1	ECKERÖ	12358t	79	19.5k	121.1m	1500P	265C	34T	BA	SE	7633155

ECKERÖ Built as the JENS KOFOED by Aalborg Værft A/S, Aalborg, Denmark for *Bornholmstrafikken*. Used on the Rønne - København, Rønne - Ystad and (until December 2002) Rønne - Sassnitz services. Rønne - København service became Rønne – Køge in September 2004. In October 2004 sold to *Eckerö Linjen* for delivery in May 2005. Renamed the ECKERÖ and substantially rebuilt before entering service in early 2006. In January 2009 transferred from the Finnish to the Swedish flag.

AG EMS

THE COMPANY *AG Ems* is a German public sector company.

MANAGEMENT Managing Director & Chief Executive Dr Bernhard Brons, **Marine Superintendent** Knut Gerdes, **Operations Manager** Hans-Jörg Oltmanns.

ADDRESS Zum Borkumanleger 6, 26723 Emden, Germany.

TELEPHONE Administration & Reservations +49 (0)1805-180182.

INTERNET Email info@ag-ems.de **Website** www.ag-ems.de *(English, German, (Dutch)*

ROUTES OPERATED Conventional Ferries Emden (Germany) - Borkum (German Frisian Islands) (2 hrs; *GRONINGERLAND, MÜNSTERLAND, OSTFRIESLAND, WESTFALEN*; up to 4 per day), Eemshaven (The Netherlands) - Borkum (55 mins; *GRONINGERLAND, MÜNSTERLAND, OSTFRIESLAND, WESTFALEN*; up to 4 per day). **Fast Ferries** Emden - Borkum (1 hr; *NORDLICH, NORDLICH II*; up to 4 per day), Eemshaven - Borkum (30 mins; *NORDLICHT, NORDLICH II*; 1 per week in summer).

1	GRONINGERLAND	1070t	91	12.0k	44.4m	621P	30C	-	BA	DE	9002465
2	MÜNSTERLAND	1859t	86	15.5k	78.7m	1200P	70C	10L	BA	DE	8601989
3p»	NORDLICHT	435t	89	33.0k	38.8m	272P	0C	0L	-	DE	8816015
4p»	NORDLICHT II	870t	21	33.0k	46.0m	450P	0C	0L	-	DE	9937490
5	OSTFRIESLAND	1859t	85	16.0k	78.7m	1200P	70C	10L	BA	DE	8324622
6p	WAPPEN VON BORKUM	287t	76	11.5k	42.8m	358P	0C	0L	-	DE	7525918
7	WESTFALEN	1812t	72	15.5k	77.9m	1200P	65C	10L	BA	DE	7217004

GRONINGERLAND Built by Husumer Schiffswerft, Husum, Germany as the HILLIGENLEI for *Wyker Dampfschiffs-Reederei Föhr-Amrum GmbH* of Germany. Operated Schlüttsiel - Halligen – Wittdün (North Frisian Islands). In 2004 laid up. In late 2005 sold to *AG Ems*. In 2006 renamed the GRONINGERLAND.

MÜNSTERLAND Built by Martin Jansen GmbH & Co KG Schiffswerft, Leer, Germany for *AG Ems*. During 2021/22 converted to LNG propulsion and a new stern section fitted by Royal Niestern Sander, Farmsum, Netherlands.

NORDLICHT Fjellstrand 38m passenger-only catamaran built at Mandal, Norway.

NORDLICHT II Built by Kim Seah Shipyard, Batam, Indonesia, a subsidiary of Penguin Shipyard International, Singapore. She is based on the Incat Crowther 46 design.

OSTFRIESLAND Built by Martin Jansen GmbH & Co KG Schiffswerft, Leer, Germany. In 2015 lengthened by 15.4 m and converted to LNG propulsion by BVT Brenn-und Verformtechnik GmbH, Bremen, Germany.

WAPPEN VON BORKUM Built as the HANNOVER by Schiffswerft Schlömer GmbH & Co KG, Oldersum, Germany for *Friesland Fahrlinie* of Germany. In 1979 sold to *AG Ems* and renamed the STADT BORKUM. In 1988 sold to *ST-Line* of Finland, operating day trips from Rauma and renamed the PRINCESS ISABELLA. In 1994 returned to *AG Ems* and renamed the WAPPEN VON BORKUM.

WESTFALEN Built by as the WESTFALEN by C Cassens Schiffswerft, Emden, Germany. Rebuilt in 1994. In 2006 renamed the HELGOLAND and inaugurated a new Wilhelmshaven - Helgoland service for subsidiary *Helgoland Linie*. In January 2016 reverted to the name WESTFALEN and used on service from Borkum.

FINNLINES

THE COMPANY *Finnlines Plc* is a Finnish private sector company owned by the Grimaldi Group. It operates three passenger brands: *Finnlines HansaLink*, *Finnlines NordöLink* and *FinnLink*.

MANAGEMENT President and CEO Emanuele Grimaldi, **Head of Passenger Services and Line Manager HansaLink & Hanko–Rostock** Kielo Vesikko, **Line Manager NordöLink, Finnlink and Russia** Antonio Raimo.

ADDRESS PO Box 197, 00181 Helsinki, Finland.

TELEPHONE Administration +358 (0)10 343 50, **Passenger Reservations** +358 9 231 43 100.

INTERNET Email info.fi@finnlines.com **Website** www.finnlines.com *(English, Finnish, German, Swedish, Russian)*

ROUTES OPERATED *Finnlines Hansalink branded routes* Helsinki (Vuosaari) - Travemünde (27 hrs; *FINNLADY, FINNMAID, FINNSTAR*; 7 per week).

Finnlines NordöLink branded route Malmö - Travemünde (9 hrs; *EUROPALINK, FINNPARTNER, FINNTRADER;* up to 4 per day).

FinnLink branded route Naantali (Finland) - Långnäs - Kapellskär (Sweden) (6 hrs; *FINNFELLOW, FINNSWAN*; 2 per day).

1	EUROPALINK	46119t	07	22.0k	218.8m	554P	-	300T	BA2	FI	9319454
2	FINNFELLOW	33769t	00	22.0k	188.3m	440P	-	220T	BA	FI	9145164
3	FINNLADY	45923t	07	22.0k	218.8m	500P	-	300T	BA2	FI	9336268
4	FINNMAID	45923t	06	22.0k	218.8m	500P	-	300T	BA2	FI	9319466
5	FINNPARTNER	33313t	94	21.3k	183.0m	280P	-	236T	A2	SE	9010163
6	FINNSTAR	45923t	06	22.0k	218.8m	500P	-	300T	BA2	FI	9319442
7	FINNSWAN	45923t	07	22.0k	218.8m	500P	-	300T	BA2	FI	9336256
8	FINNTRADER	33313t	95	21.3k	183.0m	280P	-	220T	BA2	SE	9017769
9	IGOUMENITSA	33724t	99	22.0k	188.3m	440P	-	210T	BA2	IT	9137997

EUROPALINK Built by Fincantieri-Cantieri Navali Italiani SpA, Castellamare, Italy for *Finnlines* to operate for *Finnlines NordöLink* between Travemünde and Malmö. Launched as the FINNLADY but name changed before delivery. In April 2009 transferred to *Finnlines HansaLink*. In October 2012 sold to *Atlantica Navigazione* of Italy, another company within the *Grimaldi Group*, for Mediterranean service. In January 2018 repurchased by *NordöLink* (a subsidiary of *Finnlines*) and returned to the Travemünde and Malmö service.

FINNFELLOW 'Ro-pax' ferry built as the STENA BRITANNICA by Astilleros Españoles, Cadiz, Spain for *Stena RoRo* and chartered to *Stena Line BV* to operate between Hoek van Holland and Harwich. In 2003 replaced by a new STENA BRITANNICA, sold to *Finnlines*, renamed the FINNFELLOW and placed on the Helsinki – Travemünde route. In 2004 transferred to *FinnLink*.

FINNLADY, FINNMAID Built by Fincantieri-Cantieri Navali Italiani SpA, Ancona, Italy to operate between Helsinki and Travemünde.

FINNPARTNER 'Ro-pax' vessel built by Stocznia Gdańska SA, Gdańsk, Poland for *Finnlines Oy* of Finland to provide a daily service conveying both freight and a limited number of cars and passengers on the previously freight-only route between Helsinki and Travemünde. In February 2007 replaced by the FINNLADY and placed on the Turku - Travemünde freight service; in May sent to the Remontowa Shipyard in Gdańsk for rebuilding to increase passenger capacity and allow for two-deck through loading. Currently operating on the Travemünde - Malmö and Lübeck - St Petersburg services.

FINNSWAN Built by Fincantieri-Cantieri Navali Italiani SpA, Castellamare, Italy as the NORDLINK for *Finnlines* to operate for *Finnlines NordöLink* between Travemünde and Malmö. In February 2018 renamed the FINNSWAN and in May moved to the Naantali - Långnäs - Kapellskär route.

FINNTRADER 'Ro-pax' vessel built by Stocznia Gdańska SA, Gdańsk, Poland for *Finnlines Oy* of Finland to provide a daily service conveying both freight and a limited number of cars and passengers on the previously freight-only route between Helsinki and Travemünde. In 2006/07 rebuilt to increase passenger capacity and allow for two-deck through loading. In 2007 transferred to the Malmö - Travemünde route.

IGOUMENITSA 'Ro-pax' ferry built by Astilleros Españoles, Cadiz, Spain. Ordered by *Stena RoRo* of Sweden and launched as the STENA SEAPACER 1. In 1998 sold, before delivery, to *Finnlines* and renamed the FINNCLIPPER. Entered service on the Helsinki - Travemünde route in 1999. During Winter 1999/2000 she was converted to double-deck loading. In 2003 transferred to

FinnLink. In 2007 an additional freight deck was added. In May 2018 chartered to *Baleària* of Spain and renamed the ROSALIND FRANKLIN. In November 2021 returned to *Finnlines* and in December was renamed the FINNCLIPPER. In March 2022 chartered to *Grimaldi Lines* of Italy to operate on their Brindisi-Igoumenitsa-Patras service and renamed the IGOUMENITSA.

Under Construction

10	FINNCANOPUS	64603t	22	25.0k	229.5m	1100P	-	370T	BA2	FI	9902419
11	FINNSIRIUS	64603t	23	25.0k	229.5m	1100P	-	370T	BA2	FI	9902421

FINNCANOPUS, FINNSIRIUS Under construction by CMI Jinling Weihai Shipyard, Weihai, China. To operate on the Kapellskär-Långnäs-Naantali route, replacing FINNSWAN and FINNFELLOW. When these vessels are delivered the route will have a greater passenger focus.

FJORD LINE

THE COMPANY *Fjord Line* is a Norwegian company. During 2007 most of the shares of the company were purchased by *Frode and Ole Teigen*. The company bought and merged with *Master Ferries* during December 2007 and all operations are branded as *Fjord Line*.

MANAGEMENT CEO Brian Thorsted Hansen', Communications **Director** Eva Sørås Mellgren.

ADDRESS PO Box 513, 4379 Egersund, Norway**.**

TELEPHONE Administration & Reservations +47 51 46 40 99.

INTERNET Email info@fjordline.com freight@fjordline.com **Website** www.fjordline.com *(English, Danish, German, Dutch, Norwegian)*

ROUTES OPERATED Conventional Ferry Bergen (Norway) – Stavanger - Hirtshals (Denmark) (17 hrs; ***BERGENSFJORD, STAVANGERFJORD***; daily), Langesund (Norway) - Hirtshals (4 hrs 30 mins; ***BERGENSFJORD, STAVANGERFJORD***; daily), Sandefjord (Norway) - Strömstad (Sweden) (2 hrs 30 mins; ***OSLOFJORD***; 2 per day), **Fast Ferry *May-August*** Kristiansand (Norway) **-** Hirtshals (Denmark) (2 hrs 15 min; ***FJORD FSTR***; up to 3 per day).

1	BERGENSFJORD	31678t	13	21.5k	170.0m	1500P	600C	90T	BA	DK	9586617
2»	FJORD FSTR	11888t	20	37.0k	109.0m	1200P	404C	30L	A	DK	9837339
3	OSLOFJORD	16794t	93	19.0k	134.4m	882P	350C	44T	BA	NO	9058995
4	STAVANGERFJORD	31678t	13	21.5k	170.0m	1500P	600C	90T	BA	DK	9586605

BERGENSFJORD, STAVANGERFJORD Built by Bergen Group Fosen AS, Rissa, Norway for *Fjord Line*. They operate on LNG**.**

FJORD FSTR Austal 109m catamaran built by Austal Ships, Cebu, Philippines.

OSLOFJORD Built by Fosen Mekaniske Verksteder, Rissa, Norway for *Rutelaget Askøy-Bergen* as the BERGEN and used on the *Fjord Line* Bergen - Egersund - Hanstholm service. In April 2003 chartered to *DFDS*, renamed the DUCHESS OF SCANDINAVIA and, after modifications, introduced onto the Harwich - Cuxhaven service. In 2004 sold to *Bergensfjord KS* of Norway and chartered to *DFDS*. In 2005 sub-chartered to *Fjord Line* for 5 months (with *DFDS* officers and deck-crew) and renamed the ATLANTIC TRAVELLER. In 2006 chartered directly to *Fjord Line*. In March 2008 purchased by *Fjord Line* and renamed the BERGENSFJORD. In January 2014 renamed the OSLOFJORD, rebuilt as a day ferry by STX Finland, Rauma, Finland and, in June 2014, inaugurated a new service between Sandefjord and Strömstad.

FORSEA

THE COMPANY *ForSea* (formerly *Scandlines Helsingør - Helsingborg*) is the trading name of *HH Ferries Group*, a Swedish private sector company owned by First State Investments. Previously a joint venture between *Scandlines* and *Stena Line*, it was acquired by First State Investments in January 2015 and until 2018 operated as part of the *Scandlines* network.

MANAGEMENT CEO Kristian Durhuus.

ADDRESS Bredgatan 5, 252 25 Helsingborg, Sweden.

Europalink *(Frank Lose)*

Tycho Brahe *(Richard Seville)*

TELEPHONE Administration & Reservations +46 42 18 61 00.

INTERNET Email customerservice@forseaferries.com **Website** www.forsea.dk *(Danish)*, www.forseaferries.com *(English)*, www.forsea.se *(Swedish)*.

ROUTES OPERATED Helsingør (Sjælland, Denmark) - Helsingborg (Sweden) (20 mins; *AURORA AF HELSINGBORG, MERCANDIA IV, MERCANDIA VIII, HAMLET, TYCHO BRAHE*; up to every 15 mins)

1	AURORA AF HELSINGBORG	10918t	92	14.0k	111.2m	1250P	225C	25Lr	BA	SE	9007128
2	HAMLET	10067t	97	13.5k	111.2m	1000P	244C	34L	BA	DK	9150030
3	MERCANDIA IV	4296t	89	13.0k	95.0m	420P	170C	18L	BA	DK	8611685
4	MERCANDIA VIII	4296t	87	13.0k	95.0m	420P	170C	18L	BA	DK	8611623
5	TYCHO BRAHE	11148t	91	14.5k	111.2m	1250P	240C	35Lr	BA	DK	9007116

AURORA AF HELSINGBORG Train/vehicle ferry built by Langsten Verft A/S, Tomrefjord, Norway for *SweFerry* for *ScandLines* joint *DSB/SweFerry* service between Helsingør and Helsingborg. In autumn 2018 converted to full battery electric operation with shoreside power supply. She can also operate in hybrid and diesel electric mode, although the last is only used in emergency.

HAMLET Road vehicle ferry built by Finnyards, Rauma, Finland for *Scandlines* (50% owned by *Scandlines AG* and 50% owned by *Scandlines AB* of Sweden) for the Helsingør - Helsingborg service. Sister vessel of the TYCHO BRAHE but without rail tracks.

MERCANDIA IV Built as the SUPERFLEX NOVEMBER by North East Shipbuilders Ltd, Sunderland, UK for *Vognmandsruten* of Denmark. In 1989 sold to *Mercandia* and renamed the MERCANDIA IV. In 1990 she began operating on their *Kattegatbroen* Juelsminde - Kalundborg service. In 1996 she was transferred to their *Sundbroen* Helsingør - Helsingborg service. In 1997 the service and vessel were leased to *HH-Ferries*. In 1999 she was purchased by *HH-Ferries*. She has been equipped to carry dangerous cargo.

MERCANDIA VIII Built as the SUPERFLEX BRAVO by North East Shipbuilders Ltd, Sunderland, UK for *Vognmandsruten* of Denmark and used on their services between Nyborg and Korsør and København (Tuborg Havn) and Landskrona (Sweden). In 1991 she was chartered to *Scarlett Line* to operate on the København and Landskrona route. In 1993 she was renamed the SVEA SCARLETT but later in the year the service ceased and she was laid up. In 1996 she was purchased by *Mercandia*, renamed the MERCANDIA VIII and placed on their *Sundbroen* Helsingør - Helsingborg service. In 1997 the service and vessel were leased to *HH-Ferries*. In 1999 she was purchased by *HH-Ferries*. Now reserve vessel. Between April and July 2015 she operated between Puttgarden and Rødby for *Scandlines*, following damage sustained by the PRINSESSE BENEDIKTE at Gdańsk during a refit. In summer 2018 and summer 2019 chartered to *Praamid* of Estonia to act as spare vessel.

TYCHO BRAHE Train/vehicle ferry, built by Tangen Verft A/S, Tomrefjord, Norway for DSB for the ScandLines joint DSB/SweFerry service between Helsingør and Helsingborg.

FRS GROUP

THE COMPANY *FRS (Förde Reederei Seetouristik)* a German private sector company with worldwide shipping interests.

ADDRESS Norderhofenden 19-20, 24937 Flensburg, Germany.

TELEPHONE +49 461 864-0.

INTERNET Email info@frs.de **Website** frs.world *(English, German)*

FRS BALTIC

THE COMPANY *FRS Baltic* is a trading name of *FRS*.

ADDRESS Jasmunder Landstrasse 2, 18546 Sassnitz / Neu Mukran, Germany.

TELEPHONE +49 (0)461 864-608.

INTERNET Email info@frsbaltic.com **Website** frsbaltic.com *(English, German)*

ROUTE OPERATED Sassnitz (Germany) - Ystad (Sweden) (Trelleborg from spring 2023) (2 hrs 30 mins; **SKANE JET**; 1/2 per day.

1»	SKANE JET	5619t	98	43.0k	91.3m	663P	220C	-	A	CY	9176060

SKANE JET Incat 91-metre catamaran, built speculatively by Incat, Hobart, Tasmania, Australia. In Spring 1998, following *Incat's* acquisition of a 50% share in *Scandlines Cat-Link A/S*, she was chartered by *Nordic Catamaran Ferries K/S* to that company, operating between Århus and Kalundborg and named the CAT-LINK V. She is the current holder of the Hales Trophy for fastest crossing of the Atlantic during her delivery voyage between the USA and Falmouth, UK (although this claim is disputed because it was not a genuine commercial service). In 1999 the charter was transferred to *Mols-Linien*, she was renamed the MADS MOLS and operated between Århus and Odden. Charter ended in July 2005. Laid up and renamed the INCAT 049. In 2006 sold to *Gabriel Scott Rederi (Master Ferries)* and renamed the MASTER CAT. In December 2008 purchased by *Fjord Line* renamed the FJORD CAT. Did not operate in 2009 but service resumed in 2010. In August 2020 sold to *FRS Baltic* and renamed the SKANE JET. SKANE JET to operate between Sassnitz and Ystad (Trelleborg in 2023).

FRS SYLTFÄHRE

THE COMPANY FRS Syltfähre (*Syltfærge* in Danish) is the trading name of *Römö-Sylt Linie GmbH & Co. KG*, a German private sector company, a subsidiary of *FRS*.

MANAGEMENT Managing Director RSL Birte Dettmers, Tim Kunstmann.

ADDRESS *Germany* Norderhofenden 19-20, 24937 Flensburg, Germany, ***Denmark*** Kilebryggen, 6792 Rømø, Denmark.

TELEPHONE Administration +49 (0)461 864 0, **Reservations *Germany*** +49 (0)461 864 601, ***Denmark*** +49 461 864 601.

INTERNET Email info@syltfaehre.de **Website** www.syltfaehre.de *(Danish, English, German)*

ROUTE OPERATED List auf Sylt (Sylt, Germany) - Havneby (Rømø, Denmark) (approx. 40 mins; ***RÖMÖ EXPRESS, SYLT EXPRESS***; variable - approx two-hourly). **Note**: The Danish island of Rømø is linked to the Danish mainland by a toll-free road causeway; the German island of Sylt is linked to the German mainland by the Hindenburgdamm, a rail-only causeway on which cars are conveyed on shuttle wagons.

1	RÖMÖ EXPRESS	3423t	91	15.0k	96.95m	345P	127C	-	BA	CY	9008794
2	SYLT EXPRESS	3650t	05	16.0k	88.2m	600P	80C	10L	BA	CY	9321823

RÖMÖ EXPRESS Built as the TRESFJORD by Fiskerstrand Verft A/S of Norway for *Møre og Romsdal Fylkesbåtar AS (MRF)* of Molde, Norway. In 2005 transferred to *Fjord1 MRF AS* of Molde, Norway. In October 2012 transferred to *Fjord 1 AS* of Florø, Norway. Until 2010 operated between Molde and Vestnes. She was then converted to LNG propulsion. Between February 2011 and January 2019 operated between Flakk and Rørvik. In January 2019 became a reserve vessel on the Molde and Vestnes route. In September 2019 purchased by *Römö-Sylt Linie* and renamed the RÖMÖ EXPRESS.

SYLT EXPRESS Built by Fiskerstrand Verft A/S, Aalesund, Norway for *Römö-Sylt Linie*.

HAVILA VOYAGES

THE COMPANY *Havila Voyages* is a trading name of *Havila Shipping ASA*, a Norwegian private sector company, In March 2018 it won a ten-year concession to operate, with *Hurtigruten*, the coastal route between Bergen and Kirkenes from January 2021. The start has been delayed.

MANAGEMENT CEO Bent Martini, **Marketing Manager** Tonje Alvestad Ytrebø.

ADDRESS Postboks 215, 6099 Fosnavaag, Norway.

TELEPHONE *Norway* +47 70 00 70 70. ***UK*** +44 (0)3455 280026.

INTERNET   Email office@havila.no **Website** www.havilavoyages.com *(English, German, Norwegian)*

ROUTE OPERATED Bergen - Kirkenes.

1	HAVILA CAPELLA	15800t	21	15.5k	124.1m	640P	9C	0L	S	NO	9865570
2	HAVILA CASTOR	15812t	21	15.5k	124.1m	640P	9C	0L	S	NO	9865582

HAVILA CAPELLA, HAVILA CASTOR Hybrid vessels built by by Tersan Shipyard, Yalova, Turkey. Run on LNG and batteries.

Under Construction

3	HAVILA POLARIS	15471t	22	15.5k	124.1m	640P	9C	0L	S	NO	9873759
4	HAVILA POLLUX	15471t	22	15.5k	124.1m	640P	9C	0L	S	NO	9873761

HAVILA POLARIS, HAVILA POLLUX Hybrid vessels under construction by Tersan Shipyard, Yalova, Turkey. To run on LNG and batteries.

HOLLAND NORWAY LINES

THE COMPANY *Holland Norway Lines* is a Dutch private sector company.

MANAGEMENT CEO Bart Cunnen, **General Manager Marketing & Sales** Elmer Roukema.

ADDRESS *Netherlands* Borkumkade 7, 9979 XX Eemshaven, The Netherlands, *Norway* Vestre Strandgate 31, 4611 Kristiansand, Norway.

TELEPHONE Netherlands +31 85 40 15 252

INTERNET Email info.nl@hollandnorwaylines.com **Website** hollandnorwaylines.com *(English, Dutch, German, Norwegian)*

ROUTE OPERATED Eemshaven (Netherlands) - Kristiansand (Norway) (18 hrs; *ROMANTIKA*; 3 per week).

1	ROMANTIKA	40803t	02	22.0k	193.8m	2178P	300C	82T	BA	NL	9237589

ROMANTIKA Built by Aker Finnyards, Rauma, Finland for *Tallink Grupp*. **In** June 2021 chartered to the *Tangier Med Port Authority* of Morocco and operated between Tangier and Sete. In October chartered to the *UK Government* to provide Hotel accommodation at the COP25 Conference in Glasgow. In April 2021 bare boat chartered to *Holland Norway Lines*.

HURTIGRUTEN

THE COMPANY *Hurtigruten Group AS i*s a Norwegian private sector company. The service was originally provided by a consortium of companies. By 2006, through mergers and withdrawal from the operation, there were just two companies - *Troms Fylkes D/S* and *Ofotens og Vesteraalens D/S* and in that year *Hurtigruten ASA* was formed. In September 2015 it was taken over by *Silk Bidco AS* of Norway and the company changed its name to *Hurtigruten AS*, now *Hurtigruten Group AS*. They operate as two brands: *Hurtigruten Expeditions* and *Hurtigruten Norwegian Coastal Express*. Coastal express covers the traditional route along the Norwegian coast and expeditions covers all other destinations, as well as expeditions along the Norwegian coast.

MANAGEMENT CEO Hurtigruten Group Daniel Skjeldam, **CEO Hurtigruten Norway** Hedda Felin, **CEO Hurtigruten Expedition** Asta Lassesen, **Chief Sales & Marketing Officer** Stine Steffensen Børke.

ADDRESS Hurtigruten AS, Fredrik Lamges gate 14, Postboks 6144, 9291 Tromsø, Norway.

TELEPHONE Administration +47 970 57 030, **Reservations Norway** +47 810 03 030,

UK +44 (0)2036 037112.

INTERNET Email firmapost@hurtigruten.com uk.sales@hurtigruten.com

Websites   www.hurtigruten.co.uk   *(English)*   www.hurtigruten.no   *(Norwegian)*
www.hurtigruten.de *(German)* www.hurtigruten.fr *(French)* www.hurtigruten.us *(US English)*

ROUTE OPERATED 'Hurtigruten' sail from Bergen and calls at 34 ports up to Kirkenes and takes you along one of the world's most exciting coast lines, where you will find yourself close to nature, people and traditions. The round trip takes just under 11 days.

1p	FRAM	11647t	07	18.0k	110.0m	500P	0C	0L	-	NO	9370018
2p	FRIDTJOF NANSEN	21765t	19	15k	140.0m	530P	0C	0L	-	NO	9813084
3	KONG HARALD	11204t	93	18.0k	121.8m	691P	45C	0L	S	NO	9039119
4p	MAUD	16151t	03	18.0k	135.7m	1000P	45C	0L	-	NO	9247728
5	NORDKAPP	11386t	96	18.0k	123.3m	691P	45C	0L	S	NO	9107772
6	NORDLYS	11204t	94	18.0k	121.8m	691P	45C	0L	S	NO	9048914
7	NORDNORGE	11384t	97	18.0k	123.3m	691P	45C	0L	S	NO	9107784
8p	OTTO SVERDRUP	15539t	02	18.0k	138.5m	1000P	0C	0L	S	NO	9231951
9	POLARLYS	11341t	96	18.0k	123.0m	737P	35C	0L	S	NO	9107796
10	RICHARD WITH	11205t	93	18.0k	121.8m	691P	45C	0L	S	NO	9040429
11p	ROALD AMUNDSEN	21765t	19	15k	140.0m	530P	0C	0L	-	NO	9813072
12p	SPITSBERGEN	7344t	09	16.0k	100.5m	335P	0C	0L	-	NO	9434060
13p	TROLLFJORD	16140t	02	18.0k	135.7m	822P	0C	0L	-	NO	9233258
14	VESTERÅLEN	6262t	83	18.0k	108.6m	560P	35C	0L	S	NO	8019368

FRAM Built by Fincantieri-Cantieri Navali Italiani SpA at Trieste for *Hurtigruten Group ASA* (ordered by *OVDS*). Since 2007 she has operated cruises around Greenland and Svalbad during the summer period and in South America during the winter and this has been the pattern since. She is named after Fridtjof Nansen's expedition ship FRAM and has ice class 1A/1B.

FRIDTJOF NANSEN, ROALD AMUNDSEN Built by Kleven Verft, Ulsteinvik, Norway. They are designed to cope with both polar waters (for cruising) and service on the regular routes along the Norwegian coastline.

KONG HARALD Built by Volkswerft, Stralsund, Germany for *Troms Fylkes D/S.*

MAUD Built as the MIDNATSOL by Fosen Mekaniske Verksteder, Rissa, Norway for *Troms Fylkes D/S.* From 2016 also used as an expedition ship in the Antarctic. In January 2021 converted to hybrid propulsion, moved to the company's expedition fleet and, in May 2021, renamed the MAUD.

NORDKAPP Built by Kværner Kleven Skeppsvarv, Ulsteinvik, Norway for *Ofotens og Vesteraalens D/S.* During the winters of 2005/06 and 2006/07 she operated cruises in South America but following the delivery of the FRAM she now remains on the Hurtigruten throughout the year.

NORDLYS Built by Volkswerft, Stralsund, Germany for *Troms Fylkes D/S.* In 2002 sold to *Kilberg Shipping KS* of Norway and leased back on 15 year bareboat charter with options to repurchase. She was laid up during winter 2008/09 until required to replace the damaged RICHARD WITH from the end of January. She now operates full-time on the Hurtigruten roster.

NORDNORGE Built by Kværner Kleven, Ulsteinvik, Norway for *Ofotens og Vesteraalens D/S.* During winters 2002/03 - 2007/08 she operated cruises in South America. During most of Winter 2008/09 she was used as an accommodation vessel for a liquefied natural gas field. Laid up at Bremerhaven during winter 2009/10.

OTTO SVERDRUP Built as the FINNMARKEN by Kværner Kleven Skeppsvarv, Ulsteinvik, Norway for *Ofotens og Vesteraalens D/S.* In October 2009 chartered as a support vessel for the Gorgon Project (natural gas) in Western Australia. In November 2011 returned to *Hurtigruten* and, in February 2012, returned to service. In January 2021 converted to hybrid propulsion, moved to the company's expedition fleet. In May renamed the OTTO SVERDRUP.

POLARLYS Built by Ulstein Verft A/S, Ulsteinvik, Norway for *Troms Fylkes D/S.*

RICHARD WITH Built by Volkswerft, Stralsund, Norway for *Ofotens og Vesteraalens D/S*. In 2002 sold to *Kystruten KS*, of Norway and leased back on 15 year bareboat charter with options to re-purchase. In 2022 converted to diesel/electric hybrid propulsion.

SPITSBERGEN Built as the ATLANTIDA by Estaleiros Navais de Viana do Castelo, Viana do Castelo, Portugal for *Atlanticoline* of Portugal as a ro-ro ferry to operate in the Azores. Although completed in 2009, she was never delivered because she did not meet the required specification. In June 2015 purchased by *Hurtigruten* and renamed the NORWAY EXPLORER. Taken to the Öresund Drydocks shipyard, Landskrona, Sweden for rebuilding to make her suitable for *Hurtigruten* service and cruising in polar waters. In May 2016 renamed the SPITSBERGEN and entered service on the *Hurtigruten*, running along-side the LOFOTEN. Unlike most other *Hurtigruten* vessels, no cars could be conveyed. In January 2021 moved to the company's expedition fleet.

TROLLFJORD Built by Fosen Mekaniske Verksteder, Rissa, Norway for *Troms Fylkes D/S*. In 2021 converted to hybrid propulsion and moved to the company's expedition fleet.

VESTERÅLEN Built by Kaarbös Mekaniske Verksted A/S, Harstad, Norway for *Vesteraalens D/S*. From 1987 owned by *Ofotens og Vesteraalens D/S* and from 2006 by *Hurtigruten Group ASA*.

Under Construction

15p	NEWBUILDING	21765t	-	15k	140.0m	530P	0C	0L	-	NO	9871189

NEWBUILDING Option from Kleven Verft, Ulsteinvik, Norway. Other details as FRIDTJOF NANSEN and ROALD AMUNDSEN. Delivery date is currently uncertain.

FÆRGESELSKABET LÆSØ

THE COMPANY *Færgeselskabet Læsø K/S* is a Danish public sector company, 50% owned by the county of North Jylland and 50% by the municipality of Læsø.

MANAGEMENT Managing Director Lars Ricks, **Marketing Manager** Bente Faurholt.

ADDRESS Havnepladsen 1, 9940 Læsø, Denmark.

TELEPHONE Administration & Reservations +45 98 49 90 22

INTERNET Email info@laesoe-line.dk **Website** www.laesoe-line.dk *(English, Danish, German)*

ROUTE OPERATED Læsø - Frederikshavn (Jylland) (1 hr 30 mins; *ANE LÆSØ*, *MARGRETE LÆSØ*; up 7 per day).

1	ANE LÆSØ	2208t	95	12.0k	53.8m	440P	72C	-	BA	DK	9107370
2	MARGRETE LÆSØ	3668t	97	13.5k	68.5m	586P	76C	12L	BA	DK	9139438

ANE LÆSØ Built as the VESBORG by Ørskov Stålskibsværft, Ørskov, Denmark for *Samsø Linien*. In March 2012 sold to *Læsø Færgen*. Rebuilt by Soby Yard, Aerø, Denmark and renamed the ANE LÆSØ. Between September 2014 and February 2015 she operated on the Hou - Sælvig (Samsø) service which had been taken over by *Samsø Rederi* before their new SAMSØ (now PRINSESSE ISABELLA) was delivered. She will continue to act as reserve vessel on this route.

MARGRETE LÆSØ Built as the LÆSØ FÆRGEN by A/S Norsdsøværftet, Ringkøbing, Denmark for *Andelsfærgeselskabet Læsø* of Denmark. In June 1997 renamed the MARGRETE LÆSØ. In July 1999 transferred to *Færgeselskabet Læsø*.

MOLSLINJEN

THE COMPANY *Molslinjen A/S* (formerly *Mols-Linien A/S*) is a Danish private sector company owned by *EQT Infrastructure* of Sweden.

MANAGEMENT CEO Søren Jespersen, **Communications Manager** Jesper Maack, **Marketing Manager** Mikkel Hybel.

ADDRESS Hveensgade 4, 8000 Aarhus C, Denmark.

Romantika *(Frank Lose)*

Finbo Cargo *(Frank Lose)*

TELEPHONE Administration +45 89 52 52 00, **Reservations** *Bornholmslinjen* +45 70 900 100, *Other Routes* +45 70 10 14 18 (press 1).

INTERNET   Email   molslinjen@molslinjen.dk   **Websites**   www.molslinjen.dk www.bornholmslinjen.com *(Danish)*

ROUTES OPERATED *Alslinjen* Fynshav (Als) – Bøjden (Funen) (50 mins; *FRIGG SYDFYEN, FYNSHAV*; hourly (summer) two-hourly (winter)), *Bornholmslinjen* Rønne (Bornholm, Denmark) – Køge (5 hrs 30 mins; *HAMMERSHUS*; 1 per day, Rønne – Sassnitz (Germany) (3 hrs 20 mins; *HAMMERSHUS*; 1 per day). **Fast Ferry** Rønne – Ystad (Sweden) (1 hr 20 mins; *EXPRESS 1, MAX*; up to 8 per day), *Fanølinjen* Esbjerg (Jylland) – Nordby (Fanø) (12 mins; *FENJA, MENJA, SØNDERHO*; every 20-40 mins), *Langelandslinjen* Spodsbjerg (Langeland) – Tårs (Lolland) (45 mins; *LANGELAND, LOLLAND*; hourly), *Molslinjen* **(all services fast ferry)** *All year* Århus (Jylland) – Odden (Sjælland) (1 hr 5 mins; *EXPRESS 2, EXPRESS 3, EXPRESS 4*; up to 12 per day), *April - October- weekends only* Ebeltoft (Jylland) – Odden (45 mins; *EXPRESS 2*; 1 per day), *Samsølinjen* Kalundborg – Ballen (Samsø) (1 hr 15 min; *SAMSØ*; up to 4 per day).

1»	EXPRESS 1	10504t	09	40.0k	112.6m	1200P	417C	34L	A	DK	9501590
2»	EXPRESS 2	10500t	13	40.0k	112.6m	1000P	417C	34L	A	DK	9561356
3»	EXPRESS 3	10842t	17	40.0k	109.4m	1000P	411C	34L	A	DK	9793064
4»	EXPRESS 4	11345t	19	37.0k	109.0m	1006P	425C	36L	A	DK	9824564
5	FENJA	751t	98	11.5k	49.9m	396P	34C	4L	BA	DK	9189378
6	FRIGG SYDFYEN	1676t	84	13.5k	70.1m	338P	50C	8L	BA	DK	8222824
7	FYNSHAV	3380t	98	14.5k	69.2m	450P	96C	8L	BA	DK	9183025
8	GROTTE	925t	21	11.5k	49.9m	396P	34C	4L	BA	DK	9909429
9	HAMMERSHUS	18500t	18	17.7k	158.0m	720P	-	90L	BA	DK	9812107
10	LANGELAND	4500t	12	16.0k	99.9m	600P	122C	36L	BA	DK	9596428
11	LOLLAND	4500t	12	16.0k	99.9m	600P	122C	36L	BA	DK	9594690
12»	MAX	5617t	98	43.0k	91.3m	800P	220C	-	A	DK	9176058
13	MENJA	751t	98	11.5k	49.9m	396P	34C	4L	BA	DK	9189380
14	POVL ANKER	12131t	78	19.5k	121.0m	1500P	262C	26T	BA	DK	7633143
15	SAMSØ	4250t	08	16.0k	91.4m	600P	122C	30L	BA	DK	9548562

EXPRESS 1 Incat 112m catamaran built by Incat Tasmania Pty Ltd for *MGC Chartering* of the Irish Republic. Launched as the INCAT 066. On completion, sold to for *MGC Chartering* of the Irish Republic and renamed the MGC 66. In April 2009 chartered to *LD Lines*, renamed the NORMAN ARROW and, in June, placed on the Dover - Boulogne route. In November 2009 withdrawn and laid up for the winter. In April 2010 began operating on the Portsmouth Le Havre - route. In March 2012 chartered to *Mols-Linien* and renamed the KATEXPRESS 1 (Note: in upper and lower case spelt 'KatExpress 1'). Entered service in May 2012. In January 2017 renamed the EXPRESS 1. In September 2018 moved to the *Bornholmslinjen* service.

EXPRESS 2 Incat 112m catamaran built by Incat Tasmania Pty Ltd. Launched as INCAT 067. In March 2013 chartered to *Mols-Linien* and renamed the KATEXPRESS 2 for ten years with a purchase option. (Note: in upper and lower case spelt 'KatExpress 2'). Entered service in May 2013. In March 2017 renamed the EXPRESS 2.

EXPRESS 3 Incat 109m catamaran built by Incat Tasmania Pty Ltd, Hobart, Australia.

EXPRESS 4 Austal 109m catamaran built by Austal Ships, Fremantle, Australia.

FENJA Built by Morsø Værft A/S, Nykøbing Mors, Denmark for *Scandlines Sydfyenske A/S* for the Esbjerg - Nordby service.

FRIGG SYDFYEN Built by Svendborg Skibsværft A/S, Svendborg, Denmark for *Sydfyenske Dampskibsselskab (SFDS)* of Denmark for the service between Spodsbjerg and Tårs. In June 2012 moved to the Fynshav - Bøjden route.

FYNSHAV Built as the KYHOLM by Ørskov Staalskibsværft, Frederikshavn, Denmark for *Samsø Linien* of Denmark. In October 2008 chartered to *Nordic Ferry Services* and in July 2009 sold to them. Used on the Kalundborg - Koby Kås service. In March 2015 renamed the FYNSHAV and moved to the Fynshav - Bøjden service.

GROTTE Built by Hvide Sande Shipyard, Denmark to replace the SØNDERHO on the Esbjerg - Nordby service. Of similar dimensions and capacity to the FENJA and MENJA but electrically powered.

HAMMERSHUS Built by Rauma Marine Constructions Oy, Rauma, Finland. Delivered in July 2018. She operates between Rønne and Køge (Bornholm) and Rønne and Sassnitz.

LANGELAND Built by Sietas Werft, Hamburg, Germany for the Spodsbjerg - Tårs route.

LOLLAND Built by Sietas Werft, Hamburg, Germany. She was launched as the SAMSØ and it was intended that she would be operated on the Hou - Sælvig service, being owned by *Samsø Linien* and operated by *Færgen*. However, these plans were dropped and in February 2012 she was renamed the LOLLAND. After delivery in March 2012 she was, in April, placed on the Spodsbjerg - Tårs route.

MAX Incat 91-metre catamaran, built speculatively at Hobart, Tasmania, Australia. In Spring 1998, following *Incat's* acquisition of a 50% share in *Scandlines Cat-Link A/S*, she was sold to that company and named the CAT-LINK IV. In 1999 purchased by *Mols-Linien* and renamed the MAX MOLS. In 2000 chartered to *Marine Atlantic* of Canada to operate between Port aux Basques (Newfoundland) and North Sydney (Nova Scotia). Returned to *Mols-Linien* in Autumn 2000. In Summer 2002 chartered to *Riga Sea Lines* to operate between Riga and Nynäshamn. Returned to *Mols-Linien* in Autumn 2002. In 2004 chartered to *P&O Ferries* to operate between Portsmouth and Caen. Operated under the marketing name 'Caen Express'. In November 2004 returned to *Mols-Linien* and placed on the Århus – Odden route to enhance the service. In June 2017 transferred to the Ebeltoft - Odden route. In January 2019 renamed the MAX. In April transferred to the *Bornholmslinjen* service.

MENJA Built by Morsø Værft A/S, Nykøbing Mors, Denmark for *Scandlines Sydfyenske A/S* for the Esbjerg - Nordby service.

POVL ANKER Built by Aalborg Værft A/S, Denmark for *Bornholmstrafikken*. Used on the Rønne - København (until September 2004), Rønne - Køge (October 2004-date), Rønne - Ystad and Rønne - Sassnitz services. In recent years she has operated between Rønne and Sassnitz and Rønne and Ystad in the peak summer period. In July 2016 sold to *Mols-Linien A/S* and chartered back. Delivered to *Mols-Linien* at the end of August 2018.

SAMSØ Built as the KANHAVE by Frantzis Shipyard, Perama, Greece. Used on the Hou - Sælvig route. In January 2015 transferred to the Kalundborg - Koby Kås (Samsø) service. Later in January 2015 the Samsø terminal was moved to Ballen. In August 2015 renamed the SAMSØ.

Under Construction

16»	EXPRESS 5	13859t	22	37.0k	115.0m	1600P	450C	28L	A	DK	9913286

EXPRESS 5 Austal 115m catamaran under construction by Austal Ships, Cebu, Philippines. To operate between Rønne and Ystad.

REEDEREI NORDEN-FRISIA

THE COMPANY *Aktiengesellschaft Reederei Norden-Frisia* is a German public sector company.

MANAGEMENT President/CEO C U Stegmann, **Managing Director/CFO** Prok. Harms, **Technical Manager** Prok. de Vries.

ADDRESS Am Hafen 1, 26534 Norderney, Germany.

TELEPHONE *Administration & Reservations* +49 (0)4931 987 0.

INTERNET *Email* info@reederei-frisia.de ***Website*** www.reederei-frisia.de *(German)*

ROUTES OPERATED Car Ferries & Passenger Ferries Norddeich (Germany) - Norderney (German Frisian Islands) (1 hr; ***FRISIA I, FRISIA III, FRISIA IV, FRISIA VI***; up to 15 per day), Norddeich - Juist (German Frisian Islands) (1 hr 20 mins; **FRISIA II, FRISIA VII**; up to 15 per day). **Excursion Vessels (FRISIA IX, FRISIA X, WAPPEN VON NORDENEY**; varies).

1	FRISIA I	1020t	70	12.3k	63.7m	1500P	53C	-	BA	DE	7018604
2	FRISIA II	1125t	78	12.0k	63.3m	1340P	53C	-	BA	DE	7723974
3	FRISIA III	1786t	15	12.0k	74.3m	1342P	58C	-	BA	DE	9732450
4	FRISIA IV	1574t	02	12.0k	71.7m	1342P	58C	-	BA	DE	9246839
5	FRISIA VI	768t	68	12.0k	54.9m	1096P	35C	-	BA	DE	8827179
6F	FRISIA VII	363t	84	10.0k	53.0m	12P	30C	-	BA	DE	8891807
7F	FRISIA VIII	581t	10	10.0k	54,5m	12P	35C	-	BA	DE	9578127
8p	FRISIA IX	571t	80	11.0k	57.0m	785P	0C	-	-	DE	7924310
9p	FRISIA X	187t	72	12.0k	36.3m	290P	0C	-	-	DE	7222308
10p	FRISIA XI	105t	69	12.0k	35.4m	940P	0C	-	-	DE	8137237
11p	WAPPEN VON JUIST	54t	68	10.0k	20.2m	80P	0C	-	-	DE	-

FRISIA I, FRISIA II, FRISIA VI Built by Jos L Meyer Werft, Papenburg, Germany for *Reederei Norden-Frisia*. Passenger capacities relate to the summer season. Capacity is reduced during the winter.

FRISIA III Built by Cassen-Werft, Emden, Germany.

FRISIA IV Built by Schiffswerft und Maschinenfabrik Cassens GmbH, Emden, Germany for *Reederei Norden-Frisia* to replace the FRISIA VIII.

FRISIA VII Built by Schlömer Werft, Oldersum, Germany for *Reederei Norden-Frisia*. Conveys ro-ro freight to Norderney and Juist.

FRISIA VIII Built by Sietas Werft, Hamburg, Germany for AG Reederei Norden-Frisia. Conveys ro-ro freight to Norderney and Juist.

FRISIA IX, FRISIA X Built by Schiffswerft Julius Diedrich GmbH & Co. KG, Oldersum, Germany for *Reederei Norden-Frisia*. The FRISIA IX was built to convey 9 cars at the bow end but is now used in passenger-only mode. These ships are generally used for excursions.

FRISIA XI Built by Julius Diedrich Schiffswerft, Odersum, Germany as the BALTRUM IV for *Baltrum-Linie* of Germany. In November 1982 sold to *Wyker Dampfschiffs-Reederei* and renamed the RÜM HART. In March 2014 sold to *Reederei Norden-Frisia*. In October renamed to FRISIA XI.

WAPPEN VON JUIST Built by Lübbe Voss-Werft, Westerende, Germany for private owner. Sold in April 2019 to *AG Reederei Norden-Frisia* subsidy *Cassen Tours GmbH*, Norderney. Generally used for excursions.

Under Construction

12	FRISIA V	1790t	22	12.0k	74.3m	1338P	58C	-	BA	DE	9886122

FRISIA V Under construction by Pella Sietas Werft, Hamburg. To operate on the Norddeich-Norderney service. A sister vessel of the FRISIA III.

POLFERRIES

THE COMPANY *Polferries* is the trading name of *Polska Zegluga Baltycka SA (Polish Baltic Shipping Company)*, a Polish state-owned company.

MANAGEMENT President Piotr Redmerski.

ADDRESS ul Portowa 41, 78-100 Kolobrzeg, Poland.

TELEPHONE Administration & Reservations +48 22 230 2222.

INTERNET Email info@polferries.pl **Website** www.polferries.pl *(Polish, Danish, English, German, Swedish)*

ROUTES OPERATED Świnoujście - Ystad (7 hrs; **BALTIVIA, CRACOVIA, MAZOVIA**; up to 3 per day), Gdańsk - Nynäshamn (Sweden) (18 hrs; **NOVA STAR, WAWEL**; up to 6 per week).

1	BALTIVIA	17790t	81	19.0k	146.9m	250P	30C	80L	BA	BS	7931997
2	CRACOVIA	25028t	02	22.8k	180.0m	550P	-	150T	BA	BS	9237242
3	MAZOVIA	25996t	96	21.0k	168.0m	200P	-	154T	BA2	BS	9010814
4	NOVA STAR	27744t	11	19.0k	162.0m	1215P	400C	90L	A	BS	9462067
5	WAWEL	25318t	80	19.0k	163.9m	900P	550C	75L	A2	BS	7814462

BALTIVIA Built as the SAGA STAR by Fartygsentreprenader AB, Kalmar, Sweden for *TT-Saga-Line* and, from 1982, used on freight services between Travemünde and Trelleborg/Malmö. (Originally ordered by *Rederi AB Svea* as the SAGALAND). In 1989 sold to *Cie Meridionale* of France, renamed the GIROLATA and used on *SNCM* (later *CMR*) services in the Mediterranean. In 1993 she was chartered back to *TT-Line*, resumed her original name and was used on the Travemünde - Trelleborg service. Following delivery of the ROBIN HOOD and the NILS DACKE in 1995, she was transferred to the Rostock - Trelleborg route. In July 1997 she was purchased by *TT-Line* and in 1998 passenger facilities were completely renovated to full ro-pax format; following the delivery of the TOM SAWYER she was transferred back to the Travemünde - Trelleborg route, operating additional freight sailings. Briefly transferred back to Rostock - Trelleborg when the charter of the TT-TRAVELLER ended. Withdrawn in 2002, sold to *Transmanche Ferries* and renamed the DIEPPE. In 2006 replaced by the SEVEN SISTERS, sold to *Polferries*, renamed the BALTIVIA and, in 2007, placed on the Gdańsk - Nynäshamn route. In February 2013 transferred to the Świnoujście – Ystad service.

CRACOVIA Built as the MURILLO by Astilleros Españoles SA, Seville, Spain for *Trasmediterranea* of Spain. Used mainly on the service between Cadiz and Canary Islands. In June 2014 sold to *Bulgaria West Port* of Bulgaria and renamed the DRUJBA. She operated between Bourgas, Bulgaria, Batumi (Georgia) and Novorossiysk (Russia). In March 2017 sold to *Polferries* and, in June 2017, renamed the CRACOVIA. In September 2017 introduced onto the Świnoujście - Ystad route.

MAZOVIA Built as the GOTLAND by Pt Dok Kodja Bahri, Kodja, Indonesia for *Rederi AB Gotland* for charter. In 1997 briefly chartered to *Tor Line* and then to *Nordic Trucker Line*, to operate between Oxelösund and St Petersburg (a ro-ro freight service). In June 1997 she was chartered to *SeaWind Line*, enabling a twice-daily passenger service to be operated. In late 1997 she was sold to *Finnlines* and renamed the FINNARROW. She started operating twice weekly between Helsinki and Travemünde. During Summer 1998 she was transferred to *FinnLink*; a bow door was fitted and she was modified to allow for two-level loading. In 2003 transferred to *Nordö Link*. In 2005 returned to *FinnLink*. In 2006 transferred to *Finnlines Nordö Link* again. In 2007 chartered to *Stena Line* to operate between Karlskrona and Gdynia. In December 2011 transferred to the Hoek van Holland - Killingholme route. In March 2011 returned to *Finnlines* and placed on the Travemünde - Malmö service. In October 2011 transferred to *FinnLink*. Between January and March 2013 chartered to *Stena Line* to cover Irish Sea routes during the refit period but withdrawn from service prematurely following an accident. In April 2013 chartered to *Grimaldi Line* of Italy for five years and renamed the EUROFERRY BRINDISI. In October 2014 sold to the *Grimaldi Group* of Italy. In November sold to *Polferries* and renamed the MAZOVIA. Entered service in June 2015 on the Świnoujście - Ystad service.

NOVA STAR Built as the NORMAN LEADER by St Marine Shipyard, Singapore for *LD Lines* of France. However, delivery was not taken as she did not meet the design specification. She was registered to *Singapore Technologies Marine* and remained laid up until February 2014 when she was chartered to *Nova Star Cruises* of Canada and renamed the NOVA STAR. She operated between Portland, Maine USA and Yarmouth, Nova Scotia, Canada. In October 2015 she was arrested in Portland due to unpaid bills and the service ceased. In February 2016 she was chartered to *Inter Shipping* of Morocco and placed on their Algeciras (Spain) - Tangier Morocco service. In November 2017 chartered to *Polferries* and sub-charted to *Inter Shipping* until February 2018 when she was taken over by *Polferries*. She began operating between Gdańsk and Nynäshamn in September 2018. In October 2019 purchased by *Polferries*.

WAWEL Built as the SCANDINAVIA by Kockums Varvet AB, Malmö, Sweden for *Rederi AB Nordö* of Sweden. After service in the Mediterranean for *UMEF*, she was, in 1981, sold to *SOMAT* of Bulgaria, renamed the TZAREVETZ and used on *Medlink* services between Bulgaria and the Middle East, later on other routes. In 1986 she was chartered to *Callitzis* of Greece for a service

Max *(Frank Lose)*

Akranes *(Frank Lose)*

between Italy and Greece. In 1988 she was sold to *Sealink*, re-registered in The Bahamas and renamed the FIESTA. She was then chartered to *OT Africa Line*. During Autumn 1989 she was rebuilt at Bremerhaven to convert her for passenger use and in March 1990 she was renamed the FANTASIA and placed on the Dover - Calais service. Later in 1990 she was renamed the STENA FANTASIA. In 1998 transferred to *P&O Stena Line*. In 1999 she was renamed the P&OSL CANTERBURY. In 2002, following *Stena Line's* pulling out of the joint company, she was renamed the PO CANTERBURY. In Spring 2003 replaced by the PRIDE OF CANTERBURY and laid up at Dunkerque. Later in the year sold to *GA Ferries* and renamed the ALKMINI A. In 2004 moved to Greece and, after a partial rebuild (including the welding up of the bow door) placed on the Igoumenitsa – Brindisi route. Later in 2004 sold to *Polferries* and renamed the WAWEL; rebuilt to increase the number of cabins. In 2005 placed on the Świnoujście – Ystad service. In May 2015 transferred to the Gdańsk - Nynäshamn route.

Under Construction

10	NEWBUILDING 1	39599t	24	23.0k	206.6m	650P	150L	BA	IT	-
11	NEWBUILDING 2	-	25	19.0k	195.6m	400P	250L	BA	-	-

NEWBUILDING 1 Under construction by CN Visentini, Donada, Italy. To be chartered to *Polferries*.

NEWBUILDING 2 Hybrid ferry (LNG/battery pack) under construction for *Polskie Promy* of Poland by Remontowa Shipbuilding, Gdańsk, Poland. To be chartered to *Polferries*.

PRAAMID

THE COMPANY *Praamid.ee* is the trading name of the ferry operation of the *TS Laevad*, a company owned by the Port of Tallinn (majority owned by Republic of Estonia). It took over the operation of services of regular ferry traffic between Estonia's major islands (Saaremaa, Hiiumaa) and the mainland according to the contract with the state in October 2016.

ADDRESS Sadama 25/2, Tallinn 10111, Estonia.

TELEPHONE +372 618 1310.

INTERNET Email info@praamid.ee **Website** www.praamid.ee *(Estonia, English)*

ROUTES OPERATED Virtsu-Kuivastu (Saaremaa) (28 mins; **PIRET, REGULA, TÕLL**; up to 32 per day), Rohuküla - Heltermaa (Hiiumaa) (1 hr 15 mins; **LEIGER, TIIU**; up to 11 per day).

1	LEIGER	4987t	16	10.0k	114.0m	700P	150C	-	BA	EE	9762675
2	PIRET	4987t	17	10.0k	114.0m	700P	150C	-	BA	EE	9762663
3	REGULA	3774t	71	12.5k	71.2m	580P	105C	20L	BA2	EE	7051058
4	TIIU	4987t	17	10.0k	114.0m	700P	150C	-	BA	EE	9762687
5	TÕLL	4987t	17	10.0k	114.0m	700P	150C	-	BA	EE	9762651

LEIGER, TIIU Built by Sefine Shipyard, Yalova, Turkey Vessels are Diesel – Electric propulsion with readiness for future LNG-fuel conversion and operation.

PIRET, TÕLL Built by Remontowa Shipyard, Gdańsk, Poland. Vessels are Diesel – Electric propulsion with readiness for future LNG-fuel conversion and operation. Conversion of the TÕLL into Estonia's first environmentally friendly hybrid ship by installing enhanced battery banks took place in 2020. These battery banks with a combined capacity of 600 kWh allow the TÕLL to run her diesel generators in optimum efficiency range and contribute grid power to propulsion.

REGULA Built by Jos L Meyer, Papenburg, Germany for *Stockholms Rederi AB Svea* of Sweden for the service between Helsingborg and Helsingør operated by *Linjebuss International AB* (a subsidiary company). In 1980 she was sold to *Scandinavian Ferry Lines*. During Winter 1984/85 she was rebuilt to increase vehicle and passenger capacity. In 1991 ownership was transferred to *SweFerry* and operations to *ScandLines* on the Helsingborg - Helsingør service. Ownership later transferred to *Scandlines AB*. In 1997 sold to *Saaremaa Laevakompanii*. In October 2016 chartered to *TS Laevad*, and in December 2016 purchased by them. Following delivery of new vessels, she was retained as spare vessel. However, in summer 2018-2019 she was used on regular service and the MERCANDIA VIII of *HH Ferries* (now *ForSea*) was chartered as spare vessel.

SAMSØ REDERI

THE COMPANY *Samsø Rederi* is a Danish public sector company owned by the Samsø Municipality.

MANAGEMENT Managing Director Carsten Kruse.

ADDRESS Sælvig 64, 8305 Samsø, Denmark.

TELEPHONE Administration and Reservations + 45 70 22 59 00.

INTERNET Email tilsamsoe@samsoe.dk **Website** www.tilsamsoe.dk *(Danish, German, English).*

ROUTE OPERATED Vehicle Ferry Sælvig (Samsø) - Hou (Jylland) (1 hr; ***PRINSESSE ISABELLA***; up to 7 per day), **Passenger Fast Ferry** Sælvig (Samsø) - Århus (Jylland) (1 hr; ***LILLEØRE***; up to 5 per day).

1p	LILLEØRE	338t	20	29.5k	35.0m	296P	0C	0T	-	DK	9895783
2	PRINSESSE ISABELLA	5478t	15	9.9k	100.0m	600P	160C	16T	BA	DK	9692806

LILLEØRE Built by AFAI Shipyard, Guangzhou, China to an Incat design. 75 bicycles can be carried but no vehicles.

PRINSESSE ISABELLA Built as the SAMSØ by Stocznia Remontowa, Gdańsk, Poland. In June 2015 renamed the PRINSESSE ISABELLA.

SCANDLINES

THE COMPANY In 2007, the owners of *Scandlines AG*, the Danish Ministry of Transport and Energy and Deutsche Bahn AG, decided to sell their shares. The new owner was a consortium of the 3i Group (UK), Allianz Capital Partners GmbH (Germany) (40% of the shares each) and *Deutsche Seereederei GmbH* (Germany) (20% of the shares). The company was subsequently transformed into a private limited company and traded under the name Scandlines GmbH, uniting the companies *Scandlines Deutschland GmbH* and *Scandlines Danmark A/S*. With *Deutsche Seereederei GmbH* selling its shares in *Scandlines GmbH* in 2010, 3i and Allianz Capital Partners held 50% of the shares each. During 2012 *Stena Line* took over the Travemünde - Ventspils, Travemünde - Liepaja and Nynäshamn - Ventspils routes, took full control of the joint routes - Rostock - Trelleborg and Sassnitz - Trelleborg services and took over the vessels used. The freight-only route between Rostock and Hanko passed to *SOL*. In November 2013 3i Group purchased Allianz Capital Partners' share. In March 2016 3i sold a majority share in the company to First Sentier Investments and Federated Hermes.

MANAGEMENT CEO Søren Poulsgaard Jensen, **CFO** Per Johannesen Madsen, **CFO** Michael Guldmann Petersen.

ADDRESS Havneholmen 25, 8., 1561 Copenhagen V, Denmark.

TELEPHONE Administration & Reservations *Denmark* +45 33 15 15 15, *Germany* **+49 (0)381-**77 88 77 66.

INTERNET Email servcecenter.germany@scandlines.com **Website** www.scandlines.com *(Danish, English, German, Polish, Swedish)*

ROUTES OPERATED Rødby (Lolland, Denmark) - Puttgarden (Fehmarn,Germany) (45 mins; ***DEUTSCHLAND, KRONPRINS FREDERIK, PRINS RICHARD, PRINSESSE BENEDIKTE, SCHLESWIG-HOLSTEIN***; half-hourly), Gedser (Falster, Denmark) - Rostock (Germany) (2 hours; ***BERLIN, COPENHAGEN***; every 2 hours).

1	BERLIN	22319t	16	21k	169.5m	1300P	460C	96L	BA2	DE	9587855
2	COPENHAGEN	22319t	16	21k	169.5m	1300P	460C	96L	BA2	DK	9587867
3	DEUTSCHLAND	15187t	97	18.5k	142.0m	1200P	364C	30Lr	BA2	DE	9151541

4	KRONPRINS FREDERIK	16071t	81	17k	152.0m	133P	40L	46T	BA	DE	7803205
5	PRINS RICHARD	14822t	97	18.5k	142.0m	1140P	364C	36Lr	BA2	DK	9144419
6	PRINSESSE BENEDIKTE	14822t	97	18.5k	142.0m	1140P	364C	36Lr	BA2	DK	9144421
7	SCHLESWIG-HOLSTEIN	15187t	97	18.5k	142.0m	1200P	364C	30Lr	BA2	DE	9151539

BERLIN Partly built by Volkswerft Stralsund, Stralsund, Germany for *Scandlines* to operate on the Gedser - Rostock route. The propulsion system allows for adaption to LNG. In March 2014, purchased by *Scandferries ApS* of Denmark (an associated company) and towed to Fayard Shipyard, Odense to be completed with an almost completely new superstructure. Her engines were also modified straight diesel to diesel-electric hybrid in order to reduce CO2 emissions. In May 2016 chartered to *Scandlines* and entered service on the Gedser - Rostock route. The vessels are tailor-made for the route to optimise for shallow waters. Thus, the shape of the ship hull contributes to lowering fuel consumption.

COPENHAGEN As the BERLIN. Entered service in December 2016. In May 2020, retrofitted with a custom-made Norsepower rotor sail, which harnesses wind power and provides supplementary propulsion while reducing emissions. With a weight of 42 tonnes, the rotor sail unit measures 30 metres in height and 5 metres in diameter.

DEUTSCHLAND Train/vehicle ferry built by Van der Giessen de Noord, Krimpen aan den IJssel, Rotterdam, The Netherlands for *DFO* for the Puttgarden - Rødby service. During Winter 2003/04 a new hoistable deck was added for cars by Neptun Yard Rostock, (Germany). In 2014, converted to hybrid service combining traditional diesel power with electric battery power based on large-scale use of an onboard hybrid propulsion system which stores energy in a battery package, reducing the ferries' CO2 emissions by up to 15%. In 2020, fitted with new pull thrusters, which allow a more homogeneous water flow, entailing less noise and vibration and reducing CO2 emissions by a further 10-15%.

KRONPRINS FREDERIK Train/vehicle ferry built by Nakskov Skibsværft A/S, Nakskov, Denmark for *DSB* for the Nyborg - Korsør service. Withdrawn in 1997. After conversion to a car/lorry ferry, she was transferred to the Gedser - Rostock route (no rail facilities). In March 2017, following modifications, transferred to the Rødby - Puttgarden route to provide extra capacity for lorry traffic. Also serves as reserve vessel on Gedser - Rostock service.

PRINS RICHARD, PRINSESSE BENEDIKTE Train/vehicle ferries, built by Ørskov Staalskibsværft A/S, Frederikshavn, Denmark for *Scandlines A/S* for the Rødby - Puttgarden service. During Winter 2003/04 a new hoistable deck was added for cars by Neptun Yard Rostock, (Germany). In 2013-4, converted to hybrid service combining traditional diesel power with electric battery power. New pull thrusters, which allow a more homogeneous water flow, entailing less noise and vibration and reducing CO2 emissions by a further 10-15% were fitted in 2021/22.

SCHLESWIG-HOLSTEIN Train/vehicle ferry built by Van der Giessen de Noord, Krimpen aan den IJssel, Rotterdam, The Netherlands for *DFO* for the Puttgarden - Rødby service. During Winter 2003/04 a new hoistable deck was added for cars by Neptun Yard Rostock, (Germany). In 2014, converted to hybrid service combining traditional diesel power with electric battery power. In late 2019, fitted with new pull thrusters, which allow a more homogeneous water flow, entailing less noise and vibration and reducing CO2 emissions by a further 10-15%.

Under Construction

8	NEWBUILDING	14021t	24	18.0k	147.4m	140P	-	70L	BA	DK	9966685

NEWBUILDING Under construction by Cemre Shipyard, Turkey. Hybrid diesel/electric. Will be used primarily to convey freight traffic but will also be used as a backup to the other vessels.

SMYRIL LINE

THE COMPANY *Smyril Line* is a Faroe Islands company.

MANAGEMENT Adm. Director Rúni Vang Poulsen, **Accounting and Department Manager** Nina Djurhuus.

ADDRESS Yviri við Strond 1, 110 Tórshavn, Faroe Islands.

TELEPHONE Administration (Faroes) +298 34 59 00, **Reservations (Denmark)** +45 96 55 85 00.

INTERNET Email office@smyrilline.com **Website** www.smyrilline.fo *(English, Danish, Dutch, Faroese, French, German, Icelandic, Norwegian, Swedish)*

ROUTES OPERATED *Winter/Early Spring* Tórshavn (Faroes) - Hirtshals (Denmark) (36 hrs; **NORRÖNA**; 1 per week), *Spring/Early Summer/Autumn* Tórshavn - Hirtshals (36 hrs; **NORRÖNA**; 1 per week), Tórshavn - Seyðisfjördur (Iceland) (19 hrs; **NORRÖNA**; 1 per week), **Summer** Tórshavn - Hirtshals (Denmark) (30 hrs; **NORRÖNA**; 2 per week), Tórshavn - Seyðisfjördur (Iceland) (19 hrs; **NORRÖNA**; 2 per week). *Freight services* Tórshavn - Scrabster (UK) - Hirtshals (Denmark) - St. Petersburg (Russia) (**EYSTNES**, **HVITANES**), Thorlakshöfn (Iceland) - Hirtshals (Denmark) - Tórshavn (**MISTRAL**), Thorlakshöfn (Iceland) - Tórshavn - Rotterdam (**MYKINES**), Thorlakshøfn, (Iceland) - Tórshavn - Rotterdam (**AKRANES**).

1F	AKRANES	10585t	96	20.0k	138.8m	12P	-	105T	A2	F0	9160774
2F	EYSTNES	4610t	81	15.0k	102.2m	0P	-	24T	AS	F0	7922166
3F	HVITANES	4636t	80	12.0k	77.3m	0P	-	14T	AS	F0	7915541
4F	MISTRAL	10471t	98	22.0k	153.5m	12P	-	112T	A	FI	9183788
5F	MYKINES	18979t	96	20.0k	138.5m	12P	1452C	105T	A2	F0	9121998
6	NORRÖNA	36976t	03	21.0k	164.0m	1482P	800C	134T	BA	F0	9227390

AKRANES Built as the SERENADEN by Umoe Sterkoder AS, Kristiansund, Norway for *Rederi AB Engship* of Finland and chartered to *Transfennica*. In 2006 *Rederi AB Engship* was taken over by *Rettig Group Bore*. In 2007 converted at COSCO Shipyard, Nantong, China to add a garage on top of the weather deck, renamed AUTO BANK and placed on long-term charter to *UECC*. Generally used on the Baltic or Iberian services. In December 2016 converted back to a conventional ro-ro freighter by Öresundwerft, Landskrona, Sweden and renamed the BORE BANK. Chartered to *Transfennica*. In December 2019 sold to *Smyril Line* and renamed the AKRANES.

EYSTNES Con-ro vessel (only the main deck can take trailers) built as the COMETA by Fosen Mekaniske Verksteder, Rissa, Norway for *Nor-Cargo*. Until 2010 she operated for *Sea-Cargo* between Norwegian ports and Immingham; afterwards she operated on *Nor-Cargo* Norwegian domestic services. In September 2015 sold to *Smyril Line* and renamed the EYSTNES.

HVITANES Con-ro vessel (only the main deck can take trailers) built as the TANAGER by Bergen Mekaniske Verksteder, Bergen, Norway for *NorCargo* of Norway. In September 2015 sold to *Smyril Line* and renamed the HVITANES.

MISTRAL Built by J J Sietas KG, Hamburg, Germany for *Godby Shipping AB* of Finland. Chartered to *Transfennica*. In 2003 chartered to *UPM-Kymmene Oy* of Finland and operated between Rauma and Santander. In 2005 chartered to *Finnlines*. Until the end of 2007 used on a Helsinki - Hamina - Zeebrugge service only available northbound for general traffic. From January 2008 operated on *UPM-Kymmene Seaways'* service from Hamina to Lübeck, Amsterdam and Tilbury. In June 2013 charter ended. During the ensuing period she undertook several short charters. In October 2014 chartered to *P&O Ferries* as second ship on the Zeebrugge - Middlesbrough (Teesport) service; she has also operated between Tilbury and Zeebrugge. In early June 2018 replaced by the ESTRADEN and at the end of the month sub-chartered to *Stena Line* to operate between Rotterdam and Harwich. In August 2018 returned to *P&O Ferries* and operated between Teesport and Rotterdam. In March 2019 moved to the Liverpool - Dublin route. In December 2019 charter ended. Chartered to *Balieria* of Spain and used on the 'Canary Bridge' Huelva-Tenerife-Las Palmas service until end of May. In August 2020 chartered to *Smyril Line*.

MYKINES Built as the TRANSGARD by Umoe Sterkoder, Kristiansund, Norway for *Bror Husell Chartering* of Finland for long-term charter to *Transfennica* and used between Rauma and Antwerpen and Hamina and Lübeck. Later chartered to *Finncarriers*. In 2005 she underwent conversion in Poland to add a garage on top of the original weather deck and was placed on long-term charter to *UECC*. She was generally used on the Baltic or Iberian services. In 2007 renamed AUTO BALTIC. In January 2016 chartered to *Flotta Suardiaz*. In April 2017 sold to *Smyril Line* to inaugurate a new service between Thorlakshofn (Iceland), Tórshavn and Rotterdam and renamed the MYKINES.

NORRÖNA Built by Flender Werft, Lübeck, Germany for *Smyril Line*, to replace the existing NORRÖNA. Originally due to enter service in Summer 2002, start of building was delayed by financing difficulties. She was to have been built at Flensburger Schiffbau-Gesellschaft, Flensburg, Germany, but delays in arranging finance led to change of shipyard.

STENA LINE

THE COMPANY *Stena Line Scandinavia AB* is a Swedish private sector company.

MANAGEMENT CEO Niclas Mårtensson, **Chief Operating Officer** Peter Arvidsson.

ADDRESS Danmarksterminalen, 405 19 Göteborg, Sweden.

TELEPHONE Administration +46 (0)31-85 80 00.

INTERNET Email info@stenaline.com **Website** www.stenaline.com *(various)*

ROUTES OPERATED Passenger Ferries Göteborg (Sweden) - Frederikshavn (Denmark) (3 hrs 15 mins; **STENA DANICA, STENA JUTLANDICA, STENA VINGA**; up to 6 per day), Göteborg - Kiel (Germany) (14 hrs; **STENA GERMANICA, STENA SCANDINAVICA**; 1 per day), Halmstad (Sweden) - Grenaa (Denmark) (4 hrs 35 mins; **STENA NAUTICA**; 2 per day), Karlskrona (Sweden) - Gdynia (Poland) (10 hrs 30 mins; **STENA ESTELLE, STENA SPIRIT, STENA VISION**; 2 per day), Rostock (Germany) - Trelleborg (Sweden) (7 hrs); **MECKLENBURG-VORPOMMERN, SKÅNE**; 3/4 per day), Travemünde (Germany) - Karlskrona - Liepaja (Latvia) (20 hrs; **STENA LIVIA, STENA FLAVIA**; 6 per week), Stockholm (Norvik Port) – Ventspils (Latvia) (12 hrs; **STENA BALTICA, STENA SCANDICA**; 12 per week), Stockholm (Norvik Port) - Hanko (Finland) (13 hrs; **URD**, 3 per week).

1	MECKLENBURG-VORPOMMERN	36185t	96	22.0k	199.9m	600P	445C	230Tr	A2	SE	9131797
2	SKÅNE	42755t	98	21.0k	200.2m	600P	520C	240Tr	AS2	SE	9133915
3	STENA BALTICA	35456t	05	23.5k	222.1m	970P	277C	200T	A	DK	9329851
4»•	STENA CARISMA	8631t	97	40.0k	88.0m	900P	210C	-	A	SE	9127760
5	STENA DANICA	28727t	83	19.5k	154.9m	2274P	555C	120T	BAS2	SE	7907245
6	STENA ESTELLE	48035t	22	22k	239.7m	1200P	300C	220L	BA2	CY	9862994
7	STENA FLAVIA	26904t	08	24.0k	186.5m	852P	185C	120L	A	DK	9417919
8	STENA GERMANICA	44372t	01	22.0k	240.1m	900P	-	250L	BA	SE	9145176
9F	STENA GOTHICA	13144t	82	18.0k	171.0m	186P	-	104T	AS	DK	7826867
10	STENA JUTLANDICA	29691t	96	21.5k	183.7m	1500P	550C	156T	BAS2	SE	9125944
11	STENA LIVIA	26500t	08	23.5k	186.5m	800P	185C	120L	A	CY	9420423
12	STENA NAUTICA	19504t	86	19.4k	134.0m	700P	330C	70T	BA2	SE	8317954
13	STENA NORDICA	24206t	01	25.7k	169.8m	405P	375C	90L	BA2	BS	9215505
14	STENA SCANDICA	35456t	05	23.5k	222.1m	970P	277C	200T	A	DK	9329849
15	STENA SCANDINAVICA	55050t	03	22.0k	240.1m	900P	-	260L	BA	SE	9235517
16	STENA SPIRIT	39169t	88	20.0k	175.4m	2400P	550C	120T	BAS2	BS	7907661
17	STENA VINGA	13906t	05	18.5k	124.9m	400P	342C	106T	A	SE	9323699
18	STENA VISION	39178t	87	20.0k	175.4m	2400P	550C	120T	BAS2	CY	7907659
19	URD	13144t	81	17.5k	171.0m	186P	-	104T	AS	DK	7826855

MECKLENBURG-VORPOMMERN Train/vehicle ferry built by Schichau Seebeckwerft, Bremerhaven, Germany for *DFO* for the Rostock - Trelleborg service. During Winter 2002/03 modified to increase freight capacity and reduce passenger capacity. In September 2012 sold to *Stena Line*. In July 2021 transferred to the Swedish flag.

SKÅNE Train/vehicle ferry built by Astilleros Españoles, Cadiz, Spain for an American trust and chartered to *Scandlines*. She is used on the Trelleborg - Rostock service.

STENA BALTICA Built as the MERSEY VIKING by CN Visentini, Donada, Italy for *Levantina Trasporti* of Italy. Chartered to *NorseMerchant Ferries* and placed on the Birkenhead - Belfast route. In 2008 sold to *Norfolkline*, then resold to *Epic Shipping* and chartered back. In August

Stena Germanica *(Richard Seville)*

Stena Estelle *(Stena Line)*

2010, following *Norfolkline's* purchase by *DFDS*, she was renamed the MERSEY SEAWAYS. Between January and July 2011 she was operated by *Stena Line Irish Sea Ferries*, a 'stand-alone' company pending consideration of a take-over by *Stena Line* by the UK and Irish competition authorities. In July 2011 the take-over was confirmed and in August 2011 she was renamed the STENA MERSEY. In April 2012 she sold to *Stena RoRo* and chartered back by *Stena Line*. In February 2021 replaced by the STENA EMBLA sent to the Sedef Shipyard in Tuzla, Turkey to be lengthened by 36m. In February 2021 renamed the STENA BALTICA and in autumn 2021 placed on the Stockholm (Norvik Port) – Ventspils route.

STENA CARISMA Westamarin HSS 900 craft built at Kristiansand, Norway for *Stena Line* for the Göteborg - Frederikshavn service. Work on a sister vessel, approximately 30% completed, was ceased. She has not operated since 2013.

STENA DANICA Built by Chantiers du Nord et de la Méditerranée, Dunkerque, France for *Stena Line* for the Göteborg - Frederikshavn service.

STENA ESTELLE, Lengthened vessel of E-Flexer model built by CMI Jinling Weihai Shipyard, Jinling, China for *Stena RoRo*. Operates for *Stena Line* between Karlskrona and Gdynia.

STENA FLAVIA Built by CN Visentini, Porto Viro, Italy for *Epic Shipping* of the UK. Launched as the WATLING STREET. On delivery, chartered to *ISCOMAR* of Spain and renamed the PILAR DEL MAR. In 2009 laid up until February 2010 when she was chartered to *Acciona Trasmediterranea* of Spain and operated between Barcelona and Tangiers. Later that month, chartered to *T-Link* and resumed the name WATLING STREET. In May 2011 chartered to *Scandlines* and placed on the Travemünde - Ventspils service. In April 2012, sold to *Stena RoRo*; she continued to be chartered to *Scandlines*. In September 2012 charter transferred to *Stena Line*. In April 2013 renamed the STENA FLAVIA. She operated mainly between Nynäshamn and Ventspils. To be transferred to the Travemünde - Liepaja route.

STENA GERMANICA Ro-pax ferry built as the STENA HOLLANDICA by Astilleros Españoles, Cadiz, Spain for *Stena RoRo* and chartered to *Stena Line BV* to operate between Hoek van Holland and Harwich. In 2007 lengthened by 50m at Lloyd Werft, Bremerhaven and passenger capacity increased to 900. Between May and August 2010 refurbished at Gdańsk and had 100 additional cabins added. At the end of August entered service on the Göteborg - Kiel route, renamed the STENA GERMANICA III. In September, after the previous STENA GERMANICA had been renamed the STENA VISION, she was renamed the STENA GERMANICA.

STENA GOTHICA Built as the LUCKY RIDER by Nuovi Cantieri Apuania S.P.A., Marina De Carrara, Italy, a ro-ro freight ferry, for *Delpa Maritime* of Greece. In 1985 she was acquired by *Stena Line* and renamed the STENA DRIVER. Later that year she was acquired by *Sealink British Ferries* and renamed the SEAFREIGHT FREEWAY to operate freight-only services between Dover and Dunkerque. In 1988 she was sold to *SOMAT* of Bulgaria for use on *Medlink* services in the Mediterranean and renamed the SERDICA. In 1990 she was sold and renamed the NORTHERN HUNTER. In 1991 she was sold to *Blæsbjerg* of Denmark, renamed the ARKA MARINE and chartered to *DSB*. She was then converted into a ro-pax vessel, renamed the ASK and introduced onto the Århus - Kalundborg service. Purchased by *Scandlines A/S* of Denmark in 1997. In 1999 she was, after some modification, transferred to *Scandlines Euroseabridge* and placed on the Travemünde - Klaipėda route. In 2000 she was transferred to the Rostock - Liepaja route. Lengthened by 20m in 2001 and, in late 2001, chartered to *Nordö Link* to operate between Travemünde and Malmö. In late 2002 replaced by the FINNARROW and returned to *Scandlines*. She was transferred to the Rostock - Trelleborg route whilst the MECKLENBURG-VORPOMMERN was being rebuilt. She was then transferred to the Kiel - Klaipėda route. In 2003 chartered to *Scandlines AB* to operate on the Trelleborg - Travemünde route. In April 2005 the charter ended and she returned to *Scandlines AG*. Initially she was due to replace the FELLOW on the Nynäshamn – Ventspils route during her annual refit. In Autumn 2005 moved to the Rostock - Ventspils route. In January 2009 moved to the Nynäshamn – Ventspils route. In January 2011 moved to the Travemünde - Liepaja route. In May 2011 laid up. In November introduced as second vessel. In September 2012 sold to *Stena Line*. In September 2015 moved to the Göteborg - Frederikshavn freight service and renamed the STENA GOTHICA. In September to be moved to the Travemünde - Liepaja route.

STENA JUTLANDICA Train/vehicle 'ro-pax' vessel built by Van der Giessen de Noord, Krimpen aan den IJssel, Rotterdam, The Netherlands for *Stena Line* to operate between Göteborg and Frederikshavn. She was launched as the STENA JUTLANDICA III and renamed on entry into service.

STENA LIVIA Built as the NORMAN VOYAGER by CN Visentini, Porto Viro, Italy for *Epic Shipping* of the UK and chartered to *LD Lines*. Operated between Le Havre and Portsmouth and Le Havre and Rosslare. In September 2009 sub-chartered to *Celtic Link Ferries*. Initially operated between Cherbourg and Portsmouth and Cherbourg and Rosslare but the Portsmouth service was abandoned in November 2009. In October 2011 returned to *LD Lines* and placed on the St Nazaire - Gijon route. In November moved to the Portsmouth - Le Havre service and, following the establishment of the joint *LD Lines/DFDS* venture, the charter was transferred to *DFDS*. In April 2012 sold to *Stena RoRo*; she continued to be chartered by *DFDS*. In March 2014 chartered to *Brittany Ferries* and placed on the new 'économie' services between Portsmouth and Le Havre and Portsmouth and Santander. Renamed the ÉTRETAT. In April 2021 charter ended. Chartered to *Stena Line* and renamed the STENA LIVIA. Placed on the Nynäshamn – Ventspils route. To be transferred to the Travemünde - Leipaja service.

STENA NAUTICA Built as the NIELS KLIM by Nakskov Skibsværft A/S, Nakskov, Denmark for *DSB (Danish State Railways)* for their service between Århus (Jylland) and Kalundborg (Sjælland). In 1990 she was purchased by *Stena Rederi* of Sweden and renamed the STENA NAUTICA. In 1992 she was chartered to *B&I Line*, renamed the ISLE OF INNISFREE and introduced onto the Rosslare - Pembroke Dock service, replacing the MUNSTER (8093t, 1970). In 1993 she was transferred to the Dublin - Holyhead service. In early 1995 she was chartered to *Lion Ferry*. She was renamed the LION KING. In 1996 she was replaced by a new LION KING and renamed the STENA NAUTICA. During Summer 1996 she was chartered to *Transmediterranea* of Spain but returned to *Stena RoRo* in the autumn and remained laid up during 1997. In December 1997 she was chartered to *Stena Line* and placed on the Halmstad - Grenaa route. This route ended on 31st January 1999 and she was transferred to the Varberg - Grenaa route. During Winter 2001/02 she was rebuilt to heighten the upper vehicle deck and allow separate loading of vehicle decks; passenger capacity was reduced. On 16th February 2004 she was hit by the coaster JOANNA and holed. Returned to service at the end of May 2004 after repairs at Göteborg and Gdańsk.

STENA NORDICA Built as the EUROPEAN AMBASSADOR by Mitsubishi Heavy Industries, Shimonoseki, Japan for *P&O Irish Sea* for their Liverpool - Dublin service. Service transferred to from Liverpool to Mostyn in November 2001. Also operated between Dublin and Cherbourg once a week. In 2004 the Mostyn route closed and she was sold to *Stena RoRo*. Chartered to *Stena Line* to operate between Karlskrona and Gdynia and renamed the STENA NORDICA. In 2008 transferred to the Holyhead - Dublin service. In February 2015 replaced by the STENA SUPERFAST X and chartered to *DFDS*. She was renamed the MALO SEAWAYS and, in April 2015, placed on the Dover - Calais route. Withdrawn from traffic in February 2016 and laid up. In June 2016 charter ended. Renamed the STENA NORDICA and chartered to *GNV* of Italy to operate between Sicily and the Italian mainland. In January 2017 chartered to *Stena Line* and performed refit relief duties in the Irish Sea. In April placed on the Travemünde - Liepäja service. In October 2018 moved back to the Karlskrona - Gdynia route. In March 2019 replaced the STENA EUROPE on the Fishguard - Rosslare route for six months.

STENA SCANDICA Built as the LAGAN VIKING by CN Visentini, Donada, Italy for *Levantina Trasporti* of Italy. Chartered to *NorseMerchant Ferries* and placed on the Birkenhead - Belfast route. In 2008 sold to *Norfolkline*, then resold to *Epic Shipping* and chartered back. In August 2010, following *Norfolkline's* purchase by *DFDS*, she was renamed the LAGAN SEAWAYS. Between January and July 2011 she was operated by *Stena Line Irish Sea Ferries*, a 'stand-alone' company pending consideration of a take-over by *Stena Line* by the UK and Irish competition authorities. In July 2011 the take-over was confirmed and in August 2011 she was renamed the STENA LAGAN. In April 2012 she was sold to *Stena RoRo* and chartered back by *Stena Line*. In March 2020 replaced by the STENA EDDA and lengthened by 36m at the Sedef Shipyard in Tuzla, Turkey. In March 2021 renamed the STENA SCANDICA and in July placed on the Stockholm (Norvik Port) – Ventspils route.

STENA SCANDINAVICA Ro-pax vessel built by Hyundai Heavy Industries, Ulsan, South Korea, for *Stena RoRo*. Launched and delivered in January 2003 as the STENA BRITANNICA II. Chartered to *Stena Line* for use on the Hoek van Holland - Harwich service, replacing the 2000-built STENA BRITANNICA, now the FINNFELLOW of *FinnLink*. In March 2003 renamed the STENA BRITANNICA. In 2007 lengthened at Lloyd Werft, Bremerhaven. In September 2010 renamed the BRITANNICA. Between October 2010 and April 2011 refurbished and had 100 additional cabins added at Gdańsk. In April 2011 renamed the STENA SCANDINAVICA IV and entered service on the Göteborg - Kiel route. In May, after the previous STENA SCANDINAVICA had been renamed the STENA SPIRIT, she was renamed the STENA SCANDINAVICA.

STENA SPIRIT Built as the STENA SCANDINAVICA by Stocznia i Komuni Paryski, Gdynia, Poland for *Stena Line* for the Göteborg - Kiel service (launched as the STENA GERMANICA and names swapped with sister vessel before delivery). There were originally intended to be four vessels. Only two were delivered to *Stena Line*. The third (due to be called the STENA POLONICA) was sold by the builders as an unfinished hull to *Fred. Olsen Lines* of Norway and then resold to *ANEK* of Greece who had her completed at Perama and delivered as EL VENIZELOS for service between Greece and Italy. The fourth hull (due to be called the STENA BALTICA) was sold to *A Lelakis* of Greece and was to be rebuilt as a cruise ship to be called REGENT SKY; however, the project was never completed. The hull was broken up in 2004. During the summer period on some days, the vessel arriving in Göteborg overnight from Kiel operates a round trip to Frederikshavn before departing for Kiel the following evening. During Winter 1998/99 she was modified to increase freight capacity and reduce the number of cabins. In April 2011 replaced by the former STENA BRITANNICA (renamed the STENA SCANDINAVICA IV) and entered CityVarvet in Göteborg for refurbishment. In June 2011 she was renamed the STENA SPIRIT and, in July 2011, transferred to the Karlskrona - Gydnia route.

STENA VINGA Built as the HAMMERODDE by Merwede Shipyard, Hardinxveld-Giessendam, The Netherlands for *Bornholmstrafikken*. In Winter 2010 an additional vehicle deck was added for freight and some additional cabins. In November 2017 sold to *Stena RoRo* and chartered back. In September 2018 delivered to *Stena Line*, renamed the STENA VINGA and placed on the Göteborg - Frederikshavn service, replacing the STENA GOTHICA.

STENA VISION Built as the STENA GERMANICA by Stocznia im Lenina, Gdańsk, Poland for *Stena Line* for the Göteborg - Kiel service. During the summer period on some days, the vessel arriving in Göteborg overnight from Kiel operated a round trip to Frederikshavn before departing for Kiel that evening. During Winter 1998/99 modified to increase freight capacity and reduce the number of cabins. In August 2010 replaced by the former STENA HOLLANDICA (renamed the STENA GERMANICA III initially) and entered CityVarvet in Göteborg for refurbishment. In September she was renamed the STENA VISION and, in November, transferred to the Karlskrona - Gydnia route.

URD Built as the EASY RIDER by Nouvi Cantieri Aquania SpA, Venice, Italy, a ro-ro freight ferry, for *Delpa Maritime* of Greece and used on Mediterranean services. In 1985 she was acquired by *Sealink British Ferries* and renamed the SEAFREIGHT HIGHWAY to operate a freight-only service between Dover and Dunkerque. In 1988 she was sold to *SOMAT* of Bulgaria for use on *Medlink* services in the Mediterranean and renamed the BOYANA. In 1990 she was sold to *Blæsbjerg* of Denmark, renamed the AKTIV MARINE and chartered to *DSB*. In 1991 she was converted into a ro-pax vessel, renamed the URD and introduced onto the Århus - Kalundborg service. Purchased by *Scandlines* in 1997. Withdrawn at the end of May 1999 and, after modification, transferred to the *Balticum Seaways* (later *Scandlines Balticum Seaways*) Århus - Aabenraa - Klaipėda route. In 2001 lengthened and moved to the Rostock - Liepaja route. In Autumn 2005 this route became Rostock - Ventspils. Withdrawn from Rostock - Ventspils in November 2009. Vessel inaugurated new service Travemünde - Ventspils in January 2010. Replaced by the WATLING STREET in May 2011 and moved to the Travemünde - Liepaja route. In October 2012 sold to *Sol Dru A/S* (a subsidiary of *Swedish Orient Line*) and chartered to *Stena Line*. In August 2013 sold to *Stena Line*. In February 2022 placed on a new Stockholm (Norvik Port) - Hanko (Finland) service.

Under Construction

| 20 | STENA EBBA | 48035t | 22 | 22k | 239.7m | 1200P | 300C | 220L | BA2 | CY | 9863003 |

STENA EBBA Lengthened vessel of E-Flexer model built by CMI Jinling Weihai Shipyard, Jinling, China for *Stena RoRo*. To operate for *Stena Line* between Karlskrona and Gdynia. Expected December 2022.

STRANDFARASKIP LANDSINS

THE COMPANY *Strandfaraskip Landsins* is owned by the Faroe Islands Government.

ADDRESS Sjógøta 5, Postsmoga 30, 810 Tvøroyri, Faroe Islands.

TELEPHONE Administration & Reservations +298 34 30 00.

INTERNET Email firstssl.fo **Website** www.ssl.fo *(Faroese)*

ROUTES OPERATED Passenger and Car Ferries Tórshavn (Streymoy) - Tvøroyri (Suduroy) (1 hr 50 mins; **SMYRIL**; up to 3 per day), Klaksvík - Sydradali (20 min; **SAM**; up to 6 per day), Skopun – Gamlarætt (30 mins; **TEISTIN**; up to 9 per day). **Passenger-only Ferries** Sørvágur - Mykines (1 hr 15 mins; **JÒSUP (chartered ship)**; up to 3 per day, May to August only), Hvannasund - Svínoy (40 mins) - Kirkja (20 mins) - Hattarvik (10 mins) - Svínoy (30 mins; **RITAN**; up to 4 per day), Sandur - Skúvoy (35 mins; **SILDBERIN**; up to 5 per day), Tórshavn - Nólsoy (25 mins; **TERNAN**; up to 5 per day.

1	ERLA KONGSDÓTTIR	187t	20	-	27.0m	97P	3C	0L	BA	FO	9905526
2F	HASFJORD	686t	75	8.2k	40.8m	12P	0C	0L	BA	FO	7383542
3p	RITAN	81t	71	10.5k	22.1m	125P	0C	0L	-	FO	
4	SAM	217t	75	9.7k	30.2m	115P	17C	-	A	FO	7602168
5p	SILDBERIN	34t	79	7.5k	11.2m	30P	0C	0L	-	FO	
6	SMYRIL	12670t	05	21.0k	135.0m	976P	200C	32L	A	FO	9275218
7	TEISTIN	1260t	01	11.0k	45.0m	288P	33C	2L	BA	FO	9226102
8p	TERNAN	927t	80	12.0k	39.7m	319P	0C	0L	BA	FO	7947154

ERLA KONGSDÓTTIR Catamaran built by GS Marine, Gursken, Norway.

HASFJORD Built by Einar S Nielsen Mek. Verksted AS, Harstad, Norway for *Finnmark Fylkesrederi* of Norway to operate in the Hammerfest area. In 2003 the company was sold to *Veolia Transport Norge,* a subsidiary of the French *Veolia* group. In 2007 the group's Norwegian interests became *Veolia Transport Nord* and in May 2007 *Boreal Transport Nord*. In December 2019 the HASFJORD was sold to *Strandfaraskip Landsins* and delivered in February 2020. Now operates in freight-only mode, with 12 passengers maximum.

RITAN Built by Monnickenda, Volendam, The Netherlands. Used on the Hvannasund – Svínoy-Kirkja- Hattarvik service.

SAM Built by Blaalid Slip & Mek Verksted, Raudeberg, Norway. Used on the Klaksvik - Syòradali route and the Leirvik - Syòradali route.

SILDBERIN Built in Denmark. Used on the Sandur - Skúvoy route.

SMYRIL Built by IZAR, San Fernando, Spain for *Strandfaraskip Landsins*. Operates on the Tórshavn – Tvøroyri service.

TEISTIN Built by P/F Skipasmidjan a Skala, Skala, Faroe Islands for *Strandfaraskip Landsins*. Used on the Skopun – Gamlarætt service.

TERNAN Built by Tórshavnar Skipasmidja P/f, Tórshavn, Faroe Islands for *Strandfaraskip Landsins*. Used on the Tórshavn – Nólsoy service.

TALLINK/SILJA LINE

THE COMPANY *AS Tallink Grupp* is an Estonian private sector company. *Tallink Silja Oy* is a Finnish subsidiary, *Tallink Silja AB* is a Swedish subsidiary.

MANAGEMENT *AS Tallink Grupp:* Chairman of Management Board Paavo Nõgene, **Communications Director** Katri Link, *Tallink Silja Oy* **Managing Director** Margus Schults, *Tallink Silja AB* **Managing Director** Marcus Risberg.

ADDRESSES *AS Tallink Grupp* Sadama 5, Tallinn 10111, Estonia, *Tallink Silja Oy* P.O. Box 100, 00181 Helsinki, Finland, *Tallink Silja AB* Box 27295, 10253 Stockholm, Sweden.

TELEPHONE *AS Tallink Grupp* +372 (0)640 9800, *Tallink Silja Oy* **Administration** +358 (0)9 18041, **Reservations** +49 (0)40 547 541 222.

FAX *AS Tallink Grupp* Administration + 372 (0)640 9810, *Tallink Silja Oy* **Administration** +358 (0)9 180 4262.

INTERNET Email info@tallink.ee **Websites** www.tallinksilja.com *(17 languages, see the internet page)*, www.tallink.com (corporate site) *(English)*

ROUTES OPERATED Tallink branded services *Passenger Ferries* Helsinki - Tallinn: *Shuttle* (2 hrs; *MEGASTAR, STAR*; up to 6 per day), *Cruise Ferries* (3 hrs 30 - 4hrs 30 mins; *SILJA EUROPA*; normally 2 per day - currently suspended), Stockholm - Mariehamn (Åland) - Tallinn (14 hrs; *BALTIC QUEEN*; alternate days), *Freight and Car Passengers Ferry* Helsinki (Vuosaari) - Tallinn (Muuga) (3 hrs 30 mins; *REGAL STAR* 2 per day). *Freight-only Ferry* Kapellskär - Paldiski (9 hrs - 11 hrs;, *SAILOR*; 6 per week).

Silja Line branded services Helsinki (Finland) - Mariehamn (Åland) - Stockholm (Sweden) (16 hrs; *SILJA SERENADE, SILJA SYMPHONY*; 1 per day), Turku (Finland) - Mariehamn (Åland) (day)/Långnäs (Åland) (night) - Stockholm (11 hrs; *BALTIC PRINCESS*; 1 per day).

1	ATLANTIC VISION	30285t	02	27.9k	203.3m	728P	695C	110L	BA2	CA	9211509
2	BALTIC PRINCESS	48300t	08	24.5k	212.0m	2800P	300C	82T	BA	FI	9354284
3	BALTIC QUEEN	48300t	09	24.5k	212.0m	2800P	300C	82T	BA	EE	9443255
4	GALAXY	48915t	06	22.0k	212.0m	2800P	300C	82T	BA	SE	9333694
5	ISABELLE	35154t	89	21.5k	170.9m	2420P	364C	30T	BA	LV	8700723
6	MEGASTAR	49134t	16	27.0k	212m	2800P	300C	120L	BA2	EE	9773064
7	MySTAR	50000t	22	27.0k	212.0m	2800P	750C	180L	BA2	EE	9892690
8F+	REGAL STAR	15281t	00	17.5k	156.6m	100P	-	120T	A	EE	9087116
9F+	SAILOR	20921t	87	19.0k	157.6m	119P	50C	82L	A2	EE	8401444
11	SILJA EUROPA	59912t	93	21.5k	201.8m	3000P	400C	68T	BA	EE	8919805
12	SILJA SERENADE	58376t	90	21.0k	203.0m	2800P	410C	70T	BA	FI	8715259
13	SILJA SYMPHONY	58377t	91	21.0k	203.0m	2800P	410C	70T	BA	SE	8803769
14	STAR	36249t	07	27.5k	185.0m	1900P	450C	120L	BA2	EE	9364722
15	VICTORIA I	40975t	04	22.0k	193.8m	2500P	300C	82T	BA	EE	9281281

ATLANTIC VISION Built as the SUPERFAST IX by Howaldtswerke Deutsche Werft AG, Kiel, Germany for *Attica Enterprises* for use by *Superfast Ferries*. She operated between Rostock and Södertälje from January until April 2002. In May 2002 she began operating between Rosyth and Zeebrugge (with the SUPERFAST X (now the A NEPITA)). In 2004 fitted with additional cabins and conference/seating areas. In 2005 transferred to the Rostock – Hanko (later Helsinki) route. In 2006 sold to *Tallink*. In October 2008 chartered to *Marine Atlantic* of Canada to operate on the North Sydney-Port aux Basques service and renamed the ATLANTIC VISION.

BALTIC PRINCESS Built by Aker Yards, Helsinki. A large part of the hull was built at St Nazaire, France. In August 2008 replaced the GALAXY on the Tallinn - Helsinki route. In February 2013 transferred to the Stockholm - Turku service.

BALTIC QUEEN Built by STX Europe, Rauma, Finland. Usually operates between Stockholm and Tallinn.

GALAXY Built by Aker Yards, Rauma, Finland to operate as a cruise ferry on the Tallinn - Helsinki route. In July 2008 transferred to the Stockholm - Turku route and rebranded as a

Galaxy *(Richard Seville)*

Isabelle *(Richard Seville)*

Silja Line vessel. In September 2022 chartered to *The Government of the Netherlands* for seven months to house Ukrainian refugees.

ISABELLE Built as the ISABELLA by Brodogradevna Industrija, Split, Yugoslavia for *SF Line*. Used on the *Viking Line* Stockholm - Naantali service until 1992 when she was switched to operating 24-hour cruises from Helsinki and in 1995 she was transferred to the Stockholm - Helsinki route. During 1996 she additionally operated day cruises to Muuga in Estonia during the 'layover' period in Helsinki. In 1997 she was transferred to the Stockholm - Turku route. in January 2013 she was replaced by the VIKING GRACE. After covering for the AMORELLA during her refit period she was laid up. In April 2013 sold to *Hansa Link Limited*, a subsidiary of *AS Tallink Grupp* and renamed the ISABELLE. In May placed on the Stockholm - Riga service, replacing the SILJA FESTIVAL. During 2022 used as an accommodation vessel for Ukrainian refugees.

MEGASTAR Built by Meyer Turku, Turku, Finland to operate on the Tallinn - Helsinki Shuttle. She is LNG/diesel dual powered. An option on a second vessel was allowed to lapse in March 2016.

MySTAR Built by Rauma Marine Constructions of Finland to operate on the Helsinki - Tallinn 'Shuttle' service. Due to enter service 30 September 2022.

REGAL STAR Partly built by Sudostroitelnyy Zavod Severnaya Verf, St Petersburg. Work started in 1993 (as a deep-sea ro-ro) but was never completed. In 1999 the vessel was purchased, taken to Palumba SpA, Naples and completed as a short-sea ro-ro with accommodation for 80 drivers. In 2000 she was delivered to *MCL* of Italy and placed on a route between Savona and Catania. In September of that year she was chartered by *Grimaldi Ferries* and operated on a route Salerno – Palermo – Valencia. In late 2003 she was sold to *Hansatee Shipping* of Estonia and, in 2004, placed on the Kapellskär – Paldiski route, replacing the KAPELLA. From February 2006 she was transferred to the Helsinki – Tallinn service, replacing the KAPELLA due to the hard ice conditions. She continued in this service for the summer, but the returned to the Paldiski – Kapellskär service. In June 2010 moved to the *SeaWind Line* Stockholm – Turku service for the summer seasons and returned to the Kapellskär - Paldiski route in the autumn.

SAILOR Built as the FINNSAILOR by Gdańsk Shipyard, Gdańsk, Poland for *Finnlines* of Finland for freight service between Finland and Germany. In 1996 converted to ro-pax format to inaugurate a new passenger/freight service between Helsinki and Norrköping (Sweden) for subsidiary *FinnLink*. In 1997 this service was transferred to the Kapellskär – Naantali route and passengers (other than lorry drivers) ceased to be conveyed. In 2000 she was chartered to *Nordö-Link* to operate between Travemünde and Malmö. In 2002 she returned to *FinnLink*. In 2004 transferred to *Nordö-Link*. In 2007 returned to *FinnLink* as fourth ship. In early 2009 transferred to *Finnlines'* freight service operating between Helsinki, Turku and Travemünde but in April transferred back. In March 2011 moved back to *Finnlines Nordö-Link*. In November 2013 chartered to *Navirail* of Estonia to operate between Paldiski and Hanko. In January 2014 returned to *Finnlines* and placed on the Naantali - Kapellskär route. In January 2015 time chartered again to *Navirail*. In February 2015 demise chartered to *Navirail* and renamed the SAILOR. In October 2016 time chartered to *DFDS*, following their take-over of the Hanko and Paldiski route. In May 2020 transferred to the Kapellskär-Paldiski route. In July 2020 sold to a subsidiary of *Tallink* and operated on the same route.

SILJA EUROPA Built by Jos L Meyer, Papenburg, Germany. Ordered by *Rederi AB Slite* of Sweden for *Viking Line* service between Stockholm and Helsinki and due to be called EUROPA. In 1993, shortly before delivery was due, *Rederi AB Slite* went into liquidation and the order was cancelled. A charter agreement with her builders was then signed by *Silja Line* and she was introduced onto the Stockholm - Helsinki route as SILJA EUROPA. In early 1995 she was transferred to the Stockholm - Turku service. In January 2013 she was transferred to the Helsinki - Tallinn route. In August 2014 chartered to an Australian company as an accommodation vessel. In March 2016 joined the BALTIC PRINCESS as second vessel on the Helsinki - Tallinn 'Cruise' service. In December 2016 resumed the role of sole cruise vessel on the route. Between 1 and 18 June 2021 she was chartered to The UK Government to provide accommodation during a G7 Conference in Cornwall. She was moored at Falmouth. In August 2022 chartered to The Government of the Netherlands to house Ukrainian refugees.

SILJA SERENADE, SILJA SYMPHONY Built by Masa-Yards Oy, Turku, Finland for *Silja Line* for the Stockholm - Helsinki service. In 1993, SILJA SERENADE was transferred to the Stockholm - Turku service but in early 1995 she was transferred back to the Helsinki route.

STAR Built by Aker Yards, Helsinki, Finland for *Tallink* to operate on the Tallinn - Helsinki route. In January 2017 modified at Vene Balti Shipyard, Tallinn to allow for two deck loading. Between March and April 2020 operated between Sassnitz and Paldiski, during the Covid-19 pandemic as the Polish border was shut. On 1 October 2022 to be replaced by the MySTAR.

VICTORIA I Built by Aker Finnyards, Rauma, Finland for *Tallink*. Operates between Tallinn and Stockholm. Starting in June 2020 she has operated between Helsinki and Tallinn on a temporary basis. In June 2021 chartered to *Tanger Med* of Morocco to operate between Morocco and France following Spain's closure of their ports to vessels from Morocco. 2022 chartered to the *Scottish Government* until January 2023 to house Ukrainian refugees.

TESO

THE COMPANY *TESO (Texels Eigen Stoomboot Onderneming)* is a Dutch private company, with most shares owned by inhabitants of Texel.

MANAGEMENT Managing Director Cees de Waal.

ADDRESS Pontweg 1, 1797 SN Den Hoorn, The Netherlands.

TELEPHONE Administration +31 (0)222 36 96 00, **Reservations** Not applicable.

INTERNET Email info@teso.nl **Website** www.teso.nl *(Dutch, English, German)*

ROUTE OPERATED Den Helder (The Netherlands) - Texel (Dutch Frisian Islands) (20 minutes; *DOKTER WAGEMAKER*, *TEXELSTROOM*; hourly).

1	DOKTER WAGEMAKER	13256t	05	15.6k	130.4m	1750P	320C	44L	BA2	NL	9294070
2	TEXELSTROOM	16400t	16	15.0k	135.4m	1750P	350C	44L	BA2	NL	9741918

DOKTER WAGEMAKER Built at Galatz, Romania (hull and superstructure) and Royal Schelde, Vlissingen (fitting out) for *TESO*.

TEXELSTROOM Built by La Naval Shipyard, Sestao, Spain.

TT-LINE

THE COMPANY *TT-Line GmbH & Co KG* is a German private sector company.

MANAGEMENT Managing Directors Hanns Heinrich Conzen & Jens Aurel Scharner, **Sales Manager** Dirk Lifke.

ADDRESS Zum Hafenplatz 1, 23570, Lübeck-Travemünde, Germany.

TELEPHONE +49 (0)4502 801-81.

INTERNET Email info@ttline.com **Website** www.ttline.com *(English, German, Lithuanian, Polish, Swedish)*

ROUTES OPERATED *Passenger Ferries* Travemünde (Germany) - Trelleborg (Sweden) (8 hrs 30 mins/9 hrs 30 mins; *NILS HOLGERSSON, PETER PAN*; 2 per day). *Ro-pax Ferries* Travemünde (Germany) - Trelleborg (Sweden) (7 hrs 30 mins/8 hrs 15 mins; 1 per day), Rostock (Germany) - Trelleborg (Sweden) (5 hrs 30 mins/6 hrs 30 mins/7 hrs 30 mins; 3 per day, Świnoujście (Poland) - Trelleborg (Sweden) (7 hrs; 1 per day), Trelleborg - Klaipėda (Lithuania) (15 hrs; 5 per week), Świnoujście (Poland) - Rønne (Bornholm, Denmark) (5 hrs (day), 6 hrs 30 mins (night); 1 per week) (summer only), **Note:** Other than Travemünde - Trelleborg route, ship deployment following delivery of new PETER Pan is not known.

1	AKKA	36468t	01	18.0k	190.8m	744P	-	171T	BAS2	DE	9217230
2	HUCKLEBERRY FINN	26391t	88	18.0k	177.2m	400P	280C	121T	BAS2	SE	8618358
3	MARCO POLO	14398t	93	19.0k	150.3m	130P	-	130T	A2	CY	9019080
4	NILS DACKE	26796t	95	18.5k	179.7m	300P	-	157T	BA	CY	9087465

5	NILS HOLGERSSON	56138t	22	21.0k	177.0m	900P	-	160T	BAS2	DE	9865685
6	PETER PAN	56138t	22	21.0k	177.0m	900P	-	160T	BAS2	DE	9880946
7	ROBIN HOOD	26790t	95	18.5k	179.7m	317P	-	157T	BA	DE	9087477
8	TINKER BELL	44245t	01	18.0k	220.0m	744P	-	210T	BAS2	SE	9217242
9	TOM SAWYER	26478t	89	18.0k	177.2m	400P	280C	121T	BAS2	CY	8703232

AKKA, TINKER BELL Built by SSW Fähr und Spezialschiffbau GmbH, Bremerhaven, Germany as the NILS HOLGERSSON and PETER PAN for the Travemünde - Trelleborg route. In January and February 2018 the PETER PAN was lengthened at MWB Motorenwerke Bremerhaven AG, Germany by 30 metres. In February 2022 the NILS HOLGERSSON was renamed the AKKA and in 2022 the PETER PAN was renamed the TINKER BELL.

HUCKLEBERRY FINN Built as the NILS DACKE by Schichau Seebeckwerft AG, Bremerhaven, Germany, as a ro-pax vessel. During Summer 1993 rebuilt to transform her into a passenger/car ferry and renamed the PETER PAN, replacing a similarly named vessel (31356t, 1986). On arrival of the new PETER PAN in Autumn 2001 she was renamed the PETER PAN IV. She was then converted back to ro-pax format, renamed the HUCKLEBERRY FINN and, in early 2002, transferred to the Rostock -Trelleborg route.

MARCO POLO Built as the VIA IONIO by van der Gissen de Noord, Krimpen-a d Ijssel, Netherlands at their Welgelegen shipyard for *Viamare di Navigazione SpA* of Italy. Between April and August 1993 chartered to *TT-Line* and operated between Travemünde and Trelleborg. In August, placed on Mediterranean service. In April 1994 sold to *Adriatica di Navigazione SpA* of Italy and renamed the ESPRESSO RAVENNA. Operated between Ravenna - Catania. In July 2012 sold to *Compagnia Italiana Di Navigaz* of Italy and in January 2017 renamed the BARBARA KRAHULIK. In July 2019 sold to *TT-Line* and chartered back. Operated for *Tirennia* of Italy, mainly between Naples and Catania Delivered in November 2019 and renamed the MARCO POLO. In January 2020, after a major rebuild, placed on the Trelleborg - Klaipėda service.

NILS DACKE, Ro-pax vessels built as the ROBIN HOOD by Finnyards, Rauma, Finland. She operated on the Travemünde - Trelleborg and Travemünde - Helsingborg routes. In December 2014 she was renamed the NILS DACKE and transferred to Cypriot registry. Moved to the Trelleborg - Świnoujście route.

NILS HOLGERSSON, PETER PAN Built by the CMI Jinling Shipyard, Nanjing, China. LNG Powered

ROBIN HOOD Ro-pax vessels built as the NILS DACKE, by Finnyards, Rauma, Finland. She operated on the Travemünde - Trelleborg and Travemünde - Helsingborg routes. In January 2014, she was transferred to a new Trelleborg - Świnoujście service and changed to Polish registry. In December 2014 she was renamed the ROBIN HOOD and transferred German Registry. Moved to the Travemünde - Trelleborg route.

TOM SAWYER Built as the ROBIN HOOD by Schichau Seebeckwerft AG, Bremerhaven, Germany, as a ro-pax vessel. During Winter 1992/93 rebuilt to transform her into a passenger/car ferry and renamed the NILS HOLGERSSON, replacing a similarly named vessel (31395t, 1987) which had been sold to *Brittany Ferries* and renamed the VAL DE LOIRE. In 2001 converted back to ro-pax format and renamed the TOM SAWYER. Transferred to the Rostock - Trelleborg route.

NILS HOLGERSSON, PETER PAN Under construction by the CMI Jinling Shipyard, Nanjing, China. It is likely that they will replace the HUCKLEBERRY FINN and TOM SAWYER and the existing NILS HOLGERSSON and PETER PAN will be renamed.

UNITY LINE

THE COMPANY *Unity Line* is a trading name of *Polskie Promy*, a Polish private section company, wholly owned fully owned by *Polska Zegluga Morska (PZM) (Polish Steamship Company)*. The operator manages seven ferries on two routes: Świnoujście – Ystad and Świnoujście – Trelleborg. Three ships are owned by *Euroafrica Shipping* which was previously a partner in the company; the ships continue to be operationally managed by *Unity Line*.

MANAGEMENT Managing Director Jarosław Kotarski.

ADDRESS Plac Rodla 8, 70-419 Szczecin, Poland.

TELEPHONE Administration& Reservations +48 (0)91 88 02 909.

INTERNET Email rezerwacje@unityline.pl **Website** www.unityline.pl *(English, German, Polish, Swedish)*

ROUTES OPERATED Passenger Service Świnoujście (Poland) - Ystad (Sweden) (6 hrs 30 mins (day), 9 hrs (night); *POLONIA, SKANIA*; 2 per day). **Freight Services** Świnoujście (Poland) - Ystad (Sweden) (8 hrs (day), 9 hrs (night); *JAN ŚNIADECKI*; 1 per day), Świnoujście (Poland) - Trelleborg (Sweden) (6 hrs 30 mins (day), 9 hrs (night); *COPERNICUS, GALILEUSZ, GRYF, WOLIN*; 4 per day).

1F+	COPERNICUS	14398t	96	19.0k	150.4m	50P	-	122T	A	CY	9031703
2F+	GALILEUSZ	15848t	92	17.0k	150.4m	160P	-	115L	A	CY	9019078
3F+	GRYF	18653t	90	16.0k	158.0m	180P	-	125L	BA	CY	8818300
4F+	JAN ŚNIADECKI	14417t	88	17.0k	155.1m	57P	-	70Lr	SA2	CY	8604711
5	POLONIA	29875t	95	17.2k	169.9m	920P	440C	145Lr	SA2	CY	9108350
6	SKANIA	23933t	95	22.5k	173.7m	1400P	430C	140L	BA	CY	9086588
7F+	WOLIN	22874t	86	17.5k	188.9m	370P	-	110Lr	SA	CY	8420842

COPERNICUS Built as the PUGLIA by Fincantieri-Cantieri Navali Italiani SpA, Ancona, Italy for *Tirrenia di Navigazione SpA.* of Italy. In 2016 rebranded as *Moby Cargo*. In December 2017 sold to *Euroafrica Shipping*, renamed the COPERNICUS and, in September 2018, placed on the Świnoujście - Trelleborg route.

GALILEUSZ Built as the VIA TIRRENO by Van der Giessen de Noord, Krimpen aan den IJssel, The Netherlands for *Viamare di Navigazione SpA* of Italy. Initially operated between Voltri and Termini Imerese. In 1998 transferred to the Génova - Termini Imerese route and in 2001 to the Génova - Palermo route. In 2006 sold to *Euroafrica Shipping*, renamed the GALILEUSZ and in November introduced onto the *Unity Line* Świnoujście - Ystad service. In February 2007 transferred to the new Świnoujście - Trelleborg route.

GRYF Built as the KAPTAN BURHANETTIN ISIM by Fosen Mekaniske Verksteder, Fevag, Norway for *Turkish Cargo Lines* of Turkey to operate between Trieste (Italy) and Derince (Turkey). In 2002 chartered to *Latlines* to operate between Lübeck and Riga (Latvia). In 2003 chartered to *VentLines* to inaugurate a new service between Travemünde and Ventspils. In 2004 sold to *Polsteam*, managed by *Unity Line* and renamed the GRYF. Entered service in 2005. In February 2007 transferred to the new Świnoujście - Trelleborg route.

JAN ŚNIADECKI Built by Falkenbergs Varv AB, Falkenberg, Sweden for *Polish Ocean Lines* to operate between Świnoujście and Ystad. Now operates for *Unity Line* on this route.

POLONIA Train/vehicle ferry built by Langsten Slip & Båtbyggeri A/S, Tomrefjord, Norway for *Polonia Line Ltd* and managed by *Unity Line*.

SKANIA Built as the SUPERFAST I by Schichau Seebeckwerft, Bremerhaven, Germany for *Superfast Ferries* of Greece. Operated between Patras and Ancona (Italy). In 1998 transferred to the Patras - Igoumenitsa (Greece) - Bari (Italy) route. In 2004 sold to a subsidiary of *Grimaldi Lines*, renamed the EUROSTAR ROMA and placed on the Civitavecchia (Italy) - Barcelona (Spain) service. In 2008 sold to *Polsteam* and renamed the SKANIA. After modifications, she was placed on the *Unity Line* Świnoujście - Ystad service as second passenger vessel. In during the peak summer period in 2010 operated a round trip between Ystad and Rønne for *Bornholmstrafikken*.

WOLIN Train/vehicle ferry built as the ÖRESUND by Moss Rosenberg Værft, Moss, Norway for *Statens Järnvägar* (*Swedish State Railways*) for the 'DanLink' service between Helsingborg and København. Has 817 metres of rail track. Service ceased in July 2000 and vessel laid up. In 2001 sold to *Sea Containers Ferries* and in 2002 converted at Gdańsk, Poland to a passenger ferry. She was chartered to *SeaWind Line*, renamed the SKY WIND and in Autumn 2002 replaced the STAR WIND on the Stockholm - Turku service. In 2007 sold to *Polsteam*, renamed the WOLIN and placed on the *Unity Line* Świnoujście - Trelleborg service.

Akka *(Frank Lose)*

Galileusz *(Frank Lose)*

Under Construction

| 8 | NEWBUILDING 1 | 24 | - | 19.0k | 195.6m | 400P | - | 250L | BA | - | - |
| 9 | NEWBUILDING 2 | 24 | - | 19.0k | 195.6m | 400P | - | 250L | BA | - | - |

NEWBUILDING 1, NEWBUILDING 2 Hybrid ferries (LNG/battery pack) under construction for *Polskie Promy* by Remontowa Shipbuilding, Gdansk, Poland. Two vessels will be used by *Unity Line* and one may be chartered to *Polferries*. There is an option for a fourth vessel.

VIKING LINE

THE COMPANY *Viking Line Abp* is a Finnish company Listed on the Helsinki Stock Exchange since 1995.

MANAGEMENT President & CEO Jan Hanses, **Executive Vice President/Deputy CEO and Chief Financial Officer at Viking Line Abp** Mats Engblom.

ADDRESS PO Box 166, 22100 Mariehamn, Åland, Finland.

TELEPHONE Administration +358 (0)18 270 00, **Reservations** +358 (0)600 41577.

INTERNET Email international.sales@vikingline.com **Websites** www.vikingline.com *(English)* www.vikingline.fi *(Finnish)* www.vikingline.se *(Swedish)* www.vikingline.ee *(Estonian)* www.vikingline.de *(German)*

ROUTES OPERATED *Conventional Ferries - all year* Stockholm (Sweden) - Mariehamn (Åland) - Helsinki (Finland) (14 hrs; *GABRIELLA*; alternate days), Stockholm - Mariehamn (day)/Långnäs (Åland) (night) - Turku (Finland) (9 hrs 10 mins; *VIKING GLORY, VIKING GRACE*; 2 per day), Kapellskär (Sweden) - Mariehamn (Åland) (2 hrs 15 mins; *ROSELLA*; up to 3 per day), Helsinki - Tallinn (2 hrs 30 mins; *VIKING XPRS*; 2 per day), Cruises from Stockholm to Mariehamn (21 hrs - 24 hrs round trip (most 22 hrs 30 mins; *VIKING CINDERELLA*; 1 per day).

1	GABRIELLA	35492t	92	21.5k	171.2m	2420P	400C	50T	BA	FI	8917601
2	ROSELLA	16850t	80	21.3k	136.0m	1700P	340C	40T	BA	AX	7901265
3	VIKING CINDERELLA	46398t	89	21.5k	191.0m	2500P	100C	-	BA	SE	8719188
4	VIKING GLORY	63543t	21	23.0k	225.5m	2800P	556C	90L	BA	FI	9827877
5	VIKING GRACE	57565t	13	23.0k	214.0m	2800P	556C	90L	BA	FI	9606900
6	VIKING XPRS	34000t	08	25.0k	185.0m	2500P	250C	60L	BA	EE	9375654

GABRIELLA Built as the FRANS SUELL by Brodogradiliste Industrija, Split, Croatia for *Sea-Link AB* of Sweden to operate for subsidiary company *Euroway AB*, who established a service between Lübeck, Travemünde and Malmö. In 1994 this service ceased and she was chartered to *Silja Line*, renamed the SILJA SCANDINAVIA and transferred to the Stockholm - Turku service. In 1997 she was sold to *Viking Line* to operate between Stockholm and Helsinki. She was renamed the GABRIELLA**.**

ROSELLA Built by Oy Wärtsilä Ab, Turku, Finland for *SF Line*. Used mainly on the Stockholm - Turku and Kapellskär - Naantali services until 1997. From 1997 operated 21 to 24-hour cruises from Stockholm to Mariehamn under the marketing name 'The Dancing Queen', except in the peak summer period when she operated between Kapellskär and Turku. In Autumn 2003 transferred to a new twice-daily Helsinki - Tallinn ferry service. In May 2008 placed on the Mariehamn - Kapellskär route under the Swedish flag. In 2011 she was extensively rebuilt at Balti Laevaremondi Tehas in Tallinn, Estonia. Cabin capacity was lowered from 1184 to 418 and the restaurant and shop areas were increased. In January 2014 placed under the Finnish flag.

VIKING CINDERELLA Built as the CINDERELLA by Wärtsilä Marine Ab, Turku, Finland for *SF Line*. Until 1993 provided additional capacity between Stockholm and Helsinki and undertook weekend cruises from Helsinki. In 1993 she replaced the OLYMPIA (a sister vessel of the MARIELLA) as the main Stockholm - Helsinki vessel after the OLYMPIA had been chartered to *P&O European Ferries* and renamed the PRIDE OF BILBAO. In 1995 switched to operating 20-hour cruises from Helsinki to Estonia in the off peak and the Stockholm - Mariehamn - Turku service during the peak summer period (end of May to end of August). From 1997 she remained cruising throughout the year. In Autumn 2003 she was transferred to the Swedish flag, renamed the VIKING CINDERELLA and transferred to Stockholm - Mariehamn cruises. She operates these cruises all year round.

VIKING GLORY Built by Xiamen Shipbuilding Industry Co. Ltd, Xiamen, China. She is LNG powered and replaced the AMORELLA on the Stockholm - Mariehamn - Turku service. Entered service in February 2022.

VIKING GRACE Built by STX Europe, Turku, Finland. She operates between Stockholm and Turku. She is powered by LNG. Entered service in January 2013.

VIKING XPRS Built by Aker Yards, Helsinki to operate between Helsinki and Tallinn. In January 2014 placed under the Estonian flag.

WAGENBORG

THE COMPANY *Wagenborg Passagiersdiensten BV* is a Dutch private sector company.

MANAGEMENT Managing Director Ger van Langen.

ADDRESS Reeweg 4, 9163 ZM Nes, Ameland, The Netherlands.

TELEPHONE Administration & Reservations *International* +31 88 1031000, *Netherlands* 0900 9238.

INTERNET Email info@wpd.nl **Website** www.wpd.nl *(Dutch, English, German)*

ROUTES OPERATED *Car Ferries* Holwerd (The Netherlands) - Ameland (Frisian Islands) (45 minutes; *OERD, SIER*; up to 14 per day), Lauwersoog (The Netherlands) - Schiermonnikoog (Frisian Islands) (45 minutes; *MONNIK, ROTTUM*; up to 6 per day).

1	MONNIK	1121t	85	12.2k	58.0m	1000P	46C	9L	BA	NL	8408961
2	OERD	2286t	03	11.2k	73.2m	1200P	72C	22L	BA	NL	9269673
3	ROTTUM	1121t	85	12.2k	58.0m	1000P	46C	9L	BA	NL	8408959
4	SIER	2286t	95	11.2k	73.2m	1200P	72C	22L	BA	NL	9075761

MONNIK Built by Scheepswerf Hoogezand, Hoogezand, The Netherlands for *Wagenborg Passagiersdiensten BV* as the OERD. In 2003, on delivery of the new OERD, she was renamed the MONNIK. Used on the Lauwersoog - Schiermonnikoog route.

OERD Built by Scheepswerf Bijlsma Lemmer, Lemmer, The Netherlands for *Wagenborg Passagiersdiensten BV*. Used on the Ameland - Holwerd route.

ROTTUM Built as the SIER by Scheepswerf Hoogezand, Hoogezand, The Netherlands for *Wagenborg Passagiersdiensten BV* and used on the Holwerd - Ameland route. In 1995 renamed the ROTTUM and transferred to the Lauwersoog - Schiermonnikoog route.

SIER Built by Shipyard Bijlsma, Wartena, The Netherlands for *Wagenborg Passagiersdiensten BV*. Used on the Ameland - Holwerd route.

WASALINE

THE COMPANY *Wasaline* is the trading name of *NLC Ferry Oy Ab*, a Finnish company, jointly owned by the cities of Vaasa and Umeå.

MANAGEMENT Managing Director Peter Ståhlberg.

ADDRESS *Finland:* Skeppsredaregatan 6, 65170 Vasa, Finland, *Sweden:* Blå Vägen 4, 91322 Holmsund, Sweden.

TELEPHONE Administration & Reservations *Finland* +358 (0)207 716 810, *Sweden* +46 (0)90 185 200.

INTERNET *Email* info@wasaline.com *Website* www.wasaline.com *(English, Finnish, Swedish)*

ROUTE OPERATED Vaasa (Finland) - Umeå (Sweden) (3 hrs 30 mins; *AURORA BOTNIA*; 2-4 per day).

| 1 | AURORA BOTNIA | 24037t | 21 | 20.0k | 150.0m | 800P | - | 105T | BA | FI | 9878319 |

AURORA BOTNIA Built by Rauma Marine Constructions, Rauma, Finland.

WYKER DAMPFSCHIFFS-REEDEREI

THE COMPANY *Wyker Dampfschiffs-Reederei* is a German company.

MANAGEMENT Managing Director Axel Meynköhn.

ADDRESS PO Box 1540, 25933 Wyk auf Föhr, Germany.

TELEPHONE Administration & Reservations +49 (0)**4681 800.**

INTERNET Email info@faehre.de **Website** www.faehre.de *(Danish, English, German)*

ROUTES OPERATED Dagebüll - Föhr (50min; *NORDERAUE, NORDFRIESLAND, RUNGHOLT*; *SCHLESWIG-HOLSTEIN, UTHLANDE*; up to 14 per day), Dagebüll - Amrun (90 min (120 min via Föhr); *NORDERAUE, NORDFRIESLAND, RUNGHOLT, SCHLESWIG-HOLSTEIN, UTHLANDE*; 7 per day), Föhr - Amrun (1 hr; *NORDERAUE, NORDFRIESLAND, RUNGHOLT*; *SCHLESWIG-HOLSTEIN, UTHLANDE*; up to 4 per day), Schlüttsiel - Hooge - Langeness (2 hrs; *HILLIGENLEI*; up to 2 per day).

1	HILLIGENLEI	467t	85	19.0k	38.3m	200P	22C	-	BA	DE	8411217
2	NORDERAUE	3250t	18	12.0k	75.9m	1200P	75C	-	BA	DE	9796121
3	NORDFRIESLAND	2287t	95	12.0k	67.0m	1200P	55C	-	BA	DE	9102758
4	SCHLESWIG-HOLSTEIN	3202t	11	12.0k	75.9m	1200P	75C	-	BA	DE	9604378
5	UTHLANDE	1960t	10	12.0k	75.9m	1200P	75C	-	BA	DE	9548407

HILLIGENLEI Built as the PELLWORM by Husumer Schiffswerft, Husum, Germany for *Neue Pellwormer Dampfschiffahrtsgesellschaft* of Germany and operated between Pellworm and Strucklahnungshörn. In 1996 sold to Sven Paulsen, Altwarp, Germany and renamed the ADLER POLONIA. Operated between Altwarp and Novo Warpno (Poland). In 2002 sold to *Wyker Dampfschiffsreederei* and renamed the HILLIGENLEI I. In February 2010 renamed the HILLIGENLEI.

NORDERAUE Built by Neptun Werft GmbH, Rostock, Germany for *Wyker Dampfschiffsreederei*.

NORDFRIESLAND Built by Husumer Schiffswerft, Husum, Germany for *Wyker Dampfschiffsreederei*.

SCHLESWIG-HOLSTEIN Built by Neptun Werft GmbH, Rostock, Germany for *Wyker Dampfschiffsreederei*.

UTHLANDE Built by J.J. Sietas GmbH & Co KG, Hamburg, Germany for *Wyker Dampfschiffsreederei*.

SECTION 8 - OTHER VESSELS

The following passenger vessel is, at the time of going to print, not operating and is owned by company which do not currently operate services. She is therefore available for possible re-deployment, either in the area covered by this book or elsewhere. Withdrawn vessels not yet disposed of and owned by operating companies are shown under the appropriate company and marked 'A '.

SEIM INDUSTRIES

| 1 | HONFLEUR | 42400t | 22 | 22.0k | 187.4m | 1680P | 550C | 150L | BA | CY | 9832119 |

HONFLEUR Partly constructed by Flensburger Schiffbau-Gesellschaft, Flensburg for Brittany Ferries, Germany to operate on the Portsmouth - Caen route, replacing the NORMANDIE. LNG powered. Construction was heavily delayed, with fitting out still incomplete and, in June 2020, the contract was cancelled. In July sold to Seim Industries of Norway, former owner of the yard. In October moved to Fosen Yard, Trondheim, Norway for completion. In May 2022 moved to Gdynia for further work. Future is currently uncertain.

Viking XPRS *(Richard Seville)*

Honfleur *(Ferry Publications Library)*

SECTION 9 - SISTERS – A LIST OF SISTER (OR NEAR SISTER) VESSELS IN THIS BOOK

The following vessels are sisters or near sisters. This refers to 'as built' condition; some ships will subsequently have been modified and become different from their sister vessels.

Passenger Ferries

ÆRØSKØBING, MARSTAL *(Ærøfærgerne)*

AKKA, TINKER BELL *(TT-Line)*

ARGYLE, BUTE *(Caledonian MacBrayne).*

ATHENA SEAWAYS, REGINA SEAWAYS, VICTORIA SEAWAYS *(DFDS).*

ATLANTIC VISION *(Tallink)*, STENA SUPERFAST VII, STENA SUPERFAST VIII *(Stena Line).*

AURA SEAWAYS, LUNA SEAWAYS *(DFDS Ferry)*

AURORA AF HELSINGBORG, HAMLET, TYCHO BRAHE *(ForSea).*

BALTIC QUEEN, BALTIC PRINCESS, GALAXY *(Tallink Silja Line).*

BASTØ I, BASTØ II *(Bastø Fosen).*

BASTØ IV, BASTØ V, BASTØ VI *(Bastø Fosen).*

BEN-MY-CHREE *(Isle of Man Steam Packet Company)*, COMMODORE CLIPPER *(Condor Ferries)*, STENA VINGA *(Stena Line)* (Near sisters).

BEN WOOLLACOTT, DAME VERA LYNN *(Woolwich Free Ferry).*

BERGENSFJORD, STAVANGERFJORD *(Fjord Line).*

BERLIN, COPENHAGEN *(Scandlines).*

CANNA *(Arranmore Fast Ferries)*, CLEW BAY QUEEN *(Clare Island Ferry Company)*, COLL *(Arranmore Island Ferries)*, EIGG *(Clare Island Ferry Company)*, MORVERN *(Arranmore Fast Ferries)*, RAASAY *(Inishbofin Island Discovery)*, RHUM *(Arranmore Island Ferries).*

CARRIGALOE, GLENBROOK *(Cross River Ferries).*

CATRIONA, HALLAIG, LOCHINVAR *(Caledonian MacBrayne)*

COLOR FANTASY, COLOR MAGIC *(Color Line).*

COLOR VIKING *(Color Line)*, STENA NAUTICA *(Stena Line).*

EPSILON *(Irish Ferries)*, STENA HORIZON, STENA FLAVIA, STENA LIVIA *(Stena Line).*

CÔTE D'ALBATRE, SEVEN SISTERS *(DFDS).*

CÔTE DES DUNES, CÔTE DES FLANDRES *(DFDS).*

CÔTE D'OPALE *(DFDS)*, GALICIA, SALAMANCA, SANTOÑA *(Brittany Ferries)*, STENA EDDA, STENA EMBLA, STENA ESTRID *(Stena Line).*

CROWN SEAWAYS *(DFDS)*, GABRIELLA *(Viking Line).*

DAGALIEN, DAGGRI *(Shetland Islands Council).*

DELFT SEAWAYS, DOVER SEAWAYS, DUNKERQUE SEAWAYS *(DFDS).*

DEUTSCHLAND, SCHLESWIG-HOLSTEIN *(Scandlines).*

DROTTEN *(Rederi AB Gotland)*, VISBORG *(DFDS).*

EARL SIGURD, EARL THORFINN *(Orkney Ferries).*

ECKERÖ *(Eckerö Linjen)*, POVL ANKER *(Molslinjen).*

EUROPALINK, FINNLADY, FINNMAID, FINNSTAR, FINNSWAN *(Finnlines)*.

EUROPEAN CAUSEWAY, EUROPEAN HIGHLANDER *(P&O Ferries)*.

FENJA, MENJA *(Molslinjen)*.

FINNCLIPPER, FINNEAGLE, FINNFELLOW *(Finnlines)*, STENA GERMANICA *(Stena Line)*.

FINNPARTNER, FINNTRADER *(Finnlines)*.

FRIDTJOF NANSEN, ROALD AMUNDSEN *(Hurtigruten)*

FRISIA III, FRISIA V *(Reederei Norden-Frisia)*.

GABRIELLA *(Viking Line)*, ISABELLE *(Tallink Silja Line)*, CROWN OF SCANDINAVIA *(DFDS)*.

GOTLAND, VISBY *(Destination Gotland)*.

HAVILA CAPELLA, HAVILA CASTOR, HAVILA POLARIS, HAVILA POLLUX *(Havila Kystruten)*.

HJALTLAND, HROSSEY *(NorthLink Ferries)*.

HUCKLEBERRY FINN, TOM SAWYER *(TT-Line)*.

KING SEAWAYS, PRINCESS SEAWAYS *(DFDS)*.

KONG HARALD, NORDLYS, RICHARD WITH *(Hurtigruten)*.

KRONPRINS FREDERIK, PRINS JOACHIM *(Scandlines)*.

LANGELAND, LOLLAND *(Molslinjen)*.

LEIGER, PIRET, TIIU, TÕLL *(Praamid)*

LOCH DUNVEGAN, LOCH FYNE *(Caledonian MacBrayne)*.

LOCH LINNHE, LOCH RANZA, LOCH RIDDON, LOCH STRIVEN *(Caledonian MacBrayne)*.

LYNHER II, PLYM II, TAMAR II *(Torpoint Ferries)*.

MAUD, TROLLFJORD *(Hurtigruten)*.

MEGASTAR, MySTAR *(Tallink/Silja Line)*.

MERCANDIA IV, MERCANDIA VIII *(ForSea)*.

MONNIK, ROTTUM *(Wagenborg)*.

MÜNSTERLAND, OSTFRIESLAND *(AG Ems)*.

NILS DACKE, ROBIN HOOD *(TT-Line)*.

NILS HOLGERSSON, PETER PAN *(TT-Line)*.

NORBANK, NORBAY *(P&O Ferries)*.

NORDKAPP, NORDNORGE, POLARLYS *(Hurtigruten)*.

OERD, SIER *(Wagenborg)*.

OILEAN NA H-OIGE, SANCTA MARIA *(Bere Island Ferries)*.

PRIDE OF CANTERBURY, PRIDE OF KENT *(P&O Ferries)*.

PRIDE OF HULL, PRIDE OF ROTTERDAM *(P&O Ferries)*.

PRINS RICHARD, PRINSESSE BENEDIKTE *(Scandlines)*.

RED EAGLE, RED FALCON, RED OSPREY *(Red Funnel Ferries)*.

RENFREW ROSE *(Highland Ferries)*, YOKER SWAN *(Sherkin Island Ferry)*.

ROMANTIKA *(Holland Norway Line)*, VICTORIA I *(Tallink Silja Line)*.

SILJA SERENADE, SILJA SYMPHONY *(Tallink Silja Line)*.

SOUND OF SCARBA, SOUND OF SHUNA *(Western Ferries)*.

SOUND OF SEIL, SOUND OF SOAY *(Western Ferries)*.

SPIRIT OF BRITAIN, SPIRIT OF FRANCE *(P&O Ferries)*.

STENA ADVENTURER, STENA SCANDINAVICA *(Stena Line)*.

STENA BALTICA, STENA SCANDINAVICA *(Stena Line)*.

STENA BRITANNICA, STENA HOLLANDICA *(Stena Line)*.

STENA EBBA, STENA ESTELLE *(Stena Line)*

STENA GOTHICA, URD *(Stena Line)*.

STENA SPIRIT, STENA VISION *(Stena Line)*.

SUPERSPEED 1, SUPERSPEED 2 *(Color Line)*.

WIGHT LIGHT, WIGHT SKY, WIGHT SUN *(Wightlink)*.

WILLEM BARENTSZ, WILLEM DE VLAMINGH *(Rederij Doeksen)*.

Fast Ferries

EXPRESS 1, EXPRESS 2, EXPRESS 3 *(Molslinjen)*.

MAX *(Molslinjen)*, SKANE CAT *(FRS Baltic)*.

RED JET 6, RED JET 7 *(Red Funnel Ferries)*.

WIGHT RYDER I, WIGHT RYDER II *(Wightlink)*.

Freight Ferries

ACACIA SEAWAYS *(DFDS)*, ALF POLLAK *(CLdN)*, GARDENIA SEAWAYS *(DFDS)*, MARIA GRAZIA ONORATO *(CLdN)*, TULIPA SEAWAYS *(DFDS)*.

ADELINE, WILHELMINE *(CLdN)*.AKRANES *(Smyril Line)*, BORE BANK *(Transfennica)*, BORE BAY *(Sea-Cargo)*, MYKINES *(Smyril Line)*.

AMANDINE, OPALINE *(CLdN)*.

ANVIL POINT *(Foreland Shipping)*, CADENA 3 *(CLdN)*, EDDYSTONE *(Foreland Shipping)*, HARTLAND POINT, HURST POINT *(Foreland Shipping*, NEW AMSTERDAM *(Finnlines)*.

ARROW *(Isle of Man Steam Packet)*, HELLIAR, HILDASAY *(NorthLink Ferries)*.

AUTO ACHIEVE, AUTO ASPIRE, AUTO ADVANCE *(UECC)*.

AUTO ECO, AUTO ENERGY *(UECC)*.

AUTOPRESTIGE, AUTOPROGRESS *(UECC)*.

AUTOSKY, AUTOSTAR, AUTOSUN *(UECC)*.

BALTIC ENABLER, BOTNIA ENABLER *(Wallenius SOL)*

BALTICBORG, BOTHNIABORG *(Wagenborg)*.

BELGIA SEAWAYS *(DFDS)*, MAXINE *(CLdN)*, SOMERSET *(Stena Line)*.

BEGONIA SEAWAYS, FICARIA SEAWAYS, FREESIA SEAWAYS, PRIMULA SEAWAYS *(DFDS)*.

BORE SEA *(Transfennica)*, BORE SONG *(P&O Ferries)*.

BOTNIA SEAWAYS, FINLANDIA SEAWAYS *(DFDS)*, FINNHAWK, FINNKRAFT *(Finnlines)*

BRITANNIA SEAWAYS, SELANDIA SEAWAYS, SUECIA SEAWAYS *(DFDS)*.

CAPUCINE, SEVERINE *(CLdN)*.

CELANDINE, CELESTINE, CLEMENTINE, MELUSINE, VICTORINE *(CLdN)*.

CELINE, DELPHINE *(CLdN)*.

CLIPPER PENNANT *(P&O Ferries)*, CLIPPER POINT, SEATRUCK PACE *(Seatruck Ferries)*, SEATRUCK PANORAMA *(Stena Line)*.

COLOR CARRIER *(Color Line)*, FINNMASTER *(Finnlines)*, MN PELICAN *(Brittany Ferries)*, SC CONNECTOR *(Sea-Cargo)*.

COPERNICUS, GALILEUSZ*(Unity Line)*, MARCO POLO *(TT-Line)*

CORONA SEA *(Transfennica)*, FINNBREEZE, FINNMILL, FINNPULP, FINNSEA, FINNSKY,

FINNSUN, FINNTIDE, FINNWAVE, FIONIA SEA *(Stena Line)*, HAFNIA SEA *(Transfennica)*, JUTLANDIA SEA *(Stena Line)*.

FINNECO I, FINNECO II, FINNECO III *(Finnlines)*.

FAUSTINE, SERAPHINE *(CLdN)*.

FINLANDIA SEAWAYS *(DFDS)*, FINNHAWK, FINNKRAFT, FINNMASTER *(Finnlines)*.

FLANDRIA SEAWAYS, HOLLANDIA SEAWAYS, HUMBRIA SEAWAYS, SCANDIA SEAWAYS *(DFDS)*.

GENCA, KRAFTCA, PLYCA, PULPCA, TIMCA, TRICA *(Transfennica)*.

HERMINE, LAURELINE, SIXTINE, YSALINE *(CLdN)*.

MAGNOLIA SEAWAYS, PETUNIA SEAWAYS *(DFDS)*.

MAZARINE, PALATINE, PEREGRINE, VESPERTINE *(CLdN)*.

MISANA, MISIDA *(Sea-Cargo)*.

MISTRAL *(Smyril Line)*, SEAGARD *(Transfennica)*.

NEPTUNE AEGLI, NEPTUNE DYNAMIS *(Neptune Lines)*.

NEPTUNE GALENE NEPTUNE ILIAD, NEPTUNE ITHAKI, NEPTUNE KEFALONIA, NEPTUNE ODYSSEY, NEPTUNE THALASSA *(Neptune Lines)*

NORSKY, NORSTREAM *(P&O Ferries)*.

PAULINE, YASMINE *(CLdN)*.

SC ATHELA *(Sea-Cargo)*, TRANSPORTER *(DFDS)*.

SCA OBBOLA, SCA ORTVIKEN, SCA ÖSTRAND *(SCA Transforest)*.

SEATRUCK PERFORMANCE, SEATRUCK POWER, SEATRUCK PRECISION, SEATRUCK PROGRESS *(Seatruck Ferries)*.

STENA FORERUNNER, STENA FORETELLER *(Stena Line)*.

STENA HIBERNIA, STENA SCOTIA *(Stena Line)*.

STENA TRANSIT, STENA TRANSPORTER *(Stena Line)*.

TAVASTLAND, THULELAND, TUNDRALAND *(Wallenius SOL)*.

SECTIONS 8 & 9 – OTHERS AND SISTERS

SPL Princess Anastasia *(Rob de Visser)*

GNV Spirit *(Rob de Visser)*

SECTION 10 - FERRIES 2022CHANGES SINCE FERRIES 2022 - BRITISH ISLES AND NORTHERN EUROPE

DISPOSALS

The following vessels, listed in *Ferries 2022 - British Isles and Northern Europe* have been disposed of - either to other companies listed in this book or others. Company names are as used in that publication.

AMORELLA *(Viking Line)* In October 2022 sold to *Corsica Line* of Italy. Renamed the MEGA VICTORIA.

AUTOPRIDE *(UECC)* In March 2022 sold to *OSM Ship Management PTE Ltd* of Singapore and renamed the MINCHAH. Currently chartered back.

CAP FINISTÈRE *(Brittany Ferries)* In February 2022 sold to *GNV* of Italy and renamed the GNV SPIRIT.

ELISABETH *(P&O Ferries)* In Autumn 2021 charter ended.

EUROCARGO BARI *(Grimaldi Lines)* Returned to the Mediterranean following the ending of the Belgium - Ireland service in July 2022.

EUROPEAN SEAWAY *(P&O Ferries)* In December 2021 sold to *Sea Lines* of Åland, Finland and renamed the SEA ANATOLIA.

EXPORTER *(Holman Paper)* This vessel is no longer used by the company.

FADIQ *(DFDS)* In July 2021 transferred to the company's Mediterranean operation.

GREENFERRY I *(1 Elbferry Fjord1)* In December 2021 the service ceased. Returned to *Fylkesbaatane A/S* of Norway.

KERRY *(DFDS)* In January 2022 charter ended. In February chartered to *Balearia* of Spain.

ORCADIA *(Pentland Ferries)* In November 2021 sold to *Creta Cargo Lines* of Greece.

PRINCESS ANASTASIA *(Moby SPL)* In July 2022 chartered to *Ulosoy* of Turkey renamed ULUSOY 16.

POL MARIS, POL STELLA *(Stena Line)* In January and February 2022 charter ended. Chartered to DFDS and transferred to their Eastern Mediterranean operations.

ROMANTIKA *(Tallink)* In March 2021 chartered to Holland - Norway Lines.

SARK BELLE *(Sark Shipping)* In October 2021 sold to *Forth Boat Tours* and renamed the QUEENSFERRY BELLE.

SASSNITZ *(Stena RoRo)* In October 2021 scrapped at Aliaga, Turkey.

SEA WIND *(Tallink)* In April 2022 sold to *Rudniki Shipping Ltd* of Russia and renamed the A WIND.

SHIPPER *(Holman Paper)* This vessel is no longer used by the company.

SØNDERHO *(Molslinien)* In February 2022 scrapped.

SPIKE ISLANDER *(The Little Ferry Company)* In December 2021 returned to Dutch owners following the company's not being selected to operate the service between Alderney and Guernsey in 2022.

STENA FORECASTER *(P&O Ferries)* In May 2022 returned to *Stena RoRo*. Chartered to *CMA CGM* of France to operate between France and Tunisia.

THE LISMORE *(Argyll & Bute Council)* In June 2022 sold to *Highland Ferries*.

TRANSFIGHTER *(Wallenius SOL)* In autumn 2021 charter ended. In January 2022 sold to *Mediterra Pasific*.

VALENTINE *(CLdN)* In November 2021 sold to *Rederi AB Gotland* of Sweden and immediately chartered to *KiwiRail* of New Zealand to operate between Wellington and Picton.

The following vessel has been renamed since the publication of *Ferries 2022 - British Isles and Northern Europe* without change of owner or operator.

VESSELS RENAMED

The following vessel has been renamed since the publication of *Ferries 2022 - British Isles and Northern Europe* without change of owner or operator.

FINNMERCHANT *(Finnlines)* In July 2022 renamed the NEW AMSTERDAM.

NILS HOLGERSSON *(TT-Line)* In February 2022 renamed the AKKA.

PETER PAN *(TT-Line)* To be renamed the TINKER BELL.

ROSALIND FRANKLIN *(Finnlines)* In November 2021 returned to *Finnlines* and renamed the FINNCLIPPER.

URIAH HEEP *(Gravesend - Tilbury Ferry)* In May 2022 renamed the THAMES KESTREL.

COMPANY CHANGES

Doolin2Aran The company was sold to *Doolin Ferries (O'Brien Line)* in June 2022 and the fleet absorbed.

ElbFerry This operator ceased trading in December 2021.

Flota Suardiaz No longer listed as this operator no longer serves UK or Irish ports.

Grimaldi Lines No longer listed as the Belgium - Ireland service ceased in July 2022.

Moby SPL This operator did not operate in 2020 and 2021 due to the Covid-19 pandemic and in 2022 due to the Russian invasion of Ukraine. The vessel was taken to the Mediterranean and chartered out so it sems unlikely the service will return.

The Little Ferry Company This operator has ceased trading in Autumn 2021.

LATE NEWS

Molslinjen has ordered two new electric ferries from the Cemre Shipyard, Turkey. They will operate on the Alslinjen and Samsølinjen routes. They will enter service in 2024 and 2025 respectively.

Seatruck on 20/09/22 CLdN entered into an agreement to acquire all shares in Seatruck Ferries Holding Ltd. from Clipper Group.

FERRIES ILLUSTRATED

AKKA	209	CROWN SEAWAYS	175	GNV ARIES	9
ALI CAT	68	DAME VERA LYNN	126	GNV SPIRIT	218
AKRANES	192	DELFT SEAWAYS	78,78	GREENFERRY 1	163
AURA SEAWAYS	25,175	DROTTEN	171	HAMNAVOE	88
BARFLEUR	58,62,149	DUNKERQUE SEAWAYS	81	HARTLAND POINT	147
BEN-MY-CHREE	47	EARL SIGURD	91	HEBRIDEAN ISLES	69
BOTNIA SEAWAYS	81	EILEAN DHIURA	110	HENDRA	100
BRAMBLE BUSH BAY	149	EMILY	153	HONFLEUR	213
BRETAGNE	62	EUROPALINK	181	HUMBRIA SEAWAYS	42
CHIEFTAIN	69	EYNHALLOW	91	ISABELLE	204
CLANSMAN	70	FINBO CARGO	187	ISLAND FLYER	149
CLEMENTINE	131	FINNPULP	134	ISLE OF ARRAN	65
COLOR CARRIER	171	FINNWAVE	134	ISLE OF INISHEER	6,45,87
COMMODORE CLIPPER	75	FRAZER TINTERN	120	ISLE OF INNISFREE	1,6
CONDOR LIBERATION	75	FYNSHAV	159	ISLE OF LEWIS	51,65,68
CORRAN	115	GALAXY	204	ISLE OF MULL	51
CÔTE D'ALBÂTRE	82	GALICIA	61	LEIRNA	99
CÔTE D'OPALE	82	GALILEUSZ	209	LOCH FRISA	70
CRACOVIA	166	GLENACHULISH	125	LOCH SHIRA	67
		GNV ANTARES	9	LOCH STRIVEN	67

INDEX